PROGRESSIVE WOMEN IN
CONSERVATIVE TIMES

PROGRESSIVE WOMEN IN CONSERVATIVE TIMES

*Racial Justice, Peace,
and Feminism,
1945 to the 1960s*

SUSAN LYNN

RUTGERS UNIVERSITY PRESS
New Brunswick, New Jersey

Library of Congress Cataloging-in-Publication Data

Lynn, Susan, 1945–
    Progressive women in conservative times : racial justice, peace,
and feminism, 1945 to the 1960s / Susan Lynn.
        p.   cm.
    Includes bibliographical references and index.
    ISBN 0-8135-1867-9 (cloth) — ISBN 0-8135-1868-7 (paper)
    1. Women political activists—United States—History—20th
century.   2. Women social reformers—United States—History—20th
century.   3. Feminists—United States—History—20th century.
4. Pacifists—United States—History—20th century.   5. United
States—Race relations.   6. United States—Social conditions—1945–
I. Title.
HQ1236.5.U6L96   1992
305.42′0973—dc20   92-7978
                                                                                       CIP

British Cataloging-in-Publication information available

FOR SORCA

Contents

Acknowledgments

The act of writing a book is far more a collective undertaking than I understood when I first began this project. I have gained enormously from being part of a network of scholars and friends, and I want to thank the following people for their contributions to this work. Joanne Meyerowitz's comments helped me sharpen and refine a portion of my argument in a critical way at an important stage in the development of this book. One part of this manuscript appeared as "Gender and Post–World War II Progressive Politics: A Bridge to Social Activism of the Late 1960s in the USA" in *Gender and History* 4 (1992), and in the process I benefited greatly from Nancy Hewitt's editorial assistance, as well as from readings by Charles Payne, Steven F. Lawson, and one anonymous reader. Several people read the entire manuscript at various stages and provided invaluable critiques. They include Estelle Freedman, Susan Hartmann, Sorca O'Connor, and Leila Rupp. In addition, a number of people read parts of the manuscript and gave thoughtful comments, including Sue Cobble, Dana Frank, Dee Garrison, Paula Giddings, Peggy Pascoe, Kathryn Kish Sklar, Linda Schott, and Mary Trigg. When this study was first taking shape as a dissertation, I received both emotional support and thoughtful criticism from members of the Women's History Dissertation Reading Group at Stanford, which included Sue Cobble, Liz Cohen, Gary Goodman, Yukiko Hanawa, Susan Johnson, Valerie Matsumoto, Peggy Pascoe, Penny Russell, Linda Schott, and Frances Taylor.

Librarians and archivists have also provided unstintingly of both time and information during the course of my research. I would especially like to thank Jack Sutters, archivist at the American Friends Service

Committee office in Philadelphia, and Elizabeth Norris, archivist and librarian at the office of the National Board of the YWCA of the U.S.A. in New York; both guided me through their collections, answered many questions, and provided me with missing bits of data when I was far from their collections. Jim Knox, American history bibliographer at the Stanford University Libraries, also helped immeasurably in the preliminary stages of this project.

I am grateful for support I received along the way from a variety of institutions. A position as visiting scholar for the Laurie New Jersey Chair in Women's Studies at Douglass College of Rutgers University provided me with time to work on the manuscript as well as the enriching experience of working closely with Paula Giddings, participating in a stimulating seminar on "Women, Race, and Reform," and meeting a number of participants in the vital network of women's history scholars at Rutgers. Other support came from a University of Dayton Research Council Award; a National Endowment for the Humanities Travel to Collections Grant; a Truman Fellowship from the University of Missouri, St. Louis; and a Woodrow Wilson Research Grant in Women's Studies.

The original inspiration for this book came from my contact with the generation of activists who are the subject of this study. As a participant in the civil rights, antiwar, and feminist movements of the 1960s, I received a great deal of encouragement and inspiration for my developing commitment to progressive politics from adults, both male and female, during my adolescence in the late 1950s and early 1960s. Chief among those were my parents, Gault and Margaret Lynn, whose concern for progressive social issues informed their lives; Tillie Olsen, who nurtured the person I was struggling to become, introduced a feminist perspective into my life, and has served as a continual source of inspiration with her depths of understanding of the human condition; and Jack Olsen, who sharpened my understanding of politics and taught me that the process of working for social change was a never-ending one that underwent constant transformations. I was also privileged to spend five summers at a YWCA camp where I was immersed in a women's community and movement before I had a name for it. I further benefited from attended a series of exciting conferences on social and political issues held for high school students by the AFSC San Francisco Regional Office.

Central to this study is the group of women I interviewed about their work for social change. Throughout the course of this study, my enthusiasm for writing has been constantly renewed by my interaction with these women activists. They gave willingly of their time in interviews and offered much useful information in follow-up conversations. Some read the manuscript and provided critiques of it as well. Above all, they provided me a constant incentive to keep working, for even in moments when I doubted my ability to do them justice, I never wavered in my belief that theirs was an important story that deserved to be told.

Two women have figured largely in sustaining me through the long years of this project. Estelle Freedman has given a great deal of energy to this project, first as dissertation director, later as close friend, colleague, and tireless critic. Her ability to combine rigorous scholarship and excellent teaching, while remaining true to her ideals, provided a model of the kind of women's historian I wanted to be. In the years since graduate school, she has given more unsparingly of her time and support than former graduate students have any reason to expect.

Finally, my ability to sustain through the many years this project has taken was greatly increased by the constant support of Sorca O'Connor. She has read more drafts of this manuscript than either she or I would care to remember, and her comments have been consistently challenging intellectually, as she has pushed me to clarify and sharpen my arguments. Even more important, she has shared daily life with me, giving me emotional support when I doubted my ability to sustain the long-term labor required of writing a book. I am grateful for her constant friendship and love.

PROGRESSIVE WOMEN IN
CONSERVATIVE TIMES

Introduction

In 1951, the American Friends Service Committee hired two women—Irene Osborne, who was white, and Alma Scurlock, who was black—to staff an experimental project in Washington, D.C. Their goal was to create sufficient public pressure to convince the school board and the Department of Parks and Recreation to integrate the city's schools and parks. Washington restaurants, theaters, hotels, and schools were all strictly segregated by race. A minor exception was the municipal system; the Department of Parks and Recreation had adopted a policy of gradual desegregation of playgrounds in 1949, but after three years only 30 of 140 areas were operated on an integrated basis.[1]

Osborne and Scurlock set to work to form a Joint Committee on Education from representatives of private agencies and individuals who supported integration. The committee blanketed the city with information by publishing a newsletter, sending speakers to church and civic groups and college and university classes, and sponsoring a series of mass community meetings. "It was terribly exciting," Osborne recalled. "Almost from the beginning we could feel that we were on the edge of a breakthrough." Before the project "you couldn't mention the word integration—it was so shocking it was like using a swearword. Within a few months, we created an atmosphere where we were all talking about it." When in 1954 the Supreme Court declared school segregation unconstitutional in *Brown v. Board of Education*, the Washington school board moved quickly to integrate the schools. The organization that Osborne and Scurlock had put together could claim some of the credit for the smooth transition to racial integration in the nation's capital.[2]

Osborne and Scurlock are part of a generation of middle-class women activists who worked for progressive social reform in the two decades following World War II, inspired by a vision of a new social and political world they hoped would emerge as the war drew to a close. That vision encompassed an expanded welfare state, a powerful labor movement, a strong tradition of civil liberties, the principle of racial equality, and a new international order in which nations would share economic resources more equitably and negotiate disputes through the United Nations. They worked along a variety of fronts in peace, civil rights, religious, and women's organizations and formed alliances with working-class women in progressive labor unions. Some women worked in all-female associations, others in mixed-sex organizations, and some in both. Among the most important organizations through which middle-class women promoted their political and social reform goals were the American Association of University Women (AAUW), the American Friends Service Committee (AFSC), the League of Women Voters (LWV), the National Council of Jewish Women (NCJW), the National Council of Negro Women (NCNW), the National Association for the Advancement of Colored People (NAACP), the Women's International League for Peace and Freedom (WILPF), and the Young Women's Christian Association (YWCA). Not all of these organizations shared an identical reform agenda, but all agreed on at least some elements of that agenda. For example, the YWCA, the AFSC, the AAUW, the LWV, and the WILPF all worked hand in hand for a stronger United Nations in the postwar world. But whereas the NAACP, the NCNW, the YWCA, and the AFSC all took strong stands on civil rights issues, the LWV and the AAUW did not.[3]

Women in this loose coalition of organizations committed to progressive social reform far outnumbered the tiny group of self-avowed feminists in the National Woman's Party (NWP), which has attracted considerable attention from historians studying women activists during this era. The NWP was a militant suffrage organization that advocated the passage of an Equal Rights Amendment for five decades following the passage of woman's suffrage. Most members of the progressive coalition opposed the NWP both because they feared that the ERA would undercut hard-won protection for working-class women and because they were repelled by the racist, anti-Semitic and right-wing leanings of some members of the NWP.[4]

Far from representing an insignificant chapter in women's activism, the postwar progressive coalition played a crucial role as a bridge that linked the prewar progressive work of women reformers with women's activism in the civil rights, antiwar, and feminist movements of the 1960s. That bridge was evident in both the tactics employed and the goals pursued during the 1940s and 1950s. Middle-class women created and joined voluntary organizations in large numbers in the late nineteenth and early twentieth centuries, in order to express their political concerns in the face of their exclusion from the male world of formal electoral politics. Their organizing strategies were shaped in part by their class privileges, particularly by access to education and to social reform jobs as well as by contacts with influential policymakers. Middle-class women's voluntary organizations employed a wide variety of techniques to influence public policy: the investigation of social problems, followed by education, publicity, lobbying, and the creation of direct social services through voluntary activities. After the victory of women's suffrage in 1920, women flocked to voluntary organizations in ever greater numbers as they discovered that the rewards of power and patronage that many men sought in the world of politics continued to elude their grasp.[5] By midcentury, women's participation in grassroots electoral activities was growing, and women had become the backbone of many local efforts of the two political parties. Opportunities to run as candidates in their own right, however, or to exert major influence in party councils remained slight. Thus women in the postwar coalition continued to rely on older voluntary groups to achieve change through education, publicity, and lobbying.

Postwar women also experimented with newer strategies and styles of organizing that relied on a more specifically female ethic. In the last decade feminist scholars have outlined gendered patterns in such areas as psychological and moral development and styles of learning. These studies have concluded that women tend to emphasize connectedness to others and to devote more energy toward nurturing personal relationships and building networks of support, whereas men are more comfortable emphasizing their separateness.[6] Such gendered patterns influence styles of social activism as well. In the "municipal housekeeping" efforts of women in the Progressive Era, for example, the settlement house movement built on networks of women reformers, though class and ethnic differences limited the boundaries of such networks.[7] Postwar women employed a female ethic specifically to build bridges *across* racial lines. This emphasis on the importance of personal relationships fore-shadowed the "personal politics" of the 1960s.[8]

Postwar women reformers pursued both older and newer goals, just as they employed older and newer tactics. In the decades of the 1920s and 1930s, women played a disproportionate role in the groundswell of antiwar feeling that swept across U.S. society. After World War II, women remained active in the struggle for world peace, but a new context dramatically reshaped the forms of that struggle. During the height of the McCarthy period, peace activists fought against the tide of Cold War hysteria to keep alive a critique of U.S. foreign policy against tremendous odds. Then, in the late 1950s, the peace movement revived to conduct a campaign for a ban on atmospheric nuclear testing, which culminated in the 1963 Test Ban Treaty. By the mid-1960s, the peace movement was well poised to provide support for the growing struggle to end the war in Vietnam. Feminist issues attracted the attention of some women activists, just as they had in earlier decades, although few women activists called themselves feminists, for reasons this book will explore. Yet their ongoing challenge to women's subordination helped feed the feminist revolt of the 1960s. Women also struggled to expand the provisions of the social welfare state through the extension of Social Security and the provision of national health care programs.

New issues arose in the context of the postwar world as well. The rise of McCarthyism inspired a spirited defense of civil liberties on the part of progressive women activists. Yet what differed most markedly be-tween the prewar and postwar generations was the shift in how they conceptualized social justice, from a prewar emphasis on economic injus-tice suffered by working-class women and children, as well as the working-class more generally, to a concern with the U.S. system of racial subordination. The efforts of women in the Progressive and inter-war periods centered on the "maternalist" politics of helping the weak and the unfortunate, particularly women and children, through the provision of social welfare measures and protective legislation, support for labor union organizing efforts, and efforts to improve the urban environment through improvements in sanitation and health.[9] The first glimmerings of a shift were evident during the war years, as racial justice began to emerge as the central paradigm of the struggle for social justice. The struggle for civil rights gathered momentum in the 1950s, providing the spark that would ignite the protest movements of the 1960s, including the feminist movement. The 1940s and 1950s, then, represented a watershed in women's social reform activism, one that ultimately led to more general challenges to discrimination based on race and gender in U.S. society during the 1960s.

The efforts of women in two organizations—the Young Women's Christian Association (YWCA) and the American Friends Service Committee (AFSC)—illustrate the continuities and discontinuities in women's activism before and after World War II. These organizations demonstrate several key characteristics of women's progressive social reform efforts in the post–World War II era. Both were in the forefront of the struggle for racial justice in the years after World War II, reflecting the shift in reform priorities among progressive women activists. Each relied extensively on the creation of interracial alliances in its struggle for racial justice. Both demonstrated the enduring significance of religious idealism as one important thread in social reform. The contrast between the two illuminates some of the complexities of postwar progressive activism, as well. Both organizations were concerned about creating a more peaceful world order, but the AFSC was pacifist, while the YWCA endorsed liberal internationalist approaches to world order. Finally, although both provided important opportunities for women to exert leadership in the arena of social reform, the all-female nature of the YWCA led that group to advocate measures to increase women's status, while the mixed-sex composition of the AFSC led it to ignore feminist issues altogether.

Progressive reform organizations faced a new political universe after World War II, the result of the dramatic changes in the international order wrought by war and the conservative retrenchment of the McCarthy period. Before the war, a trio of issues—economic justice, peace, and racial justice, with greater priority placed by white activists on the first two—had occupied those on the left end of the political spectrum. Now, however, the priorities shifted, with economic issues and peace declining in significance, and racial justice assuming increased importance. The shift away from economic issues is evident in both the AFSC and the YWCA.

The AFSC was established in 1917 by a group of prominent Quakers, part of a revived U.S. peace movement born of the cataclysm of war. It was a leading pacifist organization during the interwar period but expanded its focus to domestic social problems as well. During the 1930s, the AFSC responded to the crisis of the depression by collecting and distributing large quantities of clothing and by developing a self-help economic development project in the devastated Appalachian coalfields. The AFSC had devoted little attention to racial issues before World War II, but in the wake of the devastating race riots of 1943, the AFSC initiated a race relations program to confront the problems of racial injustice in U.S. society. By the 1950s the AFSC focused on the problems of poverty primarily in racial-ethnic communities.

The shifting priorities of the YWCA illustrate the same transition, though here the emphasis in both periods was specifically on the needs of women. The YWCA was among those single-sex organizations that advocated protective labor legislation and encouraged trade union organization of women throughout the first half of the twentieth century.[10] The YWCA organized the Industrial Clubs in the first decade of the twentieth century to provide a forum for working-class women to discuss wages, safety and health standards, and protective legislation. Working women flocked to the Industrial Department, which sponsored worker education programs and served as a pressure group within the larger YWCA, agitating for working-class women's interests. At its peak in 1930, the Industrial Department had close to 60,000 members.[11]

The need for such an organization for women workers became much less compelling, however, with the rise of the Congress of Industrial Organizations (CIO). During the late 1930s and early 1940s, the CIO unions became the primary locus of working-class women's efforts to improve their conditions and to work for political change. At the same time, membership in the YWCA Industrial Department dropped precipitously. Faced with a collapsing program, the YWCA abolished its separate industrial women's assemblies in 1949, despite the strenuous objections of many of the YWCA industrial secretaries.[12] Thus, after World War II, the salience of class-defined issues declined for middle-class women in the YWCA, and working-class women lost much of their former ability to influence policy decisions in the organization. Gradually, racial discrimination began to replace class oppression as the major paradigm of social inequality in the Y's program and in U.S. life.

The dramatic shift away from class issues in the postwar world resulted in part from the relative success of progressive activists in obtaining improvements in working conditions for industrial workers, both women and men, and laws to end child labor. New Deal reforms climaxed decades of struggle for government intervention to protect the U.S. working class, and the incorporation of women into the trade union movement further improved the situation for women workers. Coupled with postwar prosperity, these reforms satisfied many middle-class women that the tremendous extremes of economic inequality, at least as it affected whites, were nearly eliminated. In addition, the political repression of the McCarthy period decimated the Left and forestalled any further progress on economic reform. After an unprecedented massive strike wave in 1946–1947, the labor movement was thrown on the defensive in the face of the political resurgence of business forces, best exemplified by the passage of the 1947 Taft-Hartley Act. The CIO's expulsion of Communist-led unions in 1949 signaled the end of the labor movement's most crusading days, although certain unions remained a backbone for progressive causes. For those promoting a liberal perspective, the victories seemed satisfying enough. For those with more radical hopes, the 1940s spelled the end of a dream. Yet as their interest in class-based issues began to wane, middle-class women reformers began to address another form of inequality—that based on race. That focus would soon provide new opportunities and new difficulties for women in progressive organizations.

Progressive women activists' new sense of urgency about the nation's troubling racial problems reflected a shifting climate of public opinion in the United States. World War II and its aftermath profoundly altered the political significance of the system of racial subordination, highlighting the contradiction between the rhetoric of democracy promulgated abroad and the reality of racial oppression practiced at home. In the struggle between Communist and capitalist blocs for the allegiance of emerging third-world nations, the United States was vulnerable to charges of racism. On the domestic front, the internment of all citizens and residents of Japanese descent raised serious questions about how well the Constitution protected its citizens from wholesale violations of civil liberties based on racial classifications.

Meanwhile, black Americans were lured by burgeoning wartime job opportunities out of the South and into the North and West, thus accelerating the demographic shift that began three decades earlier. The political consequences of that shift were enormous, as black voters now constituted a critical swing vote in northern industrial states. A new spirit of militancy was evident in the threats of civil rights leaders in 1941 to bring thousands of protestors to Washington to demand equal opportunities in the rapidly expanding defense industries and the armed services; Franklin Roosevelt had responded by establishing the Fair Employment Practices Commission for defense industry. The membership rolls of the National Association for the Advancement of Colored People, the chief African-American protest organization, expanded exponentially from 50,000 in 1940 to 450,000 in 1946, and black soldiers, radicalized by their wartime experiences, returned home determined to challenge racial segregation.[13] When widespread racial violence erupted in Harlem and Detroit and other cities during the summer of 1943, white liberals expressed alarm and heightened their resolve to address the country's simmering racial problems. Thus beginning with the domestic and international transformations caused by World War II, accelerating in the mid-1950s after the Supreme Court decision in *Brown v. Board of Education*, and culminating in the civil rights movement of the 1960s, the struggle for racial equality moved to the forefront of the progressive agenda.

Liberal white support for racial equality represented a sharp break from the past. The indifference and outright hostility most white suffrage leaders displayed toward potential African-American allies throughout the late nineteenth and early twentieth centuries is a well-documented part of our feminist heritage. The exclusion of black women by white women's organizations pushed African-American women to abandon hopes for an interracial alliance for social reform and to concentrate on concerns specific to African-Americans. During the interwar years, there were several attempts at interracial cooperation among women activists in the South, the most notable of which occurred in the Woman's Division of the Commission on Interracial Cooperation and the YWCA. Such groups formulated demands for improved conditions in the African-American community, but white women proved unwilling to directly confront or challenge the practice of racial segregation. In the North, the Women's International League for Peace and Freedom welcomed a token number of African-American women into its ranks, but antiracist work was never a focus of the organization. The Communist party was one of the few organizations with an explicit and detailed program that attacked racism in U.S. society during the 1930s and that embraced (if not always equally) black and white, and male and female, members.[14]

In the years immediately after World War II, white women progressives began to directly challenge the legitimacy of the system of racial segregation and discrimination in the United States. Still, even as many endorsed racial integration as a goal, only a few organizations made concerted efforts to end racial injustice. The efforts of those that did were rooted in interracial alliances. Two of the most important organizations in this regard were the YWCA and the AFSC. The development of interracial alliances provided opportunities for African-Americans, and to some degree for women from other racial-ethnic groups, to exert leadership within predominantly white organizations. These alliances also initiated an interracial dialogue that challenged the racial assumptions of whites and drove them to develop a deeper understanding of the systematic nature of racism in U.S. society.

The history of the AFSC's and the YWCA's work for world peace, a second great cause of progressive reform, illustrates the fate of the two poles of the prewar peace movement—pacifism and liberal internationalism—in the postwar world. Americans had organized the largest peace movement yet witnessed by U.S. society during the interwar decades. But as the storm clouds of war descended over Europe and Asia in the 1930s, that movement collapsed. Pacifists were isolated as their previous liberal internationalist allies moved to endorse the principle of collective security. The dedicated pacifist minority that remained was radicalized by wartime experiences; many men entered government-sponsored camps for conscientious objectors or prisons, where they experimented with techniques of nonviolent resistance, while women supported male partners and helped keep pacifist organizations alive.

After the war the emerging Cold War consensus dismayed pacifists and internationalists alike, shattering the dream of a world characterized by harmony and peace. The threat of nuclear weapons added a greater sense of urgency to the quest for world peace. Both the AFSC and the YWCA deplored the increasing militarism underlying U.S. foreign policy. Both organizations advanced an alternative vision for the postwar world, one based on a strengthened United Nations, disarmament through negotiations, and a move by industrialized nations to share the benefits of their technology and wealth with less developed nations. The two organizations parted ways, however, over the principle of pacifism. Less sanguine than the AFSC about unilateral moves in the field of disarmament or conflict resolution, the YWCA supported a U.S. military presence in the postwar world yet cautioned against an overemphasis on military solutions to political problems. Like other liberal internationalist organizations, the YWCA tried to ride two horses, advocating more peaceful approaches to international problems and simultaneously and somewhat reluctantly endorsing many of the key Cold War policies of the U.S. government.

In the struggle for racial justice or peace the YWCA and the AFSC were often allies in the postwar era. They differed, however, in their attention to women's issues. Here, the contrast between the mixed-sex AFSC and the all-female YWCA underscores the importance of women's organizations in maintaining a feminist component of progressive politics. Historically, women's progressive social reform and feminism have often been closely intertwined. In the nineteenth century the abolitionist movement spawned the early women's rights movement; later, women played key roles in the social justice wing of the Progressive movement. More recently, the civil rights movement sparked the emergence of the radical branch of the women's liberation movement. In the post–World War II period, as in earlier decades, women's organizations were far more open to feminist perspectives than were mixed-sex organizations. The YWCA and the AFSC illustrate this point, for the Y consistently worked to advance women's status, while the AFSC remained silent on gender issues.[15]

The YWCA and the AFSC illustrate another important aspect of progressive reform, the significance of religious inspiration. Social reform became increasingly secularized in the course of the twentieth century, part of the larger secularization occurring in U.S. society. Yet religious ideals never lost their capacity to move people to action and to inspire commitment to social change. Examples of that power abound in the social reform literature. The civil rights movement found a base in the black churches of the South. Christian idealism also served as a major touchstone for progressive action within the YWCA. Religiously inspired groups played a significant role in sustaining dissent in the face of the intense political repression during the McCarthy period as well. The peace movement was kept alive largely by organizations such as the AFSC, particularly during the height of the Cold War in the late 1940s and early 1950s, for the AFSC's unquestioned commitment to peaceful change coupled with public respect for Friends' deep religious faith made the organization less vulnerable, though hardly immune, to red-baiting attacks.

In addition to tracing the history of a previously neglected generation of women reformers, this study sheds new light on the discourse of domesticity in U.S. society in the immediate postwar period. The prevalent image of women in that era is that of the suburban housewife who centered her life around marriage and children. Yet women activists in the YWCA, the AFSC, and other progressive organizations exemplify an alternative path to fulfillment selected by many middle-class women who joined the quest for social justice and a new world order based on peace and international cooperation. Women's political activism in the postwar era remains relatively unexplored, in part, because of the prevailing assumption that most women's lives were awash in a sea of domesticity. Women did, of course, embrace the joys and frustrations of family life in record numbers following the war. Yet our understanding of the meaning of domesticity in women's lives has been distorted in three distinct ways.

First, scholars who have focused on the intense post–World War II media campaign that pushed women back into the domestic sphere often assumed, rather than demonstrated, the all-pervasiveness of that ideal. The notion that domestic ideology suffused U.S. society was popularized by Betty Friedan's *Feminine Mystique* and gradually made its way into standard accounts of the period. In fact, the ideology of the period was not nearly as uniform in content as the usual surveys of that literature suggest; the most strident messages about a return to domesticity represented only the conservative edge of public discourse. An alternative and strikingly different view appeared in many popular magazines of the period: many experts urged women to combine domestic duties with paid work, community and political activities, or both.[16]

The popular postwar literature illuminates a second misunderstanding, that is, the assumption that marriage and family precluded women's involvement with social and political activities. For women who came of age after World War II, early age at marriage and close spacing of children combined to leave most married women with more years free from responsibilities for young children than any previous generation of women in the United States. One major outlet for women's energies and commitments was civic activism. Furthermore, domestic values were often employed to support women's public efforts, just as they had been at the turn of the century. A dramatic confrontation that occurred when members of Women Strike for Peace (WSP) were called to testify before the House Committee on Un-American Activities in 1962 demonstrates this point. Women of the WSP justified their opposition to the arms race and nuclear testing by portraying themselves as apolitical mothers who sought only to protect their children from the dangers of radiation.[17]

Finally, the relation of African-American women to domesticity was distinct from that of white women. Throughout the twentieth century, economic necessity had driven married black women into the labor force in much higher numbers than it had white women. During the immediate postwar years, black women were pursuing college degrees and professional careers at higher rates than were either black men or white women. Furthermore, since the Progressive Era, middle-class black women had tackled the problems of improving the social and economic conditions faced by the African-American community both to improve conditions for their own families and because they understood that their status in U.S. society was linked to that of poor blacks. Black women's activism in civic and political affairs was thus viewed as an extension of, rather than a contradiction to, dedication to family life.[18] We need to know more about working-class women's activism in the postwar world to understand the relationship of white working-class women's experience to the ideals of domesticity, but it is clear that domestic seclusion is an option only for those with a certain degree of financial resources.[19]

For a significant minority of middle-class women in the United States, then, the pull of domesticity paled in the face of the urgency they felt to address the country's social and political problems. Women activists, such as those in the YWCA and AFSC, played critical roles in sustaining a progressive critique of U.S. society during precisely those decades when so much effort was made to mute female voices. They endorsed racial integration within women's voluntary groups, lobbied for civil rights legislation, and worked in communities to open schools, housing and employment opportunities to all Americans. They raised their voices to protest U.S. Cold War foreign policies, arguing for measures that would contribute to worldwide peace. Some of them advocated a number of measures to improve women's status, aware of the conflicting demands and complex problems faced by women. Women made an important difference in both single-sex and mixed-sex organizations, bringing a female ethic to the work they did in communities and organizations.

The legacy of this generation of women political activists reminds us of the importance of sustaining women's social reform efforts during conservative eras like our own, in order to maintain and transform the traditions and ideas that younger generations of activists can build on. When the 1960s erupted into a decade of social protest, many of the young people who participated in those protests had received inspiration and guidance from an older generation of activists. The younger generation absorbed their values yet transmuted them to meet the widening political opportunities of the decade, cultivating a new movement from the solid roots of the old. The story of women progressive activists during the 1940s and 1950s is thus part of a larger story of social reform in U.S. society, one in which each generation of activists learns from the old yet strikes out on a new path of their own making.

1

*"The Changer and the Changed":
The Radicalization of Women
Activists in the Interwar
Decades*

When Dorothy Irene Height first arrived in New York City, the product of a small-town conservative African-American Baptist community, she was far from radical in her social views. Yet a perceptive observer might have glimpsed the seeds from which radicalism would later flower. An excellent student, interested in debating and public speaking, Height was active in a host of youth groups, including the YWCA, during her high school years. She had a keen interest in the Constitution and had closely examined the Thirteenth, Fourteenth, and Fifteenth amendments, which had ended slavery and granted citizenship and voting rights to black males. Growing up in the troubled coal-mining and steel industry district near Pittsburgh, she also had an avid interest in economic issues.

The year was 1929, the beginning of a decade of intense political ferment in the United States. Height had come from Rankin, Pennsylvania, to attend New York University, where she earned both a bachelor's degree and a master's degree in educational psychology in the short span of four years. Because of her profound religious orientation, Height gravitated toward the United Christian Youth Movement (UCYM), a coalition formed in 1935 of the Student YWCA, the Student YMCA, and several denominational student religious groups. Here she was introduced to the Social Gospel, with its insistence that Christian faith be

expressed in social and political action. Height's talent fc
ing, her tremendous energy and drive, and her thoughtful ability to
grasp the issues all catapulted her to leadership. She quickly rose to
prominence in UCYM, moving from leadership in the Harlem Christian Youth Council to president of the New York State chapter of
UCYM in 1937 and vice-chair of UCYM of North America. In 1937
she attended the Oxford Conference on the Life and Work of the
Churches, the major ecumenical gathering of the decade. Travel in
UCYM circles exposed her to the ideas of radical Christian thinkers of
her time: Walter Rauschenbusch, key proponent of the Social Gospel;
Reinhold Niebuhr, prominent theologian for the Christian Left; A. J.
Muste, labor radical and pacifist; and others. Swept up in the politics
of the decade, she found her Christian beliefs recast into radical social
activism.

In 1937 Dorothy Height embarked on a career with the YWCA,
becoming the assistant director of the YWCA's Emma Ransom House
in Harlem. Height had wearied of spending her days as a social worker
with the New York Welfare Department, then devoting evenings and
weekends to political activity. She welcomed the YWCA position as an
opportunity to incorporate her major personal commitments—social
justice and religious education—into her work life. The YWCA further
impressed her because it had been the first predominantly white organization to offer positions of leadership to black women, hiring its first
black woman on the national staff in 1912 and continuing to employ
black women at both the national and local levels when few other professional opportunities were available.[1]

A fateful encounter in her first year at Emma Ransom House introduced Dorothy Height to two women of towering stature who became
mentors and friends—Mary McLeod Bethune and Eleanor Roosevelt.
Bethune, the most influential African-American woman in the country,
had begun her career as an educator. In 1936 she joined Franklin Roosevelt's New Deal administration as director of Negro affairs for the
National Youth Administration, and that same year she organized the
Federal Council on Negro Affairs. (Popularly referred to as the "black
cabinet," the council was an informal group of blacks in Roosevelt's
administration who worked to advance black interests through government programs.) The previous year Bethune had also organized the
National Council of Negro Women (NCNW), a coalition of major black

women's associations. In 1937 Height was assigned to escort none other than Eleanor Roosevelt into a meeting of the NCNW at the Emma Ransom House. When Roosevelt was seated, Height turned to leave, but Bethune urged her to stay. That began Height's lifelong involvement in the NCNW. Two years later, when Height moved to Washington, D.C., to direct the Phyllis Wheatley YWCA, Bethune took her under her wing, grooming her for leadership in the NCNW. In 1942, Bethune asked Height to serve as executive secretary of the organization, a post she held until 1946. The two worked together night and day, and out of their collaboration emerged a close spiritual bond and the beginning of a lifetime friendship. For Height, Bethune was a great teacher, schooling her in the details of social reform politics. The 1937 meeting also marked the beginning of Height's long association with Eleanor Roosevelt. Along with other leaders of the student movement, Height worked closely with Roosevelt on the World Youth Congress held at Vassar College in 1938, a project Roosevelt sponsored in order to cement an alliance between the youth movement and her husband's administration. The two women maintained both a political alliance and a warm friendship until Roosevelt's death in 1962.

Height channeled her work for social justice through the YWCA and the NCNW throughout her adult life, firmly convinced that "women's voluntary organizations have been in the forefront" of the struggle for social change. In 1944 she was appointed secretary of interracial education for the National Board of the YWCA, located in New York City. She later served as the director of training from 1949 to 1963, then as head of the newly created Department of Racial Justice from 1963 until her retirement in 1970. At the same time, Height remained active in the NCNW, becoming president in 1957, two years after Bethune's death; she remains at the helm of the organization today. During the 1960s she achieved national recognition: She joined the Council for United Civil Rights Leadership, which was instrumental in organizing the 1963 March on Washington, and she served on John F. Kennedy's President's Commission on the Status of Women, as well as on a host of other boards and commissions.[2]

The outlines of Dorothy Height's story parallel those of other women activists in the YWCA and the AFSC, although not all of them achieved the same degree of prominence. Women who were active in these two organizations during the 1940s and 1950s came to political consciousness during turbulent times. Born in the last years of the nineteenth century or the first two decades of the twentieth, the oldest of them was just reaching adulthood during World War I, while the youngest matured during World War II. These women were too young, by and large, to have participated in the suffrage movement, and few had had any involvement in patriotic activities during World War I. Virtually all of them, however, lived through the profound disillusionment that followed the First World War and the relentless crescendo of international violence that led to the second. As a result, the issue of war and peace was of immense consequence to their generation. Massive worldwide depression, which spawned questions about the viability of capitalism, further shaped their political views.[3]

Social reform movements often arise during times of economic crisis or following the disruptions of war. The interwar decades were no exception, as hundreds of thousands of Americans embraced lives of social and political activism, envisioning a world free of the strife and desolation of war and firmly grounded in social justice and equality for all. Beyond these vague ideals, philosophical differences over both tactics and goals divided the social reform community. In the fluid and volatile political situation of the thirties, liberals, Communists, Socialists, and Christian leftists often formed alliances for particular goals, despite the considerable suspicion that impeded their relationships. Liberals, satisfied with the general direction of New Deal reforms, hoped to expand and extend their scope. Those on the Left wanted to push farther. The Communist party of the United States of America (CPUSA) espoused the primacy of class struggle and the eventual goal of revolution during the 1920s and the early 1930s. Without abandoning these long-term goals, the CPUSA initiated a new strategy in 1935, endorsing the New Deal and attempting to create a Popular Front alliance with other progressive organizations. The Christian Left shared with secular leftists a vision of total transformation of social institutions but parted company from the secularists both in the centrality of spiritual faith to their lives and in their belief that change must be achieved through gradual and democratic means. It is in these overlapping circles of the Christian Left and liberal social reform that the AFSC and the YWCA can be located. Whether identifying themselves as liberals or leftists, women activists in the YWCA and the AFSC looked to the Christian Left for religious and intellectual inspiration.

The Social Reform Milieu of the
Christian Left

The Christian Left drew on and developed a body of social and political thought grounded in the Social Gospel and post–World War I pacifism. The Social Gospel had transformed the face of U.S. Protestantism during the late nineteenth and early twentieth centuries. A product of impatience with the struggle for personal salvation and evangelical reform, the Social Gospel called for a spiritual transformation of humanity that would manifest itself in a reformed social order, infused with the principles of justice and love. The Social Gospel had both conservative and radical adherents; the former tended toward social settlement work, while the latter aimed at nothing less than the creation of the kingdom of God on earth.

In 1918 and 1919, many Social Gospel leaders began to move toward the Left, inspired by such figures as Walter Rauschenbusch and Harry Ward. Before World War I the central focus of the Social Gospel had been the problem of a rapidly industrializing society, torn by conflict between labor and capital and scarred by the poverty and congestion of urban slums. Liberal Social Gospel leaders suggested that the interests of labor and capital could be brought into harmony through liberal social reform. Now, however, more radical voices allied themselves firmly on the side of labor and insisted on confronting business interests as well as other defenders of the status quo. Many advocates of the Social Gospel called for the abolition of child labor and for safety regulations for industrial workers, a shorter work week, a living minimum wage, and recognition of the right to collective bargaining. By the early 1930s, increasing numbers of Social Gospel clergy advocated socialism, and many voted for the Socialist party in 1932.[4]

Walter Rauschenbusch was the most forceful spokesperson for a radical interpretation of the Social Gospel. He wrote that "approximate equality" was "the only enduring foundation of political democracy," a foundation fundamentally incompatible with capitalism. In *Christianity and the Social Order*, Rauschenbusch urged "religious men" to look to socialism for "the most thorough and consistent economic elaboration of the Christian social ideal." "It is," he maintained, "far and away the most powerful force for justice, democracy, and organized fraternity in the modern world."[5] For Rauschenbusch, socialism was part of the historical mission of Christianity, and the major task facing Christians was that of infusing spirituality into the materialistic socialist tradition. Support for this radical version of the Social Gospel gained adherents during the 1920s and 1930s. In 1932 the Northern General Conference of Methodists, one of the most radical of Protestant denominations, denounced capitalism, economic individualism, and the profit motive, calling for an economic order based on cooperation and unselfishness. The report of the 1937 Oxford Conference on the Life and Work of the Churches, the major international ecumenical conference of the decade, echoed this theme, arguing that capitalism enhanced acquisitiveness and created indefensible inequalities and forms of economic power that were not responsible to the community.[6] Not all Protestant leaders jumped on the Socialist bandwagon, of course, but the call for the creation of an economic order based on mutual cooperation rather than private gain became a common refrain in church circles.

No aspect of this vision of a world based on harmony and justice gathered more support from the liberal Protestant churches and advocates of the Social Gospel during the interwar decades than the crusade to end war. In the crucible of opposition to U.S. entry into World War I, the energies of female social reformers and male wartime pacifists had infused the moribund peace movement with new life. New organizations sprang up to take the place of established and conservative peace societies, advancing a radical perspective that linked peace to a broad program of social reform and democratization of U.S. society. Among the most important organizations in this new movement were the Fellowship of Reconciliation (FOR), a Christian pacifist organization established in Great Britain in 1914 and in the United States the following year; the Woman's Peace party, established in 1915, which became part of the Women's International League for Peace and Freedom (WILPF) in 1919; the American Friends Service Committee, established in 1917 by Quaker pacifists; and the War Resisters League (WRL), established as a home for secular pacifists in 1923.[7]

Undergirding this new organizational fervor was a newly activist Christian pacifism. Once the province of a few lonely voices calling for individual acts of moral witness in conscientious objection to war, pacifism now attempted to grapple with the social conditions that rendered war an ever-present reality. The Friends National Peace Conference of 1915 presaged the new mood, declaring, "The alternative to war is not inactivity and cowardice. It is the irresistible and constructive power of goodwill."[8]

Searching for a model of how to apply the ethic of Christian love to social change, pacifists seized on the example of Mahatma Gandhi. In his challenge to South Africa's racial order and his campaign to end British colonization of India, Gandhi pioneered in using techniques of nonviolent action as part of a mass movement to confront social and economic injustice. His direct action campaigns proceeded in orderly fashion through deliberate escalation of tactics from negotiations to mass marches, strikes, boycotts, and eventually, civil disobedience. Gandhi believed in the power of redemptive suffering; by approaching his opponents with love and a willingness to submit to physical violence without returning it in kind, he was convinced that public opinion could be aroused against injustice. He was confident that social movements based on positive good will and a refusal to take part in injustice could eventually reach the hearts of those in power and break their resistance. These ideas had a profound influence in pacifist circles in the interwar decades. In the early 1940s the Fellowship of Reconciliation and its offshoot, the Congress of Racial Equality (CORE), began to apply the techniques of nonviolent action to U.S. race relations.

Burgeoning opposition to war was fueled by revisionist interpretations of World War I. Rejecting as simplistic the notion that Germany had been solely responsible for the war, revisionists located the tangled roots of war in institutional forces such as militarism, nationalism, secret diplomacy, and economic competition. According to this perspective, the humiliating and economically devastating settlement of the Treaty of Versailles virtually guaranteed another war. Disarmament was thus a crucial step in the process of creating peace, but hardly sufficient. Because war arose in part from economic privation and gross disparities in income between nations, future wars could be avoided only if the world was reorganized "on the basis of production for use and not for profit, with the needs of the world and not of particular nations in view."[9]

These new currents of thought had a profound impact in liberal Protestant churches. Embarrassed by their support of U.S. participation in World War I, Protestant leaders determined not to repeat the same mistake, denouncing "the war-system as sin."[10] Ever-enlarging circles of antiwar sentiment rippled through the country during the decade of the 1920s. By the early 1930s pacifism was firmly established within the

Protestant churches, particularly among the ministry. Independent religious publications, various denominational church organs, and the Federal Council of Churches all propagated antiwar views. Jewish leaders and a few Catholics joined the rising chorus of protest. The prominence of outspoken pacifist clergy lent greater visibility and credence to pacifism than at any other time in U.S. history.

Kindled by these changes, a widespread movement for peace arose during the 1930s. The backbone of that movement consisted of women's organizations and the Protestant clergy, buttressed by a vigorous student antiwar movement, a broad coalition of young Communists, Socialists, and religious youth that stirred into life in the early years of the decade. In 1932 the student movement held the first large antiwar conference; the Oxford Oath, brought to the United States from England in 1933, became its rallying cry. In its U.S. formulation students pledged never to fight in a war their government might conduct, thus leaving open the possibility, important to Communists, that some wars might be acceptable. Pacifism was widespread; a nationwide poll of college students conducted in 1933 by Brown University's *Daily Herald* indicated that 39 percent of those responding were committed to absolute pacifism, 33 percent would serve only in case of an actual invasion, and only 28 percent were willing to serve in any war.[11] Along with parades and speeches and endless discussion, students also sponsored dramatic student strikes and boycotts of classes. At its height in 1935, the student antiwar movement pulled an estimated 175,000 students out of classes to participate in a student strike.[12]

Adult peace groups were equally active during this decade. Prompted by WILPF, Congress conducted the widely publicized Nye Senate committee's investigation of the role of the munitions industry in the U.S. decision to enter World War I. Antiwar activity culminated in 1936–1937, when the AFSC, FOR, WILPF, and liberal internationalist peace groups sponsored the Emergency Peace Campaign, a concerted effort designed to keep the nation out of war by educating the public about the underlying roots of war and by outlining alternatives.

By mid-decade, cracks in the unity of the peace movement presaged the widening rifts that eventually led to its demise in the years 1939–1941. The collapse of the League of Nations and the advent of the Spanish civil war sowed seeds of doubt about pacifism in peace circles. The most divisive issue was that of neutrality legislation, which the

Spanish civil war brought to a head. As Spanish Loyalists tried to stave off collapse in the face of a threatened Fascist takeover, a U.S. arms embargo indirectly aided the Fascist rebels, who were supplied with arms by Germany and Italy. Debates over neutrality legislation during 1937 and 1938 ranged pacifists and the Socialist party, committed to strict neutrality on the part of the United States, against Communists and liberals, who embraced collective security in order to combat the spread of fascism. By 1939 the peace movement had shattered over the issue of collective security. Pacifists became increasingly isolated as large numbers deserted the peace movement and endorsed war as the lesser of two evils.

In addition to the issues of economic justice and peace, a third issue—racial justice—held a less central but not insignificant place on the social reform agenda during these decades. The system of racial segregation had never been more rigid than during the late nineteenth and early twentieth centuries, and it found few challengers. During the 1920s and 1930s, however, religious liberals and the secular Left began to question this system of racial subordination. Radical critics of U.S. society contended that the problems of capitalism, war, and racism were interconnected. Some advocates of the Social Gospel, including the denominational bodies of the Northern Methodist, Northern Baptist, Presbyterian, and Congregational churches, denounced racial prejudice and discrimination.

Action was less forthcoming than rhetoric during these decades, however. The Federal Council of Churches established a Commission on Race Relations in 1921, but despite pronouncements that called for better living and working conditions for blacks, it fell short of challenging racial segregation. In the South, three Christian groups influenced by the Social Gospel—the Student YWCA, the Commission on Interracial Cooperation, and the Women's Mission Council of the Methodist Episcopal Church South—promoted interracial dialogue. Of these, only the Student YWCA began to endorse racial integration during the 1920s. During the 1930s the white Left moved more boldly to confront racial oppression. The Communist party was one of the few organizations with an explicit and detailed program that attacked racism in U.S. society during the 1930s and that embraced (if not always equally) black and white, and male and female, members.[13] The Congress of Industrial Organizations made new efforts to organize black workers in mining, steel and auto, and other unions, while Socialist party organizers brought black and white tenant farmers together in the Southern Tenant Farmers Union; the Fellowship of Reconciliation sponsored interracial conferences in the South. But a full-scale assault on racism in the United States awaited another era.[14]

The YWCA and the AFSC
as Social Reform Organizations

A number of organizations participated in the social reform movement of the interwar decades, linked by a general vision of reform but differing in particular goals and strategies. The YWCA and the AFSC were both parts of that larger movement, although they played significantly different roles. The YWCA was a large, diverse organization that included women from a range of political persuasions, not all of them consonant with interwar radicalism. The Student YWCA, however, as well as a number of leaders of the national board and some community YWCAs functioned as part of the movement. From its inception in 1917, the AFSC was a major actor in the interwar peace movement, and by the 1930s it turned its attention to domestic social problems as well.

The YWCA was an outgrowth of Protestantism in the second half of the nineteenth century, when middle-class women had formed YWCA city associations to provide housing, social opportunities, and religious instruction for the thousands of young single women flooding into the cities in search of work. A separate and distinct movement of student YWCA associations sprang up on college campuses in the last quarter of the nineteenth century, inspired by the evangelical and missionary fervor that swept through Protestant circles. In 1906, student and city organizations joined to form the YWCA of the U.S.A. The YWCA was organized into several broad divisions, the most important of which were the Community and Student divisions.[15] Community Ys, located in cities throughout the nation, were somewhat autonomous; each elected its own board of directors and executive secretary, and each relied on local funding sources. The Student Division, with chapters on college campuses, was funded by the National Board of the YWCA, which provided leadership and services for the entire organization. National conventions, composed of delegates elected from around the country, met biennially before World War II and triennially afterward to set broad policy outlines for the organization as a whole. Decisions of the national conventions were morally binding on local associations, though in practice there was considerable leeway in following national directives.

The first two decades of the twentieth century witnessed the conversion of many members of the YWCA to the Social Gospel. YWCA leaders looked for inspiration to Walter Rauschenbusch, who gave the major convention addresses for the YWCA national conventions in 1905 and 1915. Those in community YWCAs who had focused on charity and social control of the less fortunate began to shift their attention to the conflict between labor and capital. At the same time, the Student Division moved away from its enthusiasm for personal evangelical religion toward a more radical Christian social activism. The year 1920 marked the turning point in the Y's transition; at the national convention that year, the YWCA adopted the "Social Ideals of the Churches," a statement of Social Gospel principles. At the same time, the Y endorsed a strategy of pursuing legislative changes in an attempt to solve social problems. In the following two decades women in the YWCA supported a legislative and educational program that focused on labor problems, particularly those of women and children. The Y also took up the cause of world peace, and pacifism gained a significant following within its ranks, while the Student YWCA began to confront racism. By the 1930s, a number of leaders in the Student Y belonged to the Socialist party and voted for Norman Thomas for president.

This development illustrates a common aspect of the growth of social movements. New movements often arise from roots in older organizations that provide leadership, communications networks, and financial and institutional resources to the fledgling group. The YWCA absorbed the reform currents of the Social Gospel and Progressivism, and by the 1920s Social Gospel activists tended to dominate the leadership, playing key roles on the staff of the National Board, much of the Student YWCA, and in some of the community associations. As a result, the resources of the YWCA were harnessed to the crusade for social justice.[16]

From the perspective of a burgeoning social movement, those resources were extensive. The YWCA was a mass membership organization with extensive outreach into communities and campuses across the country. The Community YWCA maintained a network of age and interest groups, including clubs for adolescent girls, for business and professional workers, for industrial workers, and for women outside the labor force. Women flocked into the organization. Some were attracted by the YWCA's liberal views or Christian ethics, while others were drawn primarily by the wide range of social and recreational opportunities it offered. In any case, the Y, along with other organizations, provided an extensive associational network, replete with leadership, potential followers, and financial resources out of which a new movement for social justice could emerge.

Because of its different organizational profile, the AFSC played a different role in the social movement than did the YWCA. Unlike the YWCA, the AFSC was not a membership organization but a small band of dedicated activists, employing only a few hundred people and supplemented by perhaps several thousand additional volunteers. Because of its limited size, it was far less likely to recruit young women to social reform politics than was the Student YWCA. Once committed to at least some aspects of the movement, however, women activists often looked to the AFSC to provide an institutional home and an opportunity to work for the movement. A job with the AFSC often sustained a lifetime commitment to social reform activity.

The AFSC's origins were closely connected to the development of modern Quakerism. The Religious Society of Friends had been rent by a series of schisms in the nineteenth century, and by the end of the century Quakers were divided into evangelical and several nonevangelical groups that had little in common in terms of religious beliefs or practice. The task of rebuilding fell to several Quaker educators; the most prominent of these was Rufus M. Jones. A professor of philosophy at Haverford College, Jones revived interest in Quaker history and tradition, resuscitating in the process the once-central concept of the Inner Light, or "that of God in every man." Blending early Quaker doctrines with mysticism and the new biblical scholarship, Jones revitalized Quakerism in the early twentieth century. Jones also incorporated the Social Gospel into his religious philosophy, harkening back to an older Quaker tradition of social reform, at the same time placing a new emphasis on economic justice and the transformation of social institutions.[17]

Jones and other prominent Quakers established the AFSC in order to provide alternatives for service to men and women who rejected war. In 1917 and 1918, AFSC volunteers rebuilt French villages and hospitals. The AFSC's overseas relief and reconstruction programs continued through the next decade, as volunteers supervised the feeding of one million starving German children at the war's end and delivered relief supplies to victims of famine in the Soviet Union from 1920 to 1925. The AFSC applied the techniques it had learned in relief and reconstruction to the United States after the war, sponsoring self-help building projects and the development of local cooperative industries in the Appalachian coalfields during the 1930s.

The underlying vision for these ventures in relief and reconstruction was the attempt to demonstrate the relevance of pacifism as a way of life. To Rufus Jones, the essence of Quaker social action was to demonstrate "in the midst of the present evil the contagious power of goodness . . . which will tend to reinvigorate the social health." In its social reform activities, the AFSC affirmed the possibility of reconciliation between opposing forces through "respect for the dignity and capacity for growth of the other person, regardless of great differences."[18]

The AFSC was a key organization in the interwar peace movement. It initiated a number of educational programs and provided leadership to the movement in general. In 1926 the AFSC launched a new program, a series of summer peace caravans, led by students who traveled around the country distributing peace literature and speaking to youth, church, and farm groups about the need to eliminate war. The program soon expanded to year-round with staff members visiting colleges to establish study groups and recruit volunteers. In 1930 the AFSC initiated another major program, a series of Institutes of International Relations that brought students and other peace workers together for a few weeks of intensive study of the economic, social, and political underpinnings of war and peace. Faculty included pacifists and nonpacifist experts on international relations. In 1940 alone more than 2,000 people attended these institutes. As a result of the AFSC's many activities in the interwar period, activists in the peace movement were well aware of the organization.[19]

Recruitment into the Social Reform Movement

Individuals are rarely born into a social movement; rather, they become converts through a process of personal change. That process involves a series of steps, the first of which is to transform consciousness:

where before social problems were simply a given of the social environment, they are suddenly perceived in a new light as forms of injustice. Rather than creating a new system of beliefs altogether, the transformative vision of a social movement is often built from a commonly accepted value system, reformulated and with its significance extended by applying the underlying values to new problems. Yet the shift in vision is not enough; beyond that people must develop faith that change is possible, in order to marshall the courage and energy to join a moral crusade to transform social relations.[20]

Christianity provided that common language and set of ideals for most of those who became members of the Christian Left-liberal community. Without exception, the women in this study came from Protestant backgrounds. Among those who were white, almost all came from those religious denominations most deeply affected by the Social Gospel: Methodist, Unitarian, Episcopalian, Congregational, Baptist, Presbyterian, and the Society of Friends. Most of the black women in this study came from the major black denominations, including Baptist, Methodist Episcopal, and Methodist Episcopal Zion. Many mainline white Protestant denominations stressed the importance of world peace during the 1920s, while black churches used Old Testament images of righteousness and justice to denounce racial segregation.[21] This is not to suggest that the individual churches that women activists attended while growing up were necessarily oriented toward the Social Gospel. Most whites and blacks in the South, as well as some from the North, were far more likely to be steeped in a fundamentalist tradition.

The degree to which the churches directly translated Christian values into an injunction for social action varied. The Society of Friends and the Methodist church were most likely to urge members to take the message of the Social Gospel out into the world. Women who came from Quaker families exemplified an unusual approach to religious practice that demanded a high degree of integration of personal moral convictions and behavior in daily life. At the core of the Quaker message was its "peace testimony," which mandated abstention from any support for war, and proposed alternatives for the peaceful resolution of conflicts. Friends had a long history of involvement in social reform efforts, from opposition to slavery to prison reform and women's rights.[22] In the second half of the nineteenth century, under the influence of evangelicism, a number of Friends had turned away from this tradition. But for many Quakers, social action and religious worship were intertwined; as one female activist commented, "I never knew where the Meeting ended and the AFSC began."[23] Thus women raised as Quakers often assumed they would devote some of their energy as adults to the struggle for peace and social justice.

With the exception of Friends, none of the women in this study became converted to social activism through church involvement itself. Rather, Christian values formed a base that was reinterpreted in light of direct exposure to the social movement itself; or, in a few cases, the Christian concern with peace led women to seek active movement organizations to pursue that concern. That exposure occurred most often in the course of college education. In fact, the single characteristic most common to the women in this study, aside from their Protestant heritage, was their access to college education. All received at least some higher education; almost all were college graduates. The chance to attend college distinguished them from the vast majority of women in the United States before World War II. In 1930, for example, only 3.7 percent of all women over twenty-five years of age had completed four years of college.[24] Even more unusual for women of their generation, almost one-half of the women in this study obtained graduate training, usually acquiring master's degrees in social work, religious studies, or in the social sciences or humanities.

It is important to note here that the women active in the progressive organizations that are the focus of this study were, by and large, middle-class in status, although a few were upper-class and a handful had grown up in working-class families but had moved into the middle class as adults. That class status shaped the forms of their activism. A college education often served as a prerequisite to acquiring professional jobs in the YWCA and the AFSC or for achieving leadership as volunteers. Furthermore, married women often had husbands who provided an adequate income, which allowed them some degree of leisure time to devote to volunteer activities. Class privilege also empowered women to feel comfortable when they engaged in lobbying or other forms of influence directed at powerful figures in government or business.

In addition to opening up access to social reform jobs, college provided the perfect setting for recruitment into a social movement. There were several reasons for this. First, those most likely to join a social movement are those with the most time available and with few other major commitments. College students are thus a highly recruitable group, because they are usually young, single, and in transitional roles without major responsibilities for demanding jobs or families. Second, college opened up new intellectual and social vistas to women, many of whom came from the socially and politically homogeneous worlds of small towns. Classes in sociology and political science often discussed such topics as racial prejudice or international relations, and extracurricular activities exposed women to contemporary issues.

Most important, however, was that the social reform movement of the interwar decades was particularly active on college campuses. Liberal denominational schools, especially Quaker and Methodist institutions, purposefully introduced radical social criticism into campus life. On more conservative religious campuses or at secular institutions the Student Christian Movement and young Socialist and Communist groups recruited students. The Student Christian Movement, a powerful force for religious social activism, had emerged in the early 1920s when Sherwood Eddy, noted evangelist for the YMCA, initiated a college speaking program with opposition to war as a major theme.[25]

The student branch of the YWCA was particularly effective in persuading young women to join the social reform movement of the interwar decades. Christianity was a strong force on many college campuses during the 1920s and 1930s, and the YWCA was the largest and most extensive of the Christian organizations active among women students. In 1940, three-quarters of all colleges and universities had chapters of the Student YWCA.[26] Student YWCA leaders, already part of the movement for social justice, attempted to recruit young women into this crusade. Through educational lectures and discussion groups, the Y urged students to relate Christian values to the problems of the poverty and exploitation of the industrial work force, international tensions that might lead to war, and racism. These educational efforts often had a major impact on young women in the Student YWCA, deepening their concern with basic Christian values into a commitment to reforming the social and political world.

Such a transformation is evident in the life of Mary (Polly) Moss Cuthbertson. Polly Moss came from a prominent Georgia family descended from two grandfathers who had fought in the Civil War. She was "programmed into white supremacy" as a child. She attended Georgia State University from 1923 to 1927, where she joined the YWCA and was elected president of her chapter. The Y opened up a new social and political world to her, posing a direct threat to the system of racial subordination that was the linchpin of the southern social order. For Moss, the sudden unmasking of southern racial pretensions occurred in the YWCA. The YWCA Southern Regional Council, composed of student leaders from across the South, was an integrated group. Here for the first time, in council meetings and at conferences, she met black college students and faculty on a basis of social equality. Moss, who was initially shocked to hear black speakers address white audiences, was prodded by the Y's message about the Christian ground of racial equality to confront her racist preconceptions. These crucial experiences wrenched her away from her family upbringing, transforming her vision of her society. Once the myth of racial superiority shattered, the doors were open for southern white women to challenge their society on other grounds.

The next step in Moss's personal transformation was another gift of the YWCA: "a delightful sense of new hope about what was possible."[27] This transcendent sense of hope and inspiration could come from men, or women, or both. In a sexist society, men played the primary leadership roles in the Christian Left, usually holding positions in the ministry. Thus men, more often than women, were the principal speakers on college campuses and at movement conferences, the preeminent writers and intellectuals of the movement. Women looked to them for intellectual leadership.

To Moss and many other women activists of her generation, none could match the intellectual leadership of Reinhold Niebuhr. Moss studied with Niebuhr at Union Theological Seminary, where she earned a Master of Arts degree in 1938. Throughout the interwar period, Niebuhr was the most prominent and eloquent theologian on the Left, and a source of inspiration to many. He was an adviser to the YWCA, and a frequent speaker at Y conferences. Following the First World War, Niebuhr was an ardent pacifist, defender of the rights of labor, and critic of racial injustice. He joined and became active in the Socialist party by the end of the 1920s. Although he cautioned against what he saw as the excessive idealism of the early Social Gospel, arguing that no social order could become an absolute ideal, he nevertheless embraced an essentially Marxist view.

Later, however, Niebuhr became more cautious about hopes for change. In *Moral Man and Immoral Society*, published in 1932, Niebuhr questioned whether society could be transformed completely. Despite his chastened sense of what was possible, he insisted that the crusade for reform was an integral part of Christian faith and life. His growing pessimism was reinforced by the brewing storm on the European continent. By the mid-1930s, he turned against his former allies, denouncing the optimism and sentimental excesses of pacifism and the Social Gospel, with its naive "hope that human history would eventually see the inauguration of a community of love."[28] Despite this change of heart, his continued insistence that Christian ethics be applied to politics was a message that an entire generation of Christian leftists took to heart.

In addition to intellectual inspiration, young women activists gained courage and inspiration from more mature activists, whose examples inspired them to reexamine their lives and embrace the possibility of living out their ideals. In this intergenerational chain of learning, the crucial lesson was the possibility of living a life that transcended personal concerns and that was devoted to a larger vision of social good. To become political activists, women not only had to break away from conventional views of the larger political issues of the day but had to transcend conventional gender roles as well. For many women, the first such model was their mother; although few activists' mothers had been activists themselves, they often displayed that spark of independence, nonconformity, and inner strength that fed their daughters' spirits. During the budding activists' adolescence and young adulthood, older women activists opened larger vistas to view, giving personal examples of vision, faith, and the transformative nature of struggle. For Dorothy Height, Mary McCleod Bethune and Eleanor Roosevelt were such models. For Polly Moss, the Student YWCA secretaries provided an example of courage and vision. Student secretaries of the YWCA, who ran the Student Y programs on campuses, were often influential role models for the young women active in the programs, providing them with fresh intellectual and political insights into the burning issues of the day, as well as demonstrations of the integrity of their own personal lives.

As a result of these influences, Moss became deeply convinced of the necessity for social change. In her adult life, she took her place in the intergenerational chain, changing the lives of younger women through her work with both the YWCA and the AFSC. Garnet Guild, who was active in the college program of the AFSC, recalled that Polly Moss Cuthbertson "was the best person for working with students in situations where racial tensions ran high, employing "her best southern accent" for its full effect.[29] In 1931 she accepted a job as YWCA secretary for her alma mater, Georgia State. A warm, cordial woman with an elaborate and somewhat formal style of speaking, she had a delightful sense of humor and ability to laugh at herself. At Georgia State she brought the YWCA's message to young women, provoking a reaction from none other than Governor Herbert Talmadge. An interracial tea and discussion held in the 1934–1935 academic year that drew together students from black Fort Valley Normal College and white Georgia State College for Women, which Moss remembered as a tame event, erupted into a major incident when it was recounted in an inflammatory newspaper story that suggested that sexual improprieties had occurred. The state legislature attacked Georgia State and granted it funds the following year only on the promise that the president of the college dismiss Moss.[30]

Moss was next assigned to a position as YWCA secretary at Ohio State University. In the course of her work there she met Ken Cuthbertson, a young AFSC staff representative who was traveling to midwestern campuses to recruit students for AFSC programs. They were married in 1939 and moved to Chicago, where Ken had a job with the "Keep America Out of War" campaign. Pacifism became central to both their lives during these years, and they both joined the Religious Society of Friends; Quakers impressed Polly as "central in courage, insight, the ability to work with all kinds of differences, and bring people together."[31] Polly Moss Cuthbertson regretted her inability to have children, but this enabled her to devote all her energy to reform activity. Cuthbertson was involved in both the AFSC and the YWCA and performed a variety of jobs for each. She was on the staff of the College and University Divison for the Middle Atlantic Region of the YWCA from 1942 to 1947 and she served as acting executive director during 1948. She directed the AFSC's Institutional Service Program, a program of volunteer work in mental hospitals during the early 1950s, and directed the AFSC's College Program in the early 1960s.

Making the Connections:
Economic Injustice, War, and Racism

As women were drawn to the movement, they were often pulled in by one particular issue, only later to develop an understanding of the entire range of issues addressed by the movement and the way they interconnected to a larger whole. In the case of both white and black southerners, that issue was often racial injustice. As a poor black woman, Verneta Hill grew up with a burning desire to end racial discrimination, coupled with an acute awareness of poverty. Hill's father was a railroad worker and a Baptist preacher; her mother died shortly after Hill's birth. While still a child, Hill ran away from her home in Little Rock, Arkansas, and drifted to Chicago, where she was taken in by friends. During much of her adolescence she lived at a YWCA residence, where several women at the black branch of the Chicago YWCA looked after her, and she supported herself by working in the kitchen and on the switchboard. Hill quickly became involved in various club activities and a summer camp. A natural leader, she served as president of the Resident's Council at the Y and of her church group class; as she recalled, "Everywhere I went I somehow managed to get in charge."[32]

Hill had a passionate thirst for knowledge, reading everything she could get her hands on. She was also notably outspoken. Once she attended a lecture delivered by a Republican precinct worker who invoked Lincoln's emancipation of the slaves to convince blacks to vote for the Republican party. Hill stood up to refute his argument, citing U.S. history at length to prove that Lincoln had signed the Emancipation Proclamation only to save the Union, not out of genuine concern for the welfare of blacks. The precinct worker was so impressed by her public-speaking ability that he offered her a job on the spot; she declined, as she didn't support the Republican party.

From as early as she could remember, Hill had been a radical. She derived many of her ideas from her reading, her habit of always questioning, and her keen observations of her surroundings. The YWCA influenced her development as well. Participation in a YWCA Industrial Club sharpened her understanding of the problems of working women. She also joined the Urban League Youth Council, a group of high school students who participated in the struggles of depression-era Chicago. As quickly as the sheriff could move the furniture out of homes of evicted families on to the street, Hill and her friends carried it back in. They also converged on restaurants that did not serve black people, entering and waiting to be served.

With the help of a YWCA scholarship fund, Verneta Hill attended college. Declaring herself "a college tramp," she attended a community college, Bryn Mawr, the University of Chicago, and the George Williams School, where she finally graduated in 1940 with a degree in group social work. Although she had hoped to get a job with the YWCA upon graduating, she found a job instead with the YMCA's USO program, where she worked until 1947. In 1947 she returned to the YWCA to work for more than fifteen years as an executive director of several black branches. Through her years with the Y she became knowledgeable about international relations, was introduced to pacifist ideas, and became converted to the cause of world peace.[33]

Northern women had somewhat different initial contacts with the movement than did southerners. Some northern white women, though not all, grew up in families that stressed the importance of racial equality; still, few had much actual contact with blacks. Others remained ignorant of racial issues or concerns until the movement touched their lives. Either racial justice or peace might be the point of entry, with movement experience expanding awareness of the other issues. For Elizabeth (Betty) Mansfield the peace movement was her initial focus. Born in 1915 in Norristown, Pennsylvania, Mansfield came of parents who were white, middle-class, Republican Presbyterians, serious about their religious values. Mansfield's interest in international relations, world peace, and disarmament began during her adolescence. When a high school teacher displayed pictures of the devastated European countryside after World War I, she was shocked and horrified, and she resolved to work for an end to war.

Economic difficulties loomed large in young Betty Mansfield's life. Coming from a family whose comfortable economic status had been shattered by the depression, she was bitter about the economic disparities she saw around her and ripe for a philosophy to explain them. When Mansfield was fifteen a friend introduced her to the Socialist party platform, and she quickly adopted Norman Thomas, the Socialist candidate for president, as her hero.

Thomas had risen to leadership in the Socialist party after World War

I, becoming the presidential candidate on the Socialist ticket for two decades (from 1928 to 1948). Thomas was a liberal Protestant minister who became a pacifist during World War I, and his leadership was symptomatic of a shift within the Socialist party, as its Marxist and working-class elements were increasingly challenged by Social Gospelers and intellectuals. He was an extremely popular speaker on college and university campuses and developed a wide following among middle-class liberals. He rejected some of the key tenets of Marxism, including the belief that the class struggle led inevitably to socialism, favoring instead peaceful democratic means without totally renouncing the use of violence. This populist brand of socialism remained critical of the violence and totalitarianism characteristic of the Soviet Union. In practice, most of Thomas's reform goals were in closer sympathy with progressivism than with classical Marxism. Many of the programs he advocated were later adopted by the New Deal, such as public works projects, a shorter work week, unemployment insurance, agricultural relief, elimination of child labor, old age pensions, and higher taxes for the wealthy. His ultimate goal, however, the nationalization of basic industries, proved far too radical for the U.S. political system to incorporate.[34]

Despite limited family finances, Betty Mansfield scraped together enough scholarship money to attend the University of Pennsylvania during the middle of the depression. There her interest in international relations and peace drew her to the Student YWCA. She became president of her college chapter and arranged for Norman Thomas to speak on her campus. At conferences organized by the Student Christian Movement, Mansfield's commitment to peace was deeply enriched through contact with prominent leaders of the peace movement, including Norman Thomas, A. J. Muste, executive secretary of the Fellowship of Reconciliation, Scott Nearing, a radical Socialist, and Richard Niebuhr. These men provided the inspiration for linking religious values to social action, and "for creating a world of brotherhood that would make peace and justice possible." Peace remained her central concern; as valedictorian in 1937, she spoke about "hearing the cry of war in the world again."[35]

Mansfield had little awareness of the problems of racial discrimination before entering college. YWCA speakers, literature, and discussion groups awakened her to the impact of racial prejudice and discrimination on the lives of racial minorities in the United States, and through the Y she gradually adopted an antiracist stance. She was quick to act on her new beliefs. When a prominent black leader of the Student YWCA was scheduled to appear on campus, Mansfield invited her to speak to her sorority, lecturing her sorority sisters beforehand to behave hospitably. Following graduation, she worked for a year at the Henry Street Settlement House in New York City, where she became close friends with a black woman co-worker. The hostility the two encountered in public sobered her and deepened her awareness of racism.

By this time Mansfield's intellectual and political views had matured into a coherent perspective on social problems. As she recalled more than four decades later, "I was angry that our society was so poorly organized, so dominated by greedy, powerful men who seemed to care nothing for the general welfare of all our people, so crass in the way opportunities for education and self-improvement were limited by money." Her own anger at having to struggle for the chance to attend college was underscored by the knowledge that her father, who had longed to be a scholar, had been unable to attend college because of family financial problems. In addition, Mansfield's religious views infused her opposition to war. For her, war was incapable of achieving good ends, because destruction of human life was inherently evil. In its place she hoped that Gandhian notions of redemptive suffering might achieve what war could not.[36]

It was through her work with the student peace movement that Mansfield first learned about the American Friends Service Committee. When the AFSC's Student Peace Service offered her a job in 1937, she eagerly accepted. Her position took her to college campuses throughout New England, where she spoke with students, worked with peace groups on campus, and organized conferences. In the summer of 1938 she became the leader of a four-woman AFSC Peace Caravan, which settled in the small town of Montrose, Pennsylvania, to educate the people there about peace issues. Thus began Mansfield's fifteen years of work for the AFSC in the field of peace education.

Although the most common route to activism for women was through campus recruitment by the peace movement or the Student Christian Movement, several alternate patterns characterize some women activists. For some, conversion to the movement took place after college during young adulthood, as they sought a meaning for their lives. For a few, religious inspiration was not predominant; rather, a passionate commitment to pacifism or to racial justice, though secular or humanitarian in origin, drew them to the YWCA or the AFSC. These organizations were attractive because they were among the few that sponsored programs directly tackling the problem of racial injustice or promoting pacifist ideas.

The life of Barbara Graves illustrates both of these patterns. Graves grew up in a middle-class Republican family, prominent in their town, firmly opposed to war but not active in any movement. The major turning point in Graves's life came when she was confronted with the horrors of World War II. A competent administrator, Graves had joined the Red Cross in 1942, where she became associate field director in Britain. Her contact with German prisoners of war convinced her that not all Germans were evil. In her work with British pilots on leave, she was struck by the despair and fear that many of the airmen experienced and came to believe that war was a tragic mistake. Her wartime experiences led to a period of introspection during which she searched for a new direction for her life. Returning to the United States at the end of the war, she seriously considered a career in psychiatric social work. She decided to put her professional goals aside, however, when she learned about the work of the AFSC and became convinced that through such work she might "make a difference in the world and in my use of my own life." After immersing herself in Quaker literature, she dedicated her life to eliminating the causes of war. It was the strong pacifism of the AFSC, rather than its religious roots, that most attracted her to the organization. Thus her antiwar conviction developed through personal experience with war, which led her to seek out the AFSC as a channel to express and direct her deeply held beliefs that war was evil.

Graves was hired in 1948 to head the AFSC's central office in German reconstruction efforts. She became "spellbound, caught up in the magic of the AFSC" and underwent "a rather dramatic conversion . . . from one approach to life to another." Here was an organization that actually tried to put the values she cared about into action. The tiny community of relief workers of many different nationalities was bound together by the Quaker belief in the power of love to "cast out fear and anxiety and enmity." Each morning they gathered in silent Quaker worship, which helped inspire their daily work of attempting to communicate hope to war-weary German citizens. Graves was the administrator in charge, but the group tried to minimize distinctions based on rank, working as equal members of a team. To Graves, the dynamic of the community had "a wonderful and contagious kind of joy in it." Graves came to the job fully convinced that the social order had to be restructured, but it was the attempt to actually live out this belief that transformed her life. After a five-year stint in Germany, Graves returned to the United States, where she decided to pursue her social work degree. She continued to work with the AFSC in a number of volunteer capacities, and returned to the staff to direct the Voluntary International Service program from 1962 to 1968, which sponsored community development projects in the third world. She has served as a member of the AFSC staff in a variety of positions ever since.[37]

Each generation of social reformers builds on and modifies the legacy it inherits from the previous generation. For women who joined the YWCA or the AFSC during the interwar decades, the Social Gospel and Christian pacifism were the major wellsprings of moral passion. These women activists supported the specific accomplishments of the New Deal, but their reform goals ranged far beyond those limited incremental reforms to envision a new world based on human love and community, with social justice and equality for all and cooperation between nations. At least one historian has argued that "religious commitment, the lifeblood of the crusade for social justice, finally was drained from the American reform tradition" by World War II.[38] Although the triumph of bureaucratic liberalism of the New Deal might seem to confirm this judgment, this view discounts the continued vitality of religious inspiration in social reform efforts both before and after World War II.

If anything, the tremendous political repression of the late 1940s and early 1950s, which defeated the secular left, forced religious reform currents to carry the burden of the social reform tradition in the immediate post–World War II period. Christian pacifism lost many adherents during World War II, but it weathered the storm with moral fervor intact and at the height of the Cold War continued to voice opposition to U.S. foreign policy. As the civil rights movement unfolded, it emerged in part from religious roots. Although religious inspiration certainly affected smaller numbers of Americans as the twentieth century progressed, it in fact remained a crucial wellspring of social reform activity. Maintaining a religious base, such social reform efforts turned with comfortable reliance to state power to enact piecemeal measures yet never abandoned the utopian vision of the "beloved community" that would eventually flower. Chastened by the horrors of mass war and the Holocaust, leftist religious liberals maintained their faith in the potential for human transformation.

The larger social reform movement that had nurtured women activists in the interwar decades went into decline after World War II, with the Cold War and the accompanying hysteria of McCarthyism raising the stakes for the expression of political dissent. Yet a dedicated band of women social activists in the YWCA and the AFSC, animated by an esprit de corps, a sense of purpose, and a commitment to lifetime work in social reform, entered the postwar world with their vision intact. Their ideas led them to challenge the increasingly conservative tone of U.S. politics. Restive amid the complacency of many white Americans toward racial injustice, alarmed by the belligerence of the country's foreign policy, these women formed part of a dissident political culture, keeping alive a vision of an international and interracial human fellowship that has yet to be realized.

2

Children of One Father: The Development of an Interracial Organization in the YWCA

Alvessie Hackshaw was the first woman to challenge openly the practice of racial segregation in the Oakland, California, YWCA. Hackshaw coupled a personable and charming manner with iron-willed determination in the fight against racial discrimination. She credited her fighting spirit to her grandmother, who had helped raise her. An independent landowner in Texas, her grandmother had been a fearless leader of the black community, providing needed assistance when members of that community fell on hard times or providing support when they ran afoul of white authorities. Hackshaw had first joined the YWCA in San Diego, California, during the 1930s. When she moved to Oakland in 1939, she was hired by the black YWCA branch to run programs for teenage girls. The girls flocked enthusiastically to Hackshaw's leadership, and she found considerable satisfaction in befriending and guiding them. Forty years later she continued to treasure several lifelong friendships with women she had nurtured in their adolescence. Other aspects of the job proved more frustrating, and none more so than dealing with white YWCA colleagues. The YWCA's swimming pool and residence were closed to black members. Angered by that policy, Hackshaw requested that the Y open its facilities to black women and girls, but her demands were ignored, and the Y's executive secretary suggested to her that she might be too "aggressive" to work in the organization.[1]

The situation that Alvessie Hackshaw confronted was typical of most Community YWCAs across the country. The YWCA was unusual among national organizations, for it had included both black and white members since the turn of the century. Segregated facilities and programs were the rule, however, before World War II. This segregation took two quite different structural forms. In communities with large black populations, the YWCA had established black branches, administered by black staff members but ultimately controlled by and dependent on funding from the central white YWCAs. Of 417 community YWCAs, 73 had black branches in 1940. Virtually all branches had inferior buildings and facilities compared to the central white associations. Community associations without branches often had parallel but segregated programs and activities for racial-ethnic girls and women.[2] Facilities were usually segregated; for example, 81 percent of camping programs and fully 99 percent of YWCA residences were segregated before the war.[3]

African-American women were drawn to the YWCA for a variety of reasons. The Y offered an extensive range of social and recreational activities often unmatched by other organizations. In addition, opportunities for women to exercise leadership were more prevalent within the YWCA than in most organizations. Doubly stigmatized by the categories of race and gender, black women were excluded from most predominantly white organizations and usually relegated to subordinate positions in mixed-sex black organizations. In contrast, the YWCA's programs for black women and girls recruited leaders almost exclusively among black women. By the 1930s black women began to attain positions of leadership in racially mixed YWCA groups as well. Odille Sweeney, for example, was elected chair of the National Student Council of the YWCA during the 1930s, a position that served as a springboard for her lifelong career with the Student YWCA. Leadership councils, such as the Council of Industrial Girls, an elected body of national representatives from Industrial Girl Clubs, were often interracial in composition; in 1944 the council included nine white and five black women.[4] The YWCA also attracted black women because it had a more progressive record on interracial relations than most other predominantly white organizations.

Because the YWCA had so much to offer African-American women, approximately 10 percent of the YWCA's members were African Americans at a time when few other organizations crossed racial lines.[5] The Y also conducted programs and established centers in Japanese-American, Chinese-American, Mexican-American, and American Indian communities. This chapter will focus on black-white relationships, for they were the central concern in the YWCA's ongoing discussion of race relations before 1970.

Challenges to Racial Segregation

African-American leaders played a critical role in the development of the YWCA's progressive stance on race relations, both before and after World War II. It was black women who first insisted in the early 1920s that the Student YWCA embrace racial integration, and it was owing to their determined and persistent efforts that they gained the right to control their own programs and activities in Community YWCAs.[6]

Black students and staff maintained constant pressure for racial integration within the Student YWCA from the 1920s onward. In 1923 the Executive Committee of the Student YWCA approved the demands of black student members who called for social equality at Y conferences and meetings, with specific reference to sleeping and eating accommodations. The Student Y proceeded at a slow but steady pace to implement that decision. Summer conferences, held in nine regions of the country, were integrated during the interwar decades, with the exception of those in the South, where the Student YWCA faced tougher obstacles in challenging patterns of racial segregation.

Intercollegial activities became the primary means for creating an interracial student movement in the South, as virtually all college students there attended segregated colleges. The Student Y organized interracial councils in the region, drawing together representatives from both black and white colleges to discuss and formulate an interracial program. In addition, the Y sponsored interracial discussion groups and invited black speakers to white campuses. After 1936, the southern Student Y initiated a series of area leadership conferences, bringing together groups of fifty to one hundred black and white student YWCA leaders in each local area for extensive meetings. Yet the annual regional conferences in the South remained segregated into the mid-1930s, and black students, restive at the failure of the southern Student Y to adopt broader changes, pushed for a greater commitment to racial integration.

In 1936 a third racially integrated regional conference was established to provide an alternative to the two segregated regional conferences; two years later black students disbanded the all-black conference to join the integrated one. Not until 1944 did the southern Student YWCA withdraw its support from all segregated conferences. Yet this date put it on the cutting edge of change in the South, where interracial conferences were virtually unheard of.[7]

The National Board of the YWCA took tentative steps in the direction of building an interracial organization during the 1930s as well. In 1931 the National Board abolished the separate National Council for Colored Work and decided that all professional staff would serve the entire membership, rather than a racially designated portion of it. The National Board and its staff were racially integrated before World War II, as was the staff of the Student YWCA. In 1934 the board decreed that henceforth national meetings would be held only where all racial groups could be served on a basis of social equality, a policy that was strictly enforced and that often required extensive negotiations in order to find suitable accommodations. A somewhat vague but nevertheless significant statement of interracial intent was adopted by the national convention of the YWCA in 1936, pledging to build a fellowship "in which barriers of race, nationality, education, and social status are broken down in the pursuit of a common objective of a better life for all."[8]

Inspired and prodded by the leadership of the National Board, some community YWCAs began to embrace integration in the late 1930s and early 1940s. Alvessie Hackshaw's demands for integration, previously rebuffed, found new favor in 1941, when Helen Grant, who was white, became the executive secretary of the Oakland YWCA. Grant had joined the YWCA's Girl Reserve program at the age of twelve and had remained an active YWCA member throughout high school and college. The Y was largely responsible for shaping her lifelong conviction that all human beings, regardless of race or class, were equal. Grant attended the University of California at Berkeley and, immediately after graduation, accepted her first professional job with the YWCA. In 1941, at the age of thirty-two, she became executive director of the Oakland YWCA, a job she would hold until 1966. An able and competent administrator, admired by black and white staff alike, Grant supported Hackshaw's demand for integration and persuaded the Board of Directors to open the pool and the residence to women and girls of all races in 1941. Two years later the

Younger Girls Department was reorganized on an integrated basis, and Alvessie Hackshaw was selected to direct the teenage program for the Oakland YWCA. Not content to rest on past victories, Hackshaw pushed to integrate the YWCA's summer camp. In 1936 the Oakland, San Francisco, and Berkeley YWCAs had voted to open their camp, Gold Hollow, to all girls, regardless of race, color, or creed, but in practice only one black girl had attended. A number of white mothers were astonished when Hackshaw recruited other black girls to attend the new Camp Timbertall, which opened in 1939. They protested to the Board of Directors, but the board remained firm in its policy, and the mothers acquiesced. In the postwar period, Euro-American, African-American, Japanese-American, Chinese-American, and Mexican-American girls all attended Camp Timbertall.[9]

A similar struggle over racial integration of facilities occurred in Boston. When the Boston YWCA had opened its new building in 1929, the Student YWCA met with the City Y and insisted that all facilities open to women of all races. The City Y concurred, with one major exception: the swimming pool would open to black women who attended swimming events with specific clubs or groups but would be available only for whites during open swim times. In 1937 this policy was reevaluated, and the pool was opened to all women. In 1941 Lucy Miller Mitchell became the first black elected to the Board of Directors of the YWCA. Miller provided able leadership on the Public Affairs Committee for seven years, pushing the Boston Y to implement fully the principle of racial integration. By 1948 the diligent work of black and white women committed to racial equality saw results in a city organization that was racially integrated at all levels.[10]

In St. Louis, Missouri, a metropolitan organization was created in 1936–1937, pulling the black branch and several white branches together under a single interracial board of directors. Winifred Wygal, a staff member for the National Board, was visibly impressed after an extensive visit to St. Louis in 1939, commenting that "the present practices . . . on Negro-white relations seem far in advance of most Associations."[11] By 1943 black women in the St. Louis YWCA participated extensively in the citywide organization, voting on policies concerning the entire association, taking part in nominations and elections for the Board of Directors, serving on all metropolitan committees, and attending annual meetings, at which meals were served to interracial groups on a basis of social equality (that is, with integrated seating arrangements). The YWCA maintained a cafeteria that was open to people of all races. Classes and programs remained largely segregated, held at facilities frequented exclusively by either black or white women, although citywide special events of the Business and Professional, Industrial, and Girl Reserve programs were integrated. Thus the St. Louis YWCA was racially integrated at the leadership level and for special events, but not at the level of daily programs and activities.[12]

Despite some progress the Student YWCA remained impatient with the slow pace of change in community YWCAs. The Student YWCA was far ahead of the community YWCAs in its progress toward racial integration. During certain historical periods students display a devotion to social causes, often as an outgrowth of campus activism. This pattern was evident during the 1930s, when students were active in the peace movement, and during the 1960s, a decade of widespread social protest on the part of the young. The Student Y's radicalism was facilitated by its funding status, for the National Board provided financial support for the Student Y, while community Ys had to raise funds in their local communities and thus were more subject to local community pressures. Community YWCAs were often deeply critical of the Student YWCA for its position on racial equality, fearing that their own programs would be linked in the public mind with those of the more radical students, with a resulting loss of community support.

In an attempt to prod the Community Y to overturn racial segregation, the Student YWCA recommended at the 1936 national convention of the YWCA that the Y examine how segregation and discrimination affected the relationships between white women and women of color in the YWCA and in community life. The convention refused to address the issue, merely referring it to the National Board for study. Students pushed for change again in 1938, but once again the national convention shunted their proposal aside. Not until 1940 did the national convention honor the request, directing the National Board to appoint a commission to investigate the interracial practices of community YWCAs and to make recommendations for change.

Helen Jackson Wilkins (later Claytor) was instrumental in the development of this study. An African-American woman who had graduated with honors from the University of Minnesota in 1928, she had been active in the YWCA Girl Reserves and in the Student Division of the

YWCA during her college years. After college she worked as Girl Reserve secretary for the black branch of the Trenton, New Jersey, YWCA for several years. In 1929 she set a pattern she would follow during her second marriage to Robert Claytor as well: she married Earl Wilkins but chose to complete a second year on the job before moving to Kansas City to join her husband. Her husband was the brother of Roy Wilkins, director of the NAACP from 1955 to 1977, and Helen remained close friends with Roy until his death. In Kansas City she worked in several jobs—as a social worker, a supervisor for the Federal Emergency Relief Association, and then at the black YWCA branch in Kansas City.

After Earl Wilkins's early death, Helen Wilkins acceded to the YWCA's request that she move to New York to work as secretary for interracial education for the National Board. From 1940 to 1943 the study of interracial practices was a central focus for the work. She teamed up with Juliet Bell, who had expertise in conducting social science surveys, and together they designed a questionnaire that was sent to all community YWCAs. They also chose a number of local associations to visit and study in greater depth. The resulting study entailed the most systematic internal examination of the YWCA's practice of racial segregation to date. In 1944 a published report of the study, *Interracial Practices in Community YWCAs*, was disseminated to all YWCAs. The report confirmed that community YWCAs remained largely segregated, and it recommended complete racial integration. The study and its accompanying recommendations were slated for consideration by the 1946 national convention.

The Interracial Charter

When the YWCA met at its first national postwar convention in 1946, black and white activists believed the time was ripe to put the YWCA on record for racial equality. Wilkins's and Bell's recommendations began with the Interracial Charter, which pledged:

Wherever there is injustice on the basis of race, whether in the community, the nation or the world, our protest must be clear and our labor for its removal, vigorous and steady. And what we urge on others we are constrained to practice ourselves. We shall be alert to opportunities to demonstrate the richness of life inherent in an organization unhampered by artificial barriers, in which all members have full status and all persons equal honor and respect as the children of one Father.[13]

The report spelled out in great detail procedures to be followed in order to achieve racial integration throughout the organization, from the Board of Directors to staff, committees, volunteers, and program activities in each association. At the program level, Community YWCAs in strictly segregated communities were advised to plan interclub and intergroup activities to facilitate communication between segregated groups. In those communities where segregation was less extensive, the study urged community associations to launch integrated programs immediately. Associations with black branches were exhorted to reorganize these branches on an integrated basis. The study counseled community YWCAs to move as quickly as possible to open all facilities, including residences, cafeterias, camps, and health education departments to all participants.[14]

YWCA leaders understood that they had to prepare the groundwork carefully in order to secure endorsement of integration by the national convention. Resistance centered primarily in the South, the location of more than one hundred YWCAs. White women from many of these Ys were steeped in racist traditions and feared that the move toward integration would jeopardize their funding sources and alienate their white constituents. The South was not solid in its opposition, however. Although virtually all the initial opposition to integration came from the South, some southern YWCAs strongly endorsed that goal. To persuade reluctant and resistant community YWCAs required the cooperation and participation of thousands of women across the country. Able leadership provided by the National Board greatly facilitated that process.

In the struggle for racial integration, Dorothy Height was one of the most influential members of the National Board staff. When she accepted employment with the National Board in 1944, her first assignment was to visit community YWCAs to facilitate discussion of the study of interracial practices. Height was ideally suited to the task. Dignified, gracious, and thoughtful, she persistently spurred white women to reexamine ideas based on racial stereotypes and exhorted them to demonstrate their beliefs in the Christian ideal of equality. The job was not without its emotional costs; some groups refused to meet with Height because she was black, and she was subjected to both racial insults and more subtle racist attitudes. Her belief that she was an agent of social change enabled her to insulate herself to some degree from taking the slights personally.[15] For two years Height traveled to all parts of the country to persuade community YWCAs that the time for racial integration was at hand.

When the 1946 convention finally opened, the situation was tense. At the top of the agenda was the Interracial Charter. The momentous nature of the step to be taken was clear to all: approval of the charter and its accompanying recommendations would commit the full energies of the YWCA to create an interracial fellowship. On the convention floor some white delegates expressed reservations about the Interracial Charter. One woman from Harrisburg, Pennsylvania, stated her intention to vote for the recommendations but cautioned, "I don't know how I am going to carry them out," citing segregation as the rule in her community. A number of white women from southern associations expressed alarm at the implications of racial integration for their community YWCAs, fearing the loss of funds and support from the white community.

Black delegates demanded the end of second-class status within the YWCA, but not without conceding that integration might entail some losses as well. Black delegates questioned whether a half-hearted attempt to integrate would represent true progress for them. Mrs. C. D. Atkins, a delegate from Charlotte, North Carolina, warned, "Possibly, the minority group doubts the sincerity of the desire of the majority group for our full integration. There is a difference between 'integration' and 'representation'; in many instances, we merely sit on boards with no chance for leadership in that mixed group." Nor was this an isolated view; some black staff members of the National Board had also questioned whether a policy of racial inclusiveness, if not fully implemented, would bring major gains for them. Furthermore they resented that integration was always discussed in terms of the needs, desires, and readiness of the white members, with little attention to those of black women.[16]

Despite the reservations held by some delegates, appeals to the Christian and democratic purpose of the YWCA carried the day. Mary Shotwell Ingraham, president of the YWCA, argued persuasively that the Y had a Christian commitment to equality. In the days preceding the vote she met continually with some southern associations that were threatening to leave. Benjamin Mays, president of Morehouse College and vice-president of the Federal Council of Churches of Christ in America, entered an eloquent appeal in his address to the YWCA convention. Maintaining that those who defended the status quo forever argued that "the time is not ripe to do right," he insisted that "No one is free who must debate the question, What will happen to my organization if I live democracy and practice Christianity? . . . The future of democracy in the United States is with those who take the high road . . . the crusaders for social justice."[17] Not all the women present imagined that they were such crusaders, but they found it difficult to ignore the moral force of his message.

When President Ingraham finally called for a vote, she asked the convention delegates whether, if adopted, the Interracial Charter would be easy to implement. A resounding no arose from the audience. She then asked the delegates to raise their convention books in the air to signify aye or nay. It was an exhilarating moment when delegates realized that not a single woman had raised her book to vote no. A few southern white delegates left early to avoid the vote, and a few other associations withdrew shortly afterward. The YWCA nevertheless had pledged itself to full integration of its own organization. Many people saw it as a great victory; the YWCA had taken a major step forward in its commitment to an interracial society.[18]

Rocky Path toward Integration

As U.S. society slowly emerged from decades of a rigid castelike system of racial segregation, women from white and racial ethnic backgrounds confronted each other across a chasm of racial separation, ignorance, and hostility. It was little wonder that the first attempts at interracial dialogue within the YWCA proved tense and unnatural. Many white women returned from the 1946 convention fired with enthusiasm for integrating their community YWCAs. Inevitably, however, awkwardness plagued their first efforts at interracial contact. Although leaders of the Student YWCA and the staff of the National Board had extensive interracial experience, many women in local community YWCAs had not. Some whites smarted from previous encounters with black women who had criticized them for unwitting displays of racial prejudice. For their part, black women suspected that white women were insincere in their overtures and had little faith in the proffered openness. When an open-door policy was adopted, black participation was often minimal. One black leader commented, "You have no idea what you have to be continually doing to keep up the morale of Negro girls so that they can take the kind of things they have to meet. . . . It is not any fun to be in a mixed group; some girls do it because they think it is important, but it takes courage."[19]

During the decade and a half following the passage of the Interracial Charter, black women shouldered the burden of educating their white colleagues about racism. It was not always a pleasant task, but one under-taken out of deep conviction of its necessity. Whereas the recollections of white women in the Y convey a sense of excitement about exploring new territory through interracial contacts, black women more often viewed working with white women cautiously, as an inevitable but not entirely enjoyable part of eradicating the practice of racial segregation. In the process they were constantly affronted by the racial prejudices of white women in both direct and indirect ways. Black women resented their token status; like all tokens, they felt they had to be exceptional to gain positions that white women of only average accomplishment could easily attain.[20] Yet those who remained did so because the Y was one of the few predominantly white organizations committed to racial integration, and black women believed that racial integration was the necessary next step in the transformation of U.S. racial relationships.

The process of education percolated through all levels of the organiza-tion. On the National Board, Dorothy Height proved tremendously influential in raising the consciousness of white women. She was both "brilliant, and a wonderful teacher," recalled an influential white mem-ber of the board. Jewel Graham, prominent black leader of the YWCA in the 1970s and 1980s, described Height as someone with "presence"; her powers of analysis were exceptional, and she was able to "get to the core of issues," stating things with great clarity. Her skills enabled her to exert tremendous leadership within the YWCA. Height had a quick response ready when white board members complained that she always brought up the issue of racial justice. "That's my job," she would reply. Height sensed that many of her white colleagues were preoccupied with the question of whether they were personally free of prejudice. From

Height's perspective these women were using relationships with people of color "to test themselves, rather than to be sensitive to the needs of others." She exhorted them to take a broader view, focusing on the organizational aspects of racism and pointing out that in the YWCA this often took the form of the white domination of leadership positions. Insisting that white women could not successfully represent the interests of black women, and that if white women continued to predominate the YWCA would reflect only the priorities and goals of whites, she stressed the need for white and black women to share leadership roles.[21]

Black women often served as watchdogs for racism within the Y at the local level as well. To Verneta Hill the fight against racial prejudice was a central theme of her work in the YWCA. As executive director of several black branches in succession, she consistently pushed to integrate the Community YWCA, starting with the Board of Directors, then committees, and on through other aspects of the program. In every encounter she fought racist preconceptions. When she assumed the job of executive director of the black branch in Omaha, Nebraska, during the late 1940s, the budgeting process became the arena for combating racist stereotypes. Hill discovered that the black branch had been consistently underfunded and, as a consequence, was unable to operate within its budget. Hill's college preparation in group social work had given her especially strong training in budgeting, finance, and personnel matters. As the time to prepare the budget for the following year approached, the white finance director informed Hill that she would write it. Hill protested, arguing that she was perfectly capable of preparing her own budget and that, furthermore, she wanted to present it herself to the Council of Social Agencies, the Y's funding source. Her white colleagues were aghast; the budget for the black branch had always been presented by a white woman. The executive director, an ally of Hill's, intervened, suggesting that Hill be given the chance.

Appearing before a group of all white men, Hill carefully went through her budget, line by line, arguing that the black branch needed more money. Hill met with some skepticism at first. One of the men commented that the black branch had managed to get by on very little money in the past. "Yes, gentlemen," Hill replied, "every year you compliment the branch on getting along on so little, and at the end of every year you give them hell for being overspent. Now I have this theory that I have two feet and I need two shoes. Don't give me one shoe when I need two shoes." After guaranteeing that she would not overrun the budget she had presented, Hill received the allocation she had requested.[22]

Hill later confronted a much more complex and difficult struggle, "the hardest fight of my life," when the National Board assigned her to the post of executive director of a black branch in New Orleans, where she worked from 1952 to 1956. She was unfamiliar with the South and found the New Orleans black community riddled with caste and class distinctions, particularly between creoles and blacks. The YWCA branch conducted virtually no program activities but operated instead as a glorified social club for creole women, in Hill's eyes. At first the creoles rejected Hill because she was black. Confronting the creole leadership head-on, Hill began to bring more black women onto the board, but creole women resisted her leadership and tried to maintain control. Hill countered by arguing that she had a mandate from the National Board to implement YWCA policies, a claim that they brushed aside. Eventually, however, her persistence paid off, as she gradually won the trust of the women she worked with and was able to facilitate some changes. Most important to her, perhaps, was her ability to help the creole women overcome their fear of taking any action without prior approval by whites in town. Tentative steps toward integration were made, particularly before 1954. In response to the Supreme Court's decision in *Brown v. Board of Education*, however, new segregationist legislation enacted by the state of Louisiana made progress more difficult. Exhausted by the fight, despite the victories she had won, Hill left New Orleans in 1956.

As white women went through the process of unlearning racism, they responded in a variety of ways. Many reacted by feeling hurt or insulted by black women who pointed out their racism. But there were others, those most committed to creating an interracial organization, who were grateful for what they learned. Helen Grant credited her Y experience with enabling her to develop a deeper comprehension of what it might feel like to be born black in the United States. One notable moment of insight occurred when the Supreme Court announced its long-awaited decision in *Brown v. Board of Education*, declaring segregation in public schools unconstitutional. Ecstatic at the news, Grant mentioned to a black co-worker how wonderful it seemed. Years later she could still recall the woman's response: "Yes, but sometimes we get weary of thinking something is wonderful that other people take for granted."[23]

A number of white women within the YWCA were passionately committed to the goal of racial integration. Often a sense of comradeship developed between black and white women who accepted each other as allies in the struggle against racial injustice, and close friendships developed, linking black and white women into networks that endured for a lifetime. Many of these white women traced their convictions to their formative years in the Student YWCA. For them the transition to working in the more conservative Community YWCA could prove somewhat frustrating. Augusta Roberts is a case in point. Raised in a middle-class white family in Georgia, she had attended Agnes Scott College from 1925 to 1929. The Student YWCA transformed her world, introducing her to interracial experience and the ideal of racial equality. Slowly she took more and more courageous steps in breaking the color line, first attending interracial discussions, then conferences that included black speakers, and finally serving as a white "fraternal" delegate to a black conference. Racial justice was the burning issue in her developing worldview: economic justice and world peace had their place, but no issue had the compelling urgency of the struggle to end racial discrimination. The YWCA became the center of a lifelong career. She directed the Student YWCA at the University of Kentucky from 1931 to 1936 and at the University of Texas from 1936 to 1939 and then became a member of the National Field Staff of the Student YWCA for the Southern Region from 1939 to 1943.

In 1944 Roberts moved from the Student Y to a series of jobs with community YWCAs. She first served as associate executive in Newport News, Virginia, for two years, where she worked hard on the "Stay-at-Home Convention" (scheduled in 1944 when wartime travel restrictions prevented a national convention), which focused on a discussion of the Interracial Charter. After a three-year stint with the Student Y in the Philippines, she returned to Newport News to assume the post of executive director from 1949 to 1952. She found the resistance to integration from this cautious community YWCA frustrating. She next was appointed executive director of the Alexandria, Virginia, YWCA, where she stayed until 1956. In Alexandria, Roberts met with more success as she and several colleagues pushed to integrate the staff and the board. During her four years there she witnessed the creation of a united interracial board, an integrated adult program, integrated teenage leadership groups, and the transformation of the black branch into a regional

center open to all. The Alexandria Y continued to be partially segregated, as many local clubs continued to meet on a segregated basis, but no other community group in Alexandria at the time had achieved that degree of integration.[24]

As community YWCAs proceeded haltingly toward racial integration, black women endured some losses that white women had failed to calculate. Communities with black branches faced an extremely complex set of problems in making the transition to an integrated program. Black branches were vital community centers, the focus of dense social networks, and the setting for a wide range of interesting activities and programs. Despite the stigma of segregation, in many ways black branches served black communities far better than did central associations. Approximately 70 percent of the black membership of the YWCA participated in branches rather than in central YWCAs, and branches were able to attract a higher percentage of the black population than did single Associations. Furthermore, the branch structure facilitated the creation of challenging professional opportunities for black women, as most black YWCA staff were employed by the branches.[25] To close racial branches, or to convert them into geographical branches with an interracial membership, as a number of large city associations proceeded to do after 1946, thus threatened the position of black women. A number of black women left the Y rather than face professional demotions, and black women's participation declined as facilities and programs moved to more distant locations or became dominated by white women.[26]

The stormy transition that took place in Oakland, California, illustrates these difficulties. In 1946 well-meaning white women returned from the national convention determined to end the practice of segregation by converting the Linden Street Branch into a geographical, rather than a racial, branch. Executive Secretary Helen Grant and other white leaders attempted to discuss this move with leaders of the black community, but their efforts at communication fell short of satisfying many of the black women involved. A number of those women felt that the Linden Street Branch had been summarily taken away from them when it was converted to a geographical branch. In short order the executive secretary of the branch resigned, attendance at Y functions dropped sharply, and much of the program fell apart. Inspired by the Interracial

Charter, white women had inadvertently offended much of the black membership of the YWCA.[27]

In a world where racial distinctions cast a long shadow across virtually all human relationships, certain losses accompanied the movement from racial segregation to integration. This is not to say that black women in the Y sought to preserve segregation; the badge of inferiority that accompanied it necessitated its removal. But until the larger world would no longer view racial differences as significant, the closing of black community centers served to sunder a social fabric within the Y that was not necessarily replaced by new cloth.

Despite the rocky nature of the path toward integration, it was clear that community YWCAs had achieved a significant degree of racial integration by the mid-1950s. A 1955 survey of YWCA associations indicated substantial progress nationwide. Of the 266 community associations that responded, approximately 70 percent included 500 or more members from minority racial backgrounds. Forty percent of those associations were integrated in all of the five areas studied: volunteer leadership, staff, special activities such as camping and conferences, institutional facilities (residences, food service, swimming pool), and regular program groups; another 30 percent were integrated in four of these areas. Thus 71 percent of the associations were integrated in four or five areas, while 16 percent were integrated in only three areas and 13 percent in only one or two areas.[28] At the national level, as well, integration had proceeded apace: by 1958 10 percent of professional staff of the National Board was from racial-ethnic groups, compared to only 4 percent in 1946.[29] Differences between the South and other regions continued to be marked. In the Southern Region only 64 percent of the associations reported racial integration in at least three areas, compared to 90 percent in the other regions. Although the pattern of segregation prevailed in most southern YWCAs, the YWCA was far more likely to pursue racial integration than were other community agencies in the south; in Greensboro, North Carolina, for example, the Y opened its pool to blacks during 1952–1953, when the practice was virtually unheard of in the South.[30]

The most aggressive racial activists, however, were far from satisfied. Mary Shotwell Ingraham, who had shepherded the Interracial Charter through the 1946 convention, addressed the 1961 national convention with the warning that "progress toward including Negro women and girls in the mainstream of Association life . . . is very uneven in depth, breadth, and speed."[31] Many black branches continued to exist into the 1960s, partly a reflection of segregated housing patterns that made it difficult to create truly integrated programs. And although programs might be nominally interracial, truly comfortable interracial relationships remained an elusive goal in many communities, hardly surprising in a society whose history had been so deeply marred by racism.

Antiracist Education and Interracial Experience within the YWCA

As the stories of Verneta Hill and Augusta Roberts suggest, the YWCA was home for a dedicated band of women activists profoundly committed to racial justice. One focus for their efforts was educating the young women in the organization about racism. Those committed to antiracist education were able to employ the organizational resources of the YWCA in that process through positions of leadership within the Student YWCA, the staff of the National Board, and some community YWCAs scattered across the country. Their aim was to convert others to the cause, in order to pass the torch of activism on to a future generation.

Given the large size of the YWCA the potential for recruiting such converts seemed vast. In 1946 the YWCA community associations alone had a membership of 454,935 members. During the 1940s and 1950s the YWCA claimed to represent three million women and girls, a figure that included the combined totals of members and participants. Members were those who had signed the religious pledge of the YWCA and who presumably were active in the organization, while participants included all those who participated in YWCA activities.[32] Because of its broad outreach the YWCA included in its ranks many who had little understanding of U.S. racial problems, which provided Y activists an opportunity to educate politically unsophisticated women about ideals of racial equality. Y leaders presumed that educational strategies would be particularly effective with their youthful constituency, 75 percent of whom were under the age of twenty-five.

The YWCA's efforts to educate women and girls about racism were grounded in a Social Gospel interpretation of the religious and ethical implications of Christianity. Religious instruction in the Y emphasized the themes of social responsibility and love for all humankind. In addition to religious motivation, the Y attempted to expose women and girls to information about the subordinate status of racial minority groups in U.S. society through an examination of economic, political, and social forms of racial discrimination. Literature, speakers, educational forums, discussion groups, and conferences continually hammered home these themes. The Y thus clarified the oppressive nature of racial segregation and discrimination, producing the first glimmerings of antiracist consciousness for many young white women.[33]

The central emotional and intellectual experience in the Y's attempt to create antiracist consciousness was its conference program, which proved far more effective than didactic methods alone in shattering the myths of racial superiority imbued in most white women. The war years had provided the final blow to segregated conferences; after World War II all regional YWCA conferences, including those in the South, were integrated.[34] In areas of the country where demographic patterns produced a racially mixed population base, participation by black women and women from other racial-ethnic groups was not merely token but included significant numbers. In the Student YWCA's Southwest Region, for example, between one-third and one-half of the participants in student conferences during the mid-1950s were black. Conferences offered a chance to escape the routine of daily life and promoted social intimacy and thus were more conducive to comfortable interracial contacts than community-based events. Again and again white women reported that YWCA conferences provided their first genuine interracial experience.[35]

In a typical conference experience one young white woman reported, "I had never eaten previously at a table with a Negro—I had never gone swimming with a Negro, I had never talked to a Negro girl about dating and marriage. Before long I realized that in hundreds of little ways we felt the same whether our skin was dark or light. For the first time in my life I was talking to and working with Negro women who had as good and in many cases a better educational background than I. I had to *admit* to myself that they knew what they were talking about—that as a beginner there was much I could learn from them, and I had to accept them on my own level."[36]

Yet another young woman wrote home from a YWCA conference in Hendersonville, North Carolina, in 1944, "The only difference between us at Conference was the color of our skins and no one noticed that—we were truly all God's children and it was a grand experience. There were three Dorothys at Conference—I was the only white one and the other two put me in the shade with their talents. One of them was our leader, Dorothy Height, the other, our pianist, Dorothy Turner. I spent quite a lot of time with both of them—well spent too." For whites to be startled when they discovered that a black woman could be their social and intellectual peer or superior reveals the enormous depth of condescension for blacks that well-meaning whites could hold. Yet it is difficult to overstate the centrality of such meetings based on social equality in transforming such attitudes and in motivating young white women to challenge patterns of racial subordination. The young white Dorothy cited above returned to her community determined to change the pattern of segregation in her YWCA club program.[37]

Conferences served to break down racial stereotypes among young black women as well, as the words of one young adolescent suggest: "I learned to mix with white girls and discovered all whites are not prejudiced." Nor were these isolated voices. A study of girls who attended Y-Teen summer conferences in the Southern Region from 1958 to 1962 found that 78 percent of those attending interracial conferences responded that the most important part of their conference experience related to "race relations." Furthermore, Y records are replete with hundreds of personal testimonials to the power of personal contacts in breaking down racial preconceptions and promoting a sense of racial equality. Though such transformations of racial consciousness may have been most dramatic in the South, where the barriers of segregation were most firmly entrenched, they were powerful for young women from other parts of the country as well, most of whom had little opportunity to associate with women of different racial backgrounds in a relaxed setting.[38] As women of different racial groups learned to work and socialize together within the YWCA, they slowly built bridges of understanding across the gulf created by race.

The YWCA's emphasis on the moral values central to Christianity and democracy, and the optimistic assessment of the potential for individual change, were consonant with the predominant liberal paradigm of race relations during these years. Perhaps nothing better epitomized that approach than Gunnar Myrdal's class study, *An American Dilemma.* Published in 1944, Myrdal's work was the central text for those concerned with U.S. race relations in the immediate postwar period. Myrdal posited that race relations posed a dilemma for Americans caught between the creed of democracy and equality, on the one hand, and racist practices in the United States on the other. To Myrdal the subordinate status of black Americans was essentially a moral problem that had to be solved at the moral level, through a process of education and persuasion. Critics have argued that Myrdal's analysis was fundamentally inadequate to U.S. racial problems, pointing out that he underestimated the economic and structural factors underlying the country's racism, as well as the strength of the racist convictions of those most deeply committed to segregation as a way of life.[39]

Yet within the YWCA itself the combination of moral exhortation, information, and interracial experience was a potent mixture that sparked genuine change among many of its participants. That success can be attributed to several factors. First, the YWCA was not working with all elements of the population but was concentrating on the young, on women, and on those drawn to the Y's generally liberal image. Furthermore, bringing together people from similar social class backgrounds was critical to the success of interracial contacts. Divided as it was into student, industrial, and business and professional groups, the Y's program facilitated the process through which women of different races could find common ground in mutual interests. Within the YWCA commonalities of both class and religion encouraged a common conversation about racial divisions. Finally, the moral and educational approach may have been more effective in dealing with young women than with men, because women tended to be more deeply affected by religious values.

The Y's efforts at antiracist education had a profound impact especially on the young, who were ripe for the message. In a survey of members of the Girl Reserves (the YWCA's program for adolescents) in the early 1940s, girls were asked, "What do we most need to work on if we are to make the U.S. truly more democratic?" From all parts of the country they responded with answers such as "Securing equality of opportunity for Negroes," or "Breaking down the barriers of race."[40] Building on common religious values, the Y created changes in the hearts and minds of young women. In settings where women from different racial origins could eat, learn, play, and talk together, a sense of "fellowship" (the YWCA's term) unfolded, a rare experience in life in the United States.

Leaders of the YWCA pressed to make that sense of fellowship relevant to the larger society as well. In order to do so, YWCA staff experimented with informal direct actions that challenged racial segregation during the decade and a half following World War II. Segregation impinged directly on the activities of YWCA staff, particularly as they traveled frequently in integrated groups to attend conferences. These women devised a number of strategies to confront or bypass segregated establishments. When staff members wanted to go out to eat, they often asked one another, "Well, are we going out tonight to fight the race battle, or are we just going out to eat?" In the latter case they would go to a place where they could be assured that a racially mixed group would be served. If they felt more determined, however, they dreamed up new strategies to convince personnel in segregated restaurants to serve them.

Verneta Hill recalled one such incident that occurred when she and a white colleague entered a restaurant on a cross-country trip. After sitting for some time while the waitress ignored them, Hill's white friend requested that the waitress serve them. When the waitress replied that she wasn't allowed to serve "colored people," Hill's companion asked to see the manager. Informed that he was not there, she inquired who was in charge. "I am," the waitress admitted. "Well, if it was up to you, what would you do?" "Well, I guess I'd go ahead and serve everybody," the woman replied. "Well, then, why don't you just go ahead and serve us," the YWCA staff member suggested, which the waitress proceeded to do. Other types of public accommodations also came in for public pressure. For example, during the 1950s a small group of women from the Oakland YWCA decided to test the California civil rights law, sending integrated groups to bowling alleys to demand the right to bowl together. These actions, which presaged the more systematic endeavors of the civil rights movement, displayed the determination of committed Y members to break down racial barriers.[41]

Political Action for Civil Rights

Although they believed that interracial experience and antiracist education were critically important, women in the YWCA had no illusions about the limitations of education and moral influence in bringing about racial change. Significant as those strategies were within the Y itself, Y leaders clearly understood the need to change structural factors underlying the racist nature of society. In order to meet this need, the Y supported a major legislative agenda designed to promote the goal of racial equality.

The Public Affairs Committee of the National Board (PAC) was charged with the responsibility of formulating that agenda. At each national convention, the PAC presented a series of resolutions that endorsed specific proposals for legislation in Congress. If the national convention approved the resolutions, they became the basis for the work of both the national and local Public Affairs Committees. In the interim between national conventions, the PAC suggested specific actions to the National Board, following the general guidelines established by the Public Affairs Program. In order to implement its legislative agenda, the PAC sent representatives to Washington to lobby and present testimony; it also worked closely with other liberal organizations in support of particular legislation. Furthermore, it drew on a vast network of women, providing information packets to members about civil rights legislation and urging members to write to legislators. In an era of extensive women's volunteer activity, many Y members had the luxury of time that allowed them to respond quickly to such calls. As a result the Y was able to mobilize considerable pressure for the passage of progressive legislation.

The PAC represented an opportunity for women concerned about racial equality to work to promote that goal. Mildred Persinger took advantage of that opportunity, fashioning a career out of volunteer work with the PAC. A liberal white southerner, Persinger arrived in New York City in 1942 from Atlanta, where she had been teaching courses on race relations at Auburn University. She thought of herself as a "social change" person, with racial justice her central focus. At the urging of a friend she joined the Race Relations Committee of the National Board's PAC, where her first task was a study of black peonage in the Florida turpentine camps. In her mid-twenties, Persinger was both younger and more secular in orientation than most of her colleagues. In fact, she represented a broader trend within the Y, for younger members who joined the YWCA after World War II were less likely to be profoundly affected by the Social Gospel. Yet Persinger had enormous admiration for the older women on the board, and from them she absorbed some of the flavor of the Social Gospel, particularly the conviction that it was the mandate of Christianity to work for social justice. She felt that the YWCA gave her "a marvelous opportunity to see that these issues (related to social justice) were given attention" by bringing the weight of a large organization to bear in Washington.

Persinger's position as a volunteer on the National Board developed into a full-time career. She was elected to a full term on the PAC in 1944. During the late 1940s she pulled back from active work while her children were born, but she rejoined the national board in 1952 and became chair of the Public Affairs Committee in 1958, a position she held until 1970. Her job involved preparing statements, delivering testimony, lobbying members of Congress, and writing educational material in support of civil rights and other legislation. By the 1960s her expertise was widely sought, as evidenced by the number of commissions and conferences of which she was a member: President Kennedy's conference of women leaders on civil rights legislation, the President's Commission on the Status of Women, the President's Commission for the United Nations in 1970, and the World Disarmament Conference in 1970, where she represented the World YWCA.[42]

From the 1930s to the 1960s, the YWCA lobbied for and educated its members about progressive civil rights legislation and administrative actions. The Y had taken its first stand on an issue related to racial equality in 1932, when the national convention of the YWCA endorsed a federal antilynching bill, the top priority for those battling racial injustice during the interwar decades. Four years later, the national convention resolved "to initiate and support efforts to assure Negroes an equitable share in economic opportunities," and in 1940 the YWCA advocated an end to the poll tax.[43]

The war years quickened the pace of the YWCA's efforts to secure racial equality, and the organization redoubled its efforts to educate the public about civil rights. After President Franklin Roosevelt created the Fair Employment Practices Commission, the Y served as a watchdog in local communities to press for enforcement, reporting specific instances of discrimination and putting pressure on government officials responsible for implementing the order. The Y endorsed the effort to establish the FEPC on a permanent basis and protested segregation and discrimination in the armed services and in interstate travel.

Although much of the Y's emphasis on racial justice focused on African Americans, other racial and religious minorities received attention as well. The crisis of wartime events elevated two such concerns to major importance—the situation of Jews in Europe and of Japanese Americans in the United States. When Hitler's persecution of Jews intensified in 1938, YWCA statements expressed dismay and horror about such treatment, and the National Board strongly urged the government to ease immigration restrictions in order to allow all Jewish refugees to enter the United States.[44]

The YWCA also responded with alarm when President Roosevelt issued the evacuation order that forced all Japanese Americans to leave the West Coast in February 1942. The National Board issued a strong condemnation of this action, questioning the constitutionality of forced detention of citizens "on the basis of racial origin alone, without any pretense of judicial hearings." The Y offered support to Japanese Americans, establishing programs in relocation camps in an attempt to maintain the morale of internees, setting up a reception center in Denver to help those relocated from the West Coast with employment, housing, and recreation needs, and cooperating with the AFSC and other organizations in the Japanese Student Relocation Program, a program designed to find college placements for Japanese-American students who were evacuated from the West Coast.[45]

After the war the Y continued to focus on support for the trio of proposals that constituted the highest priority of the major civil rights groups for some years—antilynching legislation, abolition of the poll tax, and creation of a permanent FEPC. In addition, the Public Affairs program endorsed the more comprehensive goals of securing constitutional rights and providing equal economic opportunities for all racial minorities. At its 1949 national convention the YWCA adopted virtually all of the recommendations of Truman's President's Commission on Civil Rights.[46]

The YWCA had eagerly anticipated the Supreme Court's decision in *Brown v. Board of Education* that declared school segregation unconstitutional. After the Supreme Court's announcement, a number of community YWCAs in the South held open community meetings to discuss how to facilitate implementation of the order. In one community women went from door to door to persuade residents to support the decision. The Student YWCA wrote to all southern governors to urge them to comply with the *Brown* decision by opening all college and university campuses to all racial groups. Money was allocated to the College and University Division in order to strengthen student and faculty leadership to work more effectively for integration on college campuses.[47]

As southern resistance to school desegregation escalated in the Deep South, the YWCA recognized that voluntary compliance alone would not suffice. Turning to the power of the federal government, the Y endorsed the Douglas-Celler bills in Congress, which offered technical assistance to state and local governments working toward compliance and empowered the attorney general to institute civil proceedings in behalf of those deprived of their rights.[48] Thus, from World War II on, the YWCA endorsed virtually every item on the agenda of the major civil rights organizations.

The Context of Racial Activism in the Postwar World

As this chapter illustrates, the YWCA put itself on the line in the struggle for racial justice far more than did most predominantly white organizations. A complex set of factors interacted to create that progressive agenda within the YWCA in the postwar world: the influence of the Social Gospel and of radical ideas of social and political transformation; the common religious purpose within the organization; the influence of the Student YWCA, which pushed for racial equality within the larger adult organization; and the leadership of black women. To understand the significance of these factors, it is important to place the YWCA in the larger organizational context of the postwar world.

Those on the left end of the political spectrum had a far more progressive stance on racial justice than those of other political persuasions. The organizations that offered the most consistent support for civil rights legislation and activities in the postwar world included secular organizations heavily influenced by left or liberal ideas, such as progressive labor unions or Americans for Democratic Action, and liberal religious groups, such as the Federal Council of Churches and the Anti-Defamation League of B'nai B'rith. Thus it is not surprising that when the National Council of Negro Women in 1944 sought support from white women's organizations in the Co-ordinating Committee for Building Better Race Relations, it was the National Council of Jewish

Women, the National Council of Catholic Women (NCCW), the YWCA, and the National Women's Trade Union League (NWTUL), that heeded the call.[49]

In contrast to religiously inspired women's groups, other generally liberal white women's organizations such as the American Association of University Women (AAUW) and the Business and Professional Women's Clubs (BPW) ignored racial issues. The AAUW, for example, endorsed many items on the liberal agenda in the immediate postwar era, such as federal housing programs, support for the United Nations, expanded social security benefits, and consumer legislation, but its stand on racial justice was weak. Despite the passage of a mild resolution endorsing the elimination of discrimination against minority groups at its 1947 national convention, the AAUW never made civil rights a major priority. Some branches sponsored study groups on race relations in the 1940s and 1950s, but the national organization carefully avoided taking a stand. A debate over proposed legislation to establish a permanent Fair Employment Practices Commission from 1946 to 1948 was resolved by the AAUW's refusing to support the proposal. It is striking that no endorsement of the Supreme Court's 1954 decision on school integration was forthcoming from an organization whose primary interest was education.[50]

Religious ideals were a critical force in persuading moderates to support the struggle for racial justice within the YWCA. The official statement of purpose of the YWCA, pledging all members "to build a fellowship of women and girls devoted to the task of realizing in our common life those ideals of personal and social living to which we are committed by our faith as Christians" and to "share his [Jesus's] love for all people," served as both a touchstone and an inspiration for attempts to bring about integration. Women took the pledge seriously and were inspired to assess their actions in terms of the Christian belief in equality, giving them strength to stand up for principles that might otherwise have been sacrificed. This mutual commitment to Christian ideals often led white women who harbored reservations about racial equality to agree to sponsor integrated events and programs despite their personal reluctance. The serious attempt to live out religious ideals in social relations provided much of the impetus for the YWCA's work on race relations.[51]

The leadership provided by the Student YWCA on the issue of racial justice was also critical. Throughout the four decades from the 1920s to the 1960s, the Student Y was often a center of social activism and social awareness on college campuses. Students with an incipient social conscience were drawn to the Student Y, and participation in the organization tended to sharpen their political instincts. The Student YWCA often led the way in moving the YWCA toward greater commitment to racial justice. In the 1920s it was the Student YWCA that first endorsed the principle of racial integration; in the late 1930s the Student Y prodded the community Ys to examine their racial relationships; and in the 1960s the Student Y's involvement in the sit-in movement aroused the entire organization to greater zeal in pursuit of racial justice. Few other organizations included a large and partially autonomous student program within an adult women's organization. Students have not always played the role of catalysts for progressive social change, but during these decades they were often in the forefront of change.

In the final analysis it may have been the leadership exerted by black women that was the most significant factor in the YWCA's strong stand on racial justice. The Social Gospel perspective of the Community YWCA had led it to initiate programs in the black community as early as the turn of the century. This legacy created an unusual organizational pattern, that of a predominantly white organization with a significant number of black women within it. Black leaders were thus in a position to educate white colleagues about racism and to guide the organization toward a greater commitment to racial equality. At each crucial juncture in the YWCA's progress toward racial integration, black women took the lead, pressing for an interracial conference in 1915, demanding that the southern Student YWCA integrate at the leadership level in the early 1920s, pushing for racial integration in community YWCAs during the years of World War II, and providing important leadership in the struggle to implement the Interracial Charter after the war. These women were not alone and could not have been successful without significant support from white women committed to racial integration. Nevertheless, black women, working from positions within an organization at least nominally committed to racial equality, made a critical difference in the progressive stance of the YWCA on racial justice.

The years 1945 to 1960 were transitional ones in the history of the civil rights movement, as the political power of blacks increased in the north and the Cold War gave the discrepancy between egalitarian ideals and racist practices a new international significance. With the dawning of the 1960s four black college students in Greensboro, North Carolina, sparked a sit-in movement that spread like wildfire across the South. One of the resources that the civil rights movement brought to bear in the new phase of the struggle to change the face of the South was an aroused northern conscience. The patient work of many women in the YWCA holds a significant place among the efforts that had helped lay the groundwork for the new era. A highly respected organization that reached many women and girls through its services and activities, the YWCA played an important role in creating a groundswell of public opinion that demanded an end to racial segregation and discrimination in U.S. life, as well as in preparing fertile ground in which racial activism could flourish.

3

Speaking Truth to Power: The AFSC and the Struggle for Racial Justice

When the U.S. government ordered the evacuation of all persons of Japanese descent from the Pacific Coast in March 1942, the action constituted a wholesale violation of civil liberties on the basis of a racial classification. Wartime hysteria fueled fears that Japanese Americans would serve as a fifth column for Japan to such a degree that few of the liberal organizations usually quick to defend against injustice protested the order. Among the few to vociferously protest was the AFSC, which responded immediately to the crisis of the evacuation, denouncing it as a "direct violation of our heritage of social and racial justice," and suggesting that the action "would only serve to intensify racial tensions."[1] The AFSC assumed a major role in helping the Japanese Americans deal with the impact of the evacuation order, thus launching its first major venture in the struggle against racial injustice.

AFSC volunteers, predominantly women, took on many tasks in hopes of smoothing the transition for the Japanese and providing moral support for them in a time of crisis. The evacuation order required that all those of Japanese descent move first to temporary relocation centers, where they were transported to ten concentration camps outside the Western Defense Command area. Volunteers from the AFSC and the Society of Friends assisted internees in the myriad details involved in the painful process of uprooting, helping them settle their business and home affairs, serving as conservators of property, storing personal posses-sions, and working out deferments for the elderly or pregnant. Members of the Society of Friends provided transportation for families as they came to the relocation centers; they collected and distributed food, toys, books, and games for children, as well as sewing and knitting supplies for the women at the relocation centers.

At the heart of all this activity at the relocation center at Tanforan Racetrack near San Francisco was Josephine Whitney Duveneck. The daughter of a wealthy Boston family, Duveneck and her husband had moved to the West Coast where she joined the Society of Friends in 1934 and soon spearheaded many Friends and AFSC activities in northern California. Duveneck deserved much of the credit for the relatively smooth operation at Tanforan. A co-worker recalled that she "herded everyone around like a benevolent mother hen—army, WCCA [War-time Civil Control Administration], and Japanese alike—persuaded peo-ple to sit down and have another cup of tea instead of standing endlessly in line waiting for buses—persuaded the officials to route the families with babies and young children to buses ahead of the rest, poured tea and passed sandwiches to the army and told them quite frankly when they expressed appreciation, that we were there because we disapproved so very strongly of what the army was doing and that she certainly didn't envy them their job."[2]

Duveneck and other AFSC volunteers continued to play an active role after the Japanese Americans were sent to concentration camps, collect-ing supplies for the schools that were established, sending Christmas packages, notes and letters, gifts of food, magazines, and clothes, and making visits to the camps. The AFSC staff also aided Japanese and Japanese Americans with the transition to a new life during and after the war. The War Relocation Authority permitted those of Japanese descent to take jobs outside the Western Defense Command area, and Friends tried to locate jobs and to prepare communities to accept the Japanese. As the war ended, the work shifted to resettling the internees into old or new communities. The AFSC established hostels in Des Moines, Iowa, Cincinnati, Ohio, and Los Angeles and Pasadena, California, to ease the adjustment process. AFSC workers found sympathetic whites in the new communities who could help the returning evacuees establish new lives by finding them jobs and housing and by assuring them of a welcome. Duveneck and other AFSC workers attempted to defuse potential hostility against the returning Japanese by countering racist propaganda. On a visit to a young acquaintance in an army hospital in Auburn, California, Josephine Duveneck noticed many "Jap keep out" signs in town, and she urged the young soldier she was visiting to deal with the situation. He responded by gathering a group of white veterans and visiting store owners in town, requesting that they remove the signs, arguing that as soldiers they had fought side by side with Nisei soldiers. The signs were removed in a short space of time.[3]

Largely women volunteers attended to the organizational details of collecting supplies, visiting, and sending letters and cards to those in the internment camps. Such activities flowed out of women's traditional roles of running households and attending to the daily details of life. Such details might have seemed insignificant, yet they made a difference to those undergoing the trauma of relocation. Perhaps most important, women's ability and willingness to nurture personal relationships enabled some of the internees to keep their spirits up, allowing them to preserve ties with caring people in the outside world during their internment and easing their bitterness at their treatment. As one internee wrote from camp to AFSC worker Grace Nichols Pearson, "When things like injustice and exploitation and selfish race baiting is rampant I always feel most enthused and encouraged by unselfish generous attitudes and practices of folks like yours."[4] The work of the AFSC won the respect, gratitude, and loyalty of many Japanese Americans, a number of whom flocked to the AFSC to work as volunteers and staff after the war.

Women's ways of working were thus characterized by attention to minute organizational details and a focus on building personal connections. This is not to suggest that men were incapable of similar approaches, but only that, given patterns of socialization, it is more likely that women will easily adopt such approaches, which emerge from lifetime patterns of behavior. Women's style of working helps account for the remarkable record they compiled as effective community organizers in race relations projects (called community relations after 1950) undertaken by the AFSC in the postwar years, helping to build networks of activists in local communities that sustained efforts at social change.[5]

Origins of the AFSC'S
Race Relations Program

Like the YWCA, the AFSC underwent a profound transformation in the early 1940s, moving for the first time to pursue the goal of racial justice with vigor. In the process the largely white Society of Friends began to address racism within its ranks. In 1940 the Philadelphia yearly meeting of the Society of Friends urged the AFSC to develop a program in race relations, noting that the changing international scene mandated that whites could no longer view themselves as "trustees of a weaker race"; rather, they had to learn to work cooperatively with people of different races in the solution of mutual problems. The AFSC sponsored several conferences to discuss "race relations" in 1941 and 1942. Then, in the wake of the devastating race riots in Detroit and other U.S. cities in 1943, the AFSC initiated a Race Relations Program to directly confront the problems of racial segregation and discrimination in U.S. society.[6]

The AFSC focused on creating social change in society at large, tackling the problems of job discrimination, school integration, and housing discrimination as major priorities. The AFSC brought to the task the resources of a small but cohesive and highly effective organization. In the postwar world the AFSC consisted of a central office in Philadelphia and an expanding network of regional offices, which totaled a dozen by 1960. It employed 350 staff members nationwide in 1955 and engaged an additional 1,000 people in advisory committees that supervised each program, at both the national and local levels.[7] Like the Society of Friends, the AFSC was a predominantly white organization, but during the 1940s, 1950s, and 1960s it hired increasing numbers of staff members from racial-ethnic backgrounds, particularly in the Community Relations Division. Many but not all staff and committee members were members of the Religious Society of Friends, and all staff members were committed to the AFSC's mission of demonstrating Quaker philosophy through social action.

The Society of Friends had a long tradition of "speaking truth to power" by forthrightly criticizing those who wielded power in government and other major institutions for social injustice or militarism, and by refusing to cooperate with policies that were contrary to the group's deeply held religious beliefs. Historically that tradition was most widely known in the Friends' peace testimony, the belief that war was an instrument incapable of achieving good ends because it embraced evil means.[8] In the tradition of speaking truth to power, the AFSC's first programs in "race relations" addressed employers and administrators in educational institutions in the hope of convincing them to end segregation in their own institutions. The AFSC did not eschew the need for legal change but maintained that social and political change was a far more fundamental process than could be achieved through legal change alone, and that such change must be achieved by transforming the values of individual members of society. In order to achieve that goal, AFSC programs were designed to maintain communication with both sides in situations of conflict; the AFSC communicated with those in power in order to confront them with their complicity in supporting structures of injustice and to urge them to change. From the 1940s through the 1960s AFSC staff members devised ever bolder measures to achieve that end.[9]

One of the first projects adopted by the AFSC's Race Relations Program was the Job Opportunities Program (later called Employment on Merit). In 1952 Thelma Babbitt became the first woman hired by the program. Babbitt, a white New Englander, had no background in the field of race relations but she had learned about the AFSC through contact with a Quaker woman she met in the League of Women Voters. Babbitt applied for a job with the AFSC after the death of her second husband in 1951. She worked briefly with Anna Brinton, head of the Institutes of International Relations program in the Philadelphia office. Through Brinton she became impressed with a core Quaker tenet, that "love expressed through creative action can overcome hatred, prejudice, and fear." In 1952 Babbitt was assigned to the Merit Employment Program in Columbus, Ohio, one of several cities that had such projects. The goal of the program was to convince management in various industries to practice nondiscriminatory employment, focused at first on fields open to college graduates and professionals, but later on blue-collar and secretarial work. The AFSC also offered workshops to people from racial-ethnic minority backgrounds to prepare them to successfully make it through the job application process.[10]

Babbitt visited employers in such fields as banking, insurance, and retail trades to convince them to open to racial-ethnic applicants jobs that were traditionally reserved for whites. During 1952 and 1953 Babbitt succeeded in persuading two insurance companies and the largest department store in Columbus to integrate their sales and office positions. A dramatic incident quickly impressed upon her the difficulty of maintaining an attitude of love so central to Quaker philosophy. Soon after she began her work in Columbus, Babbitt called on the principal of a secretarial school to convince him to admit black students to his school. He responded, "You ought to go down South where they know how to treat niggers." Babbitt lost her temper, replying sharply, "How can a person who is a deacon of the Baptist church talk like that?" The conversation ended in acrimonious debate, and Babbitt, completely distraught by this encounter, reported her experience to the regional director of the AFSC. The next work day Babbitt learned that the principal had suddenly dropped dead of a heart attack. The AFSC regional director gently admonished her, "Thelma, my dear, that is not the Quakerly approach." Vowing to renounce righteous indignation in the future, Babbitt tried to learn more quietly persuasive techniques.[11]

The difficulties of convincing those in power to endorse racial integration slowly pushed women and men in the AFSC to contemplate other strategies. In 1953, when Babbitt assumed the directorship of the Employment on Merit Program for the entire country, she assessed the results of the program to date. Staff members had conducted more than 4,000 interviews with employers across the country. Babbitt found that approximately 20 percent of those interviewed were strongly opposed to a racially integrated work force; another 20 percent favored the idea and were eager for the help of the AFSC in the process; and the remaining 60 percent supported racial integration in principle but were unwilling to initiate change without the backing of public policy. The voluntary approach, Babbitt concluded, was helpful only for those already convinced.[12]

Working for School Integration

Quiet persuasion, coupled with community organization, continued to be the hallmark of most AFSC community relations programs throughout the 1940s and 1950s, but by the late 1950s a more activist stance was evident. In addition to employment, a second major focus in the AFSC's efforts to challenge racial discrimination was school desegregation. The AFSC first attempted to tackle the issue in higher education immediately after World War II, when AFSC staff recruited black faculty to visit white campuses as speakers or visiting faculty. Garnet Guild, who was white, engaged in such persuasive efforts when she worked as a college secretary for the AFSC's regional office in Des Moines, Iowa, from 1948 to 1958. She had attended Pacific College, a Quaker school in Oregon. Graduating in the midst of the depression, she received a scholarship to attend Pendle Hill, a Quaker retreat near Philadelphia. The program at Pendle Hill included work projects, and Guild worked at an American Indian school in South Dakota and did relief work for coal miners on strike in Appalachia. At the AFSC's suggestion she accepted a work/study fellowship that took her to the Middle East during World War II. In 1948 Guild became the AFSC college secretary for the North Central Region.

Here Guild found herself deeply involved in the struggle for racial integration. Her assignment required traveling to the various colleges and universities in the Upper Midwest to meet with faculty and students. The Student YWCA was her main contact on many campuses, and she often met with groups of students, recruiting them to summer service projects in the United States or abroad, as well as discussing social and political issues. Most of her time was spent talking to faculty and administrators, particularly about the need to break down racial barriers in college teaching. For example, Guild tried to convince faculty and administrators to oppose quotas for Jewish faculty and to advocate bringing faculty from black colleges to white campuses as visiting speakers in their respective areas of expertise in order to undermine racist stereotypes that blacks were not capable of being competent faculty. Guild loved her work, which gave her a great deal of freedom and allowed her to work with students and faculty. After ten years as college secretary, she was promoted to regional executive secretary for the AFSC's South Central Regional Office, the first woman to hold such a post. She served in that position from 1959 to 1969.[13]

By 1950 many activists in the struggle for racial justice looked to school integration as the linchpin for racial reform. According to historian Harvard Sitkoff, "It had become an article of faith that a Supreme Court decision ruling school segregation unconstitutional would cause the quick death of Jim Crow in America," and that decision seemed near at hand in the early 1950s.[14] In anticipation of the Supreme Court's *Brown v. Board of*

Education ruling the AFSC undertook an experimental project in Washington, D.C., to exert pressure on public officials to initiate school integration, a campaign described briefly in the Introduction.

Irene Osborne and Alma Scurlock, staff members for the project, brought complementary skills and experience to the job. Osborne's parents had moved from the rural South to Ohio, and they clung to overtly racist views. But the poverty of Osborne's childhood led her to develop an acute consciousness of the injustice of poverty and eventually to identify with other disadvantaged groups. She attended college in the late 1930s and found sociology, particularly the new field of race relations, very exciting. She was also exposed to left-wing politics, and gradually her nascent feelings about injustice were transformed into principled activism. When she graduated, she worked briefly for the Vanguard Association, a civil rights group in Columbus, Ohio. She also got involved in the Congress of Racial Equality, which was just forming; in 1945 she was elected a vice-president of CORE. During the late 1940s she taught sociology at the college level. Osborne thus had experience in the fields of civil rights and education.

Alma Scurlock was a native of Washington. She had attended Howard University and then received an masters of arts degree in social work at Columbia University, specializing in community organization. For six years she worked for the juvenile court system in Washington, D.C. She brought skills in community organizing to the project, coupled with extensive contacts with Washington's African-American community.

Irene Osborne and Alma Scurlock coupled traditional Quaker methods of friendly persuasion with community organizing techniques. They scheduled many individual conferences with school board members and other government officials to try to persuade them to desegregate the schools. At the same time they pulled together teachers, professionals, and government workers to put pressure on the school board. Irene Osborne recalled that the supervisory staff members in the AFSC national office were "a little nervous at first," when she and Alma Scurlock insisted on reaching out to the larger community rather than confining themselves to conferences with officials.[15] The two women worked closely with the Joint Committee on Education, the group they had organized, to prepare statements directed to Congress and to the commissioner of the District of Columbia, urging the adoption of a school desegregation plan. As the litigation that was to culminate in the

Brown decision moved through the courts, the Board of Education requested advice from the AFSC project. Osborne, who had primary responsibility for dealing with school issues, met frequently with officials of the school board, offering suggestions and pressing for change. Scurlock concentrated her efforts on the Department of Parks and Recreation, which was moving more quickly toward integration.

Osborne also set up a series of seminars that brought together teachers from the racially segregated school system, providing the first opportunity for many black and white teachers to meet across racial lines to discuss their fears and concerns and to explore methods for defusing the problems they anticipated in newly integrated classrooms. Led by people familiar with schools in transition, the seminars provided an atmosphere that fostered honest communication, and they proved so popular that they were repeated many times with high school students, PTA groups, and community leaders.

When the Supreme Court announced its historic school integration decision, change followed quickly. In part because the community had been galvanized in support of integration, Washington's school board was ready to move. On 25 May 1954, eight days after *Brown*, the board of education announced a plan to integrate the school system. By September 1954 about two-thirds of the city's schoolchildren were attending integrated schools, and the Board of Education had called for full integration by 1960. AFSC staff members had been working within a context where many forces supported progressive and peaceful change. The Eisenhower administration made significant moves to encourage desegregation in Washington, D.C., and the Coordinating Committee for the Enforcement of the D.C. Anti-Discrimination Laws provided grass-roots support for desegregation of theaters and restaurants. Nevertheless, Osborne and Scurlock and the joint committee they created could claim considerable credit for facilitating a smooth transition to racial integration of schools in the nation's capital.[16]

Following the successful experiment in Washington, the AFSC initiated efforts in many southern communities to encourage integration of the schools. Heading these efforts was Jean Fairfax. An African American with ten years experience in the AFSC, Fairfax was hired in 1957 as national representative of southern programs, a new position that reflected the AFSC's increasing focus on school integration. Fairfax was responsible for setting "the framework for the work we did in the south . . . for the next decade or twenty years," according to Barbara Moffett, secretary of the AFSC's Community Relations Division.[17] Fairfax had been born and raised in Cleveland, Ohio. After attending the University of Michigan she obtained her master's degree at Union Theological Seminary, where she studied with the theologians Paul Tillich and Reinhold Niebuhr. Niebuhr was "by far the greatest teacher I ever had," declared Fairfax, and from him she gained "the courage to act without waiting for all the evidence to be in." Deeply interested in applying the ideas of Christian pacifism to concrete social problems, she was attracted to the AFSC "because it offered the best opportunity at the time to bring a religious nonviolent approach to bear on social issues."[18]

Fairfax was recruited by the AFSC to join its relief efforts in Europe in 1946, and her first experience with AFSC personnel policies proved to be a bitter one. She had been assigned to a position in Germany, but when she arrived at Pendle Hill, Pennsylvania, where the teams were assembling to go overseas, she was shocked to learn that racist objections to her assignment had surfaced. German Friends had questioned the decision of the British army, which was in charge of the arrangements, to send a black person to Germany. The British army decided to oppose her appointment and so informed British Friends, who were serving as the conduit for AFSC workers being assigned to Europe. Fearing that a principled stand might jeopardize other relief programs in Germany, British Friends agreed.[19]

A storm of controversy ensued within the ranks of the U.S. workers and staff. Clarence Pickett, executive secretary of AFSC, argued that no one should go to Germany if Fairfax was not allowed to go. G. James Fleming, secretary of the Race Relations Program, argued, "If the AFSC acquiesces in a policy of racial discrimination solely because some German functionaries may not want to work with non-Aryans, it seems to me we are taking over Hitler's Aryan program." Although Pickett and Fleming both took strong stands, a number of other American Friends made "patronizing and insensitive remarks" that jarred Fairfax. After extensive discussion, the Executive Committee of the Foreign Service Section of the AFSC decided to acquiesce in the British decision but to request a different policy in the future. Fairfax was assigned to Austria instead, where she served for several years. When she returned to the United States, she took a job with the AFSC as college secretary in the New England Region from 1949 to 1955.[20]

In 1957, following a year-long trip to Africa, Fairfax accepted the job of national representative of southern programs for the AFSC, a position she held until 1965. Fairfax's task involved the direction of the AFSC's work in the South, where the AFSC had several Merit Employment Projects and was shifting focus to concentrate on school integration. Before the decade was out, the AFSC was involved in school integration projects in nine states and over 200 school districts. These projects provided support to black parents attempting to enroll their children in integrated schools, while simultaneously putting pressure on white officials and community leaders to endorse school integration.

A major testing ground of this strategy occurred in Little Rock, Arkansas. The AFSC assigned Thelma Babbitt to promote racial integration in the violence-torn city, which had been catapulted to national and international attention in 1957 when Governor Orval Faubus used the National Guard to prevent the entrance of nine black students into Central High School. Incited by the governor's action, white mobs employed violence to prevent students from attending school despite a court order to that effect. As the violence escalated, President Eisenhower federalized the Arkansas National Guard to restore order, and under armed escort, black students entered Central High. In a final stratagem to prevent integration, Governor Faubus closed all the public schools in Little Rock for the 1958–1959 school year.

During the summer of 1958, several members of the Little Rock Friends Meeting requested that the AFSC send a community worker to help reduce tensions and restore communication in the city, and in September 1959 Thelma Babbitt was sent to Little Rock. Daisy Bates, president of the local chapter of the NAACP, was actively involved in providing support to the black students and their families, but there was virtually no communication between blacks and sympathetic whites; the latter were intimidated by fear of reprisals. Babbitt set out to change that situation. Relying on Bates for contacts in the black community, Babbitt went to work contacting church groups and individuals in both the black and white communities. She found a number of white ministers who were sympathetic, and she organized supporters of school integration, black and white, into the interracial Committee of Community Unity (CCU).

The CCU sponsored a series of unprecedented interracial conferences to promote dialogue across racial lines. The first conference, which drew more than 150 participants, about one-third black and two-thirds white, "was a very moving experience for everybody, so that at the end of the day people were . . . stunned and couldn't quite realize what happened," Babbitt recalled. Additional conferences and interracial seminars for high school students followed. Out of these conferences emerged a program to support parents of black children who wanted to serve as the advance shock troops in integrating schools, which was undertaken jointly by the NAACP, the National Urban League, and the Arkansas Council on Human Relations.

When illness forced Babbitt to resign in December 1960, the vigorous alliance she had organized between blacks and whites continued to function, working successfully to defeat proposed state legislation that would allow local communities to close the schools. After Faubus's defeat at the polls in 1960, the schools reopened. Babbitt's most important contributions had been to encourage white liberals to speak out in the face of reprisals and to cement an alliance between those whites and the black community that would remain in place when the civil rights revolution swept through Little Rock in the early 1960s.[21]

AFSC school integration projects in many communities in the South encountered massive white resistance to school integration in the late 1950s. In Prince Edward County, Virginia, for example, public schools were closed in September 1959 in order to avoid compliance with a court order to integrate, and they remained closed for five years. The AFSC initially assigned Irene Osborne to work in the county to develop some creative response to this move. Osborne gathered a group of young people together to conduct an educational census to determine the number of children remaining in the county and what plans, if any, they had for schooling in the coming year. After Osborne completed her work, the AFSC hired Helen Baker, who was black, and Nancy Adams, who was white, to direct the project in Prince Edward County. Helen Baker had been an employee of the AFSC for more than ten years, often working with her husband, Percy. She had most recently directed a poverty program for the AFSC in southern New Jersey.

The AFSC instituted an Emergency Placement Program in Prince Edward County that located host families willing to take in black children and that placed junior and senior high students in homes where they could attend good public schools and be exposed to interracial experiences and cultural opportunities. Almost seventy children, ages thirteen to eighteen, were placed, primarily on the East Coast and in the Midwest. This show of support greatly lifted morale in the black community, yet approximately 1,000 children still remained without any provision for schooling. Although the AFSC established activity centers to provide students with enjoyable educational experiences, these centers were not designed to fulfill the functions of schools, for staff members were determined that the community must once again shoulder the responsibility for schooling all its children.[22]

Barbara Moffett was a driving force behind much of the work done by the AFSC's Community Relations staff. Moffett had a background in journalism, and she had begun working for the AFSC on a temporary assignment during a newspaper strike shortly after World War II. She quickly became engaged in the spirit of the AFSC's work and embarked on a lifetime career with the organization. As secretary of the Community Relations Division, she was very supportive of her staff, willing to talk with them openly about any problems they had in the field, or ideas they had for future work. She applied her skills in journalism as well, with her ability "to listen carefully to ideas of staff people, flesh them out and write them down." "She was not the kind of person to make a speech," but excelled at "synthesizing and putting things in words so others could understand," recalled Garnet Guild. Jean Fairfax credited Moffett with "setting professional standards" for the AFSC's community relations work. "She had great respect for the written record, and for documentation," which proved invaluable when the AFSC interacted with public officials in Washington. She worked smoothly with the larger decision-making community in the AFSC, keeping people posted on developments in the field, and convincing them of the need for the AFSC to remain firmly committed to supporting black communities in the South on the front lines of integration battles. Thus her influence and guidance were felt in all the work of the AFSC's Community Relations Division.[23]

Presaging the Politics of the 1960s

Activists in the AFSC, both male and female, had moved from fearless but quiet attempts at confronting public officials and persuading employers to endorse racial integration to bolder attempts at marshalling communities to demand change in their efforts to break down racial segregation during the 1940s and 1950s. But by 1959 the AFSC had begun to reevaluate its community relations programs. When the AFSC first began work on school integration in North Carolina in 1957, many local Friends and AFSC staff believed that change could come relatively easily in the "progressive" upper South. But experience proved otherwise. The strategy of applying moral suasion had failed to have any impact on the views of hardened segregationists. Attempts to organize supporters of racial integration to demand change through conventional channels had brought only modest gains at best. For four years AFSC staff members had encouraged black parents to initiate transfers of their children to white schools under the pupil placement acts enacted by southern states. The results had produced only a meager handful of black students attending racially integrated schools. These strategies were clearly inadequate in the face of massive resistance to racial integration mounted even in the upper South.

At a community relations staff retreat in early 1960 Jean Fairfax questioned the effectiveness of moral suasion in the present situation, arguing that the legal framework would have to change before substantial change on the school desegregation front could be achieved. "Perhaps we have kidded ourselves that officials would welcome the help of a private organization concerned to help them with the orderly transition to integration," she reflected. Controversy erupted among the staff and committee members; some were committed to the traditional Quaker methods, while others argued that the urgency of opposing racism justified the destruction of the social fabric in order to create something new. Barbara Moffett, secretary of the Community Relations Division of the AFSC, summarized the discussion in the following words: "We are now questioning whether our activities are strong enough to challenge a wrong law. . . . We need to look at our ability to confront leadership on the evasiveness of token desegregation." By the late 1950s and early 1960s, then, the concept of moral persuasion began to give way to an emphasis on helping racial ethnic communities exercise power. AFSC staff looked increasingly to the techniques of nonviolent resistance that had proven so effective in the 1955–1956 Montgomery bus boycott to provide an alternate model for racial change. When the sit-in movement erupted in the early 1960s, the AFSC was quick to rally behind this more confrontational approach, offering support to high school and college students engaged in the struggle.[24] During the early 1960s the AFSC played an important role in the civil rights struggle, serving as a "movement halfway house" according to scholar Aldon Morris.[25]

The strategies and tactics employed by women activists in the AFSC in the struggle for racial justice in the postwar world drew on the heritage of the past, yet transformed women's progressive politics as well. AFSC staff put pressure on government and private individuals deemed to have the power to bring about change, thus working through established channels of influence, although not directly engaged in lobbying activities. But as women activists in the AFSC also sought to mobilize larger groups in the community to demand change, they moved in the direction of the larger-scale protests that would characterize the social movements of the 1960s. The massive nonviolent protests of the civil rights movement increased the degree of pressure exerted on officials by mobilizing entire African-American communities in massive demonstrations that directly challenged the laws of segregation, and the AFSC would provide important support in those battles during the height of the civil rights movement.

Empowering
Racial-Ethnic Communities

In addition to projects that directly challenged racial segregation and discrimination, the AFSC also experimented in the late 1940s and 1950s with another approach to the country's racial problems—community organization in racial-ethnic communities. The AFSC's approach to community organization owed a great deal to the work of Saul Alinsky, foremost proponent of community organizing in the United States. Alinsky had learned his techniques from observing the Congress of Industrial Organizations campaign to unionize the Chicago meat-packing industry in the 1930s. Alinsky believed that low-income communities should organize around their own interests and needs and confront the local power structure when necessary to achieve their goals. The AFSC adopted many of Alinsky's principles in their community-organizing efforts: an outside organization should be invited into the community in order to work there; the community itself should define the issues of concern; local leaders should be developed from the community; and the purpose of organizing should be to raise the confidence among residents in poor communities to enable them to tackle their own problems. Thus, rather than provide services for racial-ethnic communities, the goal of AFSC community-organizing projects was to generate a spirit of initiative and cooperation and political participation in a community, to get people to help themselves. Social and recreational activities, self-help projects, work camps, and community organization all helped build connections between members of the community, build self-confidence and interest in the outside world, and convince people that they might have an impact on the larger political process that helped determine the nature of their lives.

In one important respect, however, some AFSC community development projects parted company from Alinsky. Alinsky insisted that community organizations must have an "enemy" to battle against and emphasized the importance of conflict. Many AFSC staff members also recognized that social change was often produced only by instigating creative conflict, yet at the same time, they argued, much as Gandhi did, it was important to maintain the Christian principle of love. Only by refusing to objectify and render evil those one opposed could communication occur among highly polarized groups within communities.[26]

At first glance the slow process of community organizing might seem to have little relevance to changing the structural patterns of racism. Yet the process could serve to sufficiently empower those who had been subordinated by racial discrimination and segregation to enable them to demand and, in some cases, to achieve significant change. Thus community organizing was a route to challenging patterns of subordination and domination that typified the relationship between racial-ethnic and white communities. One of the AFSC's greatest success stories was the discovery of Cesar Chavez, who later organized the United Farm Workers of America. Fred Ross, one of Alinsky's close associates, worked for the AFSC as a community organizer in the Mexican-American community in San Jose, California, in the late 1940s. Ross met Chavez in the course of his work and trained him in the principles of community organization. Ross's primary contact with the AFSC's San Francisco Regional Office was Josephine Whitney Duveneck, who was the guiding force in most of the community-organizing work done by that office throughout the 1940s and 1950s. Hers is a remarkable story of a determined and powerful woman committed to social reform politics.[27]

Josephine Duveneck:
AFSC Work in Community Organization

Unlike many other women activists who worked for the AFSC, Josephine Whitney was born to a life of extreme privilege. Her father, Henry M. Whitney, came from a wealthy Boston family, and during his lifetime he expanded the family fortune by investing in electric streetcar lines, iron, steel, and coal. Her mother, Margaret Green, used her marriage to Whitney to gain entrance into Boston high society, where she enjoyed the world of art, literature, and education. Josephine was born in 1891, the fifth of five children. Since her siblings were considerably older than she, she grew up essentially alone. Her mother was a cold and commanding figure who neglected and ignored Josephine, and in return Josephine regarded her with a degree of dread. Her father, on the other hand, showered her with attention and companionship, reading her stories and taking her on visits to his farm, activities he much preferred to attending the formal dinners her mother sponsored.[28]

The young girl was educated at home by governesses until the age of twelve, when she began to attend a private girls' school in Boston. She excelled at her schoolwork and established a number of close friends. In midadolescence Josephine's life changed dramatically when her parents, long unhappy in their marriage, decided to separate. Josephine and her mother left for Europe, where Josephine attended school in Paris. On their return to Boston Josephine "came out" as a debutante, a process that she endured without a great deal of enthusiasm. More interesting to her were the two courses she enrolled in at Radcliffe College. In 1910 her mother again decided to take her to Europe, where she attended lectures at Oxford University. Despite her exposure to elite educational experiences, Josephine Whitney never completed college.

When Josephine Whitney returned to Boston, she met her future husband, Frank Duveneck. Duveneck was the son of a famous bohemian artist; after his mother's death when he was a young boy, he had been raised by his mother's relatives, the Boston Brahmin family of Arthur Lyman. Frank Duveneck had just completed an engineering degree at Harvard when he began to court Whitney. The two were married in 1913. Although both came from wealthy families, they shared a rejection of the values of high society. Their relationship would prove to be a close and happy partnership for six decades, one based on mutual commitment to family life, religious devotion, and progressive social change.

The young couple moved to the West Coast shortly after their marriage. Josephine Duveneck bore four children between the years 1915 and 1922. During these same years she organized and helped found Peninsula School, a progressive school where for sixteen years she served in many roles—organizer, director, teacher, and fund-raiser. Frank Duveneck joined her in her work with the school, but in this as in other activities, she was clearly the leader. In 1924 the couple bought Hidden Villa Ranch, a thousand-acre tract in the foothills of Palo Alto, California, where they eventually settled. Although Hidden Villa was a perfect spot for a private refuge, the Duvenecks instead turned it into a center of progressive activities. Hidden Villa was the cite for the first youth hostel on the West Coast; an interracial summer camp (begun in 1945); and a meetingplace and conference grounds for numerous community and social action groups. Josephine Duveneck thus located herself at the center of a whirlwind of social activism.

That activism was centered in religious faith. Duveneck's parents had displayed little interest in religious ideas or education, but as a young girl Josephine began to read the Bible and to attend a variety of churches, from Episcopalian to Catholic, to satisfy her growing spiritual urge. In her adult life, she engaged in a profound search for faith that led her to explore Christian mysticism as well as the insights of Eastern religions. But Duveneck found her religious home in the Society of Friends, which she joined in 1934.

She quickly established herself as the most powerful figure in the Palo Alto Friends Meeting and the dominant influence in northern California Friends circles. She was admired for her spiritual insight, her energy, and her ability to get things done. As one member of Palo Alto Friends Meeting recalled, "She was cleverer than most people; she also had amazing reserves of energy; and she normally had a clearer picture of what she wanted than the rest of us. It was a potent combination."[29] Much of that boundless energy and leadership was directed toward her passion for social justice. For her, concern with social problems flowed from her religious beliefs; there was no separation between inner faith and social concern.

Duveneck's first active work with the AFSC came in the late 1930s, when the Philadelphia office asked Friends in California to help refugees from Hitler's Germany settle in the United States. Duveneck and Gerda Isenberg, who had immigrated from Germany in the 1920s, worked closely together, providing contacts for refugees to enable them to get jobs, housing, and counseling. Out of this work a regional office of the AFSC was established in San Francisco in 1942. Duveneck was the driving force in that office during its early years. Because of her personal wealth she chose to serve as a volunteer rather than as a paid employee. In 1943 she served as associate executive secretary, and throughout the 1940s and 1950s she frequently held the position of clerk (chair) of the Executive Committee, the most powerful nonstaff position in the AFSC structure. She usually chaired the Social Industrial Committee as well, which was responsible for race relations programs, and she initiated most of the AFSC's efforts in that area. From the time that Duveneck joined the Society of Friends, "her imagination, wisdom, and energy has irradiated every Service Committee activity in Northern California," wrote Stephen Thiermann, executive secretary of the San Francisco Regional Office.[30]

Following her work with Japanese Americans in the concentration camps, Duveneck next turned her attention to the problems faced by black migrants to the West Coast. The huge influx of black workers seeking wartime jobs had created overcrowding, deteriorating housing conditions, and strained recreational facilities. One community that confronted particularly difficult conditions was North Richmond, across the bay from San Francisco. The city of Richmond had burgeoned during the war, flooded by black migrants drawn by jobs in the shipping industry. Workers crowded into the North Richmond area, where, unable to obtain loans for housing, residents set up trailers and collected materials to build makeshift houses. Provisions for sanitation were minimal, and many homes lacked toilet facilities. With the collapse of the shipbuilding industry at the close of the war, an increase in drinking, gambling, narcotics, and prostitution exacerbated the economic and material problems facing the community.[31]

Duveneck's role in North Richmond was aptly described by her husband, who referred to her as a "spark plug" for many activities, generating enthusiasm and involvement on the part of others.[32] She often initiated ideas and approaches, working with other staff and volunteers to implement them. Duveneck enlisted the aid of staff worker Margaret Deuel and several members of the AFSC's San Francisco Race Relations Committee to begin investigating conditions in North Richmond. In 1947 the AFSC assigned its interracial secretary, Clotild Ferguson, a black woman, to begin working two days a week in Richmond. Ferguson helped to organize the Council of Social Agencies to coordinate social work services in the area. The AFSC also sponsored a series of work camps in 1948, with students building recreational facilities and helping residents repair their homes. In theory work camps were supposed to involve members of the community in their projects, so that volunteers worked with, rather than for, the residents. The AFSC had difficulty implementing this goal at first, as black residents expressed suspicion of the predominantly white students who attended the work camps. Nevertheless, the work camps continued, providing recreation, child care, help with home repairs, and sewing and quilting classes. [33]

In 1948 and 1949 Duveneck established a committee that planned further AFSC activities in North Richmond, exploring the possibilities for a self-help housing project and a community center. Eliza Smith, director of the weekend work camp program, insisted that a self-help housing project was premature; she argued that the community was not yet ready to cooperate with such a venture and feared that it become merely a service to residents, rather than an experience in cooperation. The AFSC decided instead to establish a community center as a vehicle for developing a greater sense of initiative and cooperation among residents. Duveneck and Red Stephenson, the Social Industrial secretary, raised funds to pay for two AFSC staff workers to live and work in the community. [34]

The North Richmond Neighborhood House opened its doors in 1949. Percy and Helen Baker had been hired as directors (the same Helen Baker who later worked for the AFSC in Prince Edward County, Virginia). The Bakers organized a neighborhood council to help plan and direct programs, while the AFSC maintained control of policy and funding decisions. The first programs established included recreation programs for children, a group for homemakers, singing, community dinners, meetings, discussion groups, and speakers. Advice was extended to those who needed to contact government services. Eventually, the Neighborhood House undertook more ambitious programs, such as a public health clinic, a children's library, a nursery program, a woodworking studio, and a playground that was built next to North Richmond Neighborhood House under the auspices of a neighborhood recreation council. [35]

The AFSC walked a narrow line between doing things for people and getting people to work to help themselves. The first approach seemed necessary in order to nurture the second. As time passed, however, the emphasis slowly shifted from the initiation of activities by Neighborhood House staff to suggestions and participation by community residents, who would bring their ideas to the staff for help with implementation. By 1953 some progress had been made. The Social Industrial Committee reported, "We have attempted to move only in response to the expressed wishes of the community. . . . There has been a remarkable growth of individual initiative in North Richmond, with people showing more ability or willingness to handle their own problems." Children began to attend day and summer camps. Residents from North Richmond attended meetings of the Richmond City Council, the Planning Commission, and the Board of Supervisors to discuss their concerns about local community problems. The goals of raising morale and developing cooperation and responsibility had been achieved, at least to a reasonable degree.[36] Throughout the process, Duveneck had been one of the guiding spirits. Her tremendous interest in people was compelling, and others responded to her spirit, strength, vision, and understanding. Furthermore, she had a practical head for details and proved tough and aggressive in her attempts to influence and change others.

In 1954, the Service Committee began to plan for the termination of its connection with Neighborhood House. The proposed change was consistent with AFSC philosophy, which called for the AFSC to initiate small-scale projects where it supplied some creative leadership and demonstrated the possibility of solving social problems, and once that mission was accomplished, devolved the project to local leadership. The AFSC did not wish to remain in communities indefinitely as a paternalistic social service organization, but to work for several years, stimulating residents to take the initiative to operate community programs themselves. Barbara Moffett argued that such devolvement should occur whenever "significant inroads have been made in the problem areas, the community has come to widely share concern for problems, there is no major need that we alone are needed for, and where we might stifle local leadership."[37] Those conditions had been met in North Richmond, and the AFSC moved to establish an independent board of trustees composed of local community members in 1955. Neighborhood House continued to operate many successful programs, including study halls and a voter registration drive that registered some 90 percent of North Richmond residents, of whom close to 90 percent went to the polls.[38]

Josephine Duveneck next turned her attention to the problems of Native Americans in California. The 1950s were a troubled time for Native Americans. During the New Deal, Commissioner of Indian Affairs John Collier had reversed the federal government's policy of assimilation, which had allotted lands to individuals, encouraged Native Americans to become independent farmers, and sold "surplus lands" to whites, decreasing the Native American land base by over half in a period of fifty years.[39] The Indian Reorganization Act of 1934 sought to restore tribal sovereignty and to preserve native culture. A group of western members of congress took up the cause of assimilation again after World War II, pushing for termination of federal supervision and of services to Native Americans. Their aim was to integrate Native Americans into the dominant culture and to substitute private for tribal ownership of land. President Truman's appointment of Dillon Myer as Commissioner of Indian Affairs in 1950 was a political victory for western land interests. Myer purged the Bureau of Indian Affairs (BIA) of most of John Collier's appointees and moved ahead on the agenda of termination. The 1954 House Concurrent Resolution 108 outlined the goals for the new policy: an end to wardship status and the reservation system; transfer of tribal assets to private title of individuals, partnerships, or corporations; and the phasing out the services of the BIA.[40]

Josephine Duveneck was deeply concerned with the potential impact of the new federal policy on California Native American groups. The AFSC studied the problem of U.S. policy toward Native Americans and published a pamphlet that was sharply critical of government policy. The authors argued that Native American tribes should be free to manage their own affairs rather than "hurried or forced into fuller participation in American society." The AFSC called on the federal government to provide greater resources in the form of technical assistance and funds in order to develop tribal resources and to provide educational opportunities to individuals.[41]

Duveneck opposed the policy of termination, but she felt she lacked detailed information about the particular needs of California Native Americans. She set out on a long trek to visit rancherias, the tiny scattered reservations that had been established throughout the state. On this fact-finding mission she established contacts, investigated the needs and conditions of different tribal groups, and tried to assess the potential impact of termination. At the conclusion of her journey, Duveneck recommended that the AFSC undertake the responsibility for providing help to Native Americans during this transition and proposed that two field-workers be established in the state.[42] The AFSC was only able to secure funding for a single field-worker for the Northern California area, and in 1954 the San Francisco Regional Office hired Frank Quinn, who was white.

Duveneck and Quinn, working closely together, quickly concluded that Native Americans needed greater representation in the formulation of government policy. The two set to work to encourage Native Americans to participate in the political process, informing them about the impact of various governmental policies and encouraging them to represent their own needs to school boards, government agencies, and Congress. Many Native Americans preferred the protection and support of the government and wanted to maintain the tribal nature of reservation life, and they began to make those views known to government personnel. Duveneck organized several statewide Native American conferences and an Intertribal Council that facilitated intertribal cooperation on mutual problems. She also educated influential and prominent citizens about the problems that Native Americans faced, organizing white supporters into the California League for American Indians, which pushed for an end to the policy of termination. Opposition to termination slowly mounted throughout the country among Native Americans and their white allies. In the fall of 1958 the government responded to that pressure; Secretary of Interior Fred Seaton announced that no group would be terminated unless it both understood and supported such action.[43]

During the 1950s the AFSC also launched a nationwide effort to promote community development on Native American reservations. The AFSC hoped that community development programs would build a sense of confidence in seriously demoralized Native American communities and would develop strategies for meeting specific needs and solving problems. On reservations across the country, AFSC sent staff members to live and work with tribal groups that requested aid. Serving as facilitators, staff worked with members of the tribe to define specific problems and to devise strategies to overcome them. The emphasis was often on economic development projects.

The potential for paternalism was endemic to projects where white and/or middle-class organizers worked in poor racial-ethnic communities. During the 1950s most AFSC staff who worked on Indian reservations were white men, often accompanied by their wives who served informally as staff members as well. Yet the AFSC did make an increasingly assertive attempt to hire people from racial-ethnic backgrounds to work in their own communities during the 1950s and 1960s. For example, Tillie Walker was hired in 1957 as the national representative of Indian programs; Walker was a Native American who had grown up on the Fort Berthold Reservation in South Dakota. But as long as a large majority of the staff were white, white allies faced a dilemma. They believed they were working for the goal of self-determination and independence of their client groups, but that independence often threatened those very allies.

Josephine Duveneck struggled with these contradictions. Duveneck established rapport fairly easily across the gulf of race and class, particularly but not exclusively with other women. As she reflected in her autobiography, "I discovered that if one offers a sincere desire for friendliness with sufficient simplicity the barriers fade away. . . . Humility, compassion, humor, openness, sympathy, all the intuitive qualities seemed to do away with barriers and we found ourselves accepted as potential friends." She was quite aware of the difficulties involved in cross-class relationships and had always been critical of "Lady Bountiful" types doing things for "the lower classes."[44]

Yet because of the tremendous strength of her personality, coupled with her class privilege, Duveneck found it difficult to give up control. She was used to setting the agenda for the projects she initiated. She had built networks of personal relationships among those she worked with, using her personal influence to guide others toward the goals she sought. She tended to select the people that she worked with and through, and she supported people as long as she could exert considerable influence over their actions. She was accustomed to leadership, and found it painful to have that leadership challenged. As one observer reported, "By the mid-1950s she had been the guiding spirit both at Peninsula School and at the Palo Alto Friends Meeting for a long generation, and she never expected not to get her way on anything of importance to her."[45]

When Duveneck was challenged by her allies, she reacted with anger. One major challenge to her leadership occurred at the Intertribal

Friendship House (IFH) in Oakland, California. Established under Duveneck's instigation by the AFSC in 1955 in order to help Native Americans who were being relocated by the BIA from rural reservations to Oakland, the IFH was intended to help Native Americans who were suffering from bewildering culture shock in the painful adjustment to urban life. The house offered counseling services, social activities, and recreation programs and encouraged the preservation of Native American arts and crafts. The house was run by a council composed of eight Native Americans and three representatives from the AFSC. During the late 1950s, when a rising tide of ethnic consciousness was transforming Native American communities, the Native American members of the council decided that they wanted to assume full responsibility for staffing, programming, and financing the center. Duveneck was offended and believed that the Native Americans were making a huge mistake in alienating their white allies.[46] As she reflected later, "I think for so many years we worked to build people up so they would help themselves . . . but when it started to happen some of us felt— . . . our nose was out of joint because they were doing these things themselves and they didn't want any advice."[47]

The difficulties Duveneck encountered were typical of the problematic relationships between liberal whites and members of racial-ethnic groups, although her class background and forceful personality exacerbated the problem. Not all AFSC staff members had such a strong need to exert leadership and to establish control; many tried assiduously to encourage leadership among grass-roots leaders. The 1940s and 1950s served as a transition in the changing relationship between white and middle-class activists and poor communities: for the first time to any significant degree, alliances were formed between liberal whites, working in conjunction with middle-class individuals from racial-ethnic backgrounds, and poor racial-ethnic communities in attempts to empower those communities. Those alliances may have been helpful for the development of poor communities during the 1940s and 1950s, for such communities were sufficiently powerless to need the resources that white and middle-class activists could draw upon. Yet inevitably the power relationships within those alliances were slowly transformed as racial-ethnic individuals and communities began to exert a greater sense of self-determination and power over their own lives. By the mid-1950s whites accustomed to positions of leadership and domination in these interracial alliances began to face challenges.

That challenge would intensify by the mid-1960s, as the black power movement and other racial-ethnic pride movements emerged. By the late 1960s the work of the AFSC reflected this shifting power balance in heated discussions of the difference between community organizing and community development. According to its proponents, community development focused on enabling people to set an agenda and take steps to create change, whereas community organization was characterized as a manipulative process in which community organizers had preconceived notions of the goals and means to achieve change in communities.[48] The two terms, however distinct, may be less useful than an examination of the spirit in which staff workers approached their work: enabling a community to set an agenda required that the organizer set aside personal ego. Civil rights workers faced the same choices and entered the same debate in the mid-1960s, when staff for the Student Nonviolent Coordinating Committee (SNCC) accused Martin Luther King and the Southern Christian Leadership Conference (SCLC) of setting their own agenda in communities rather than working with and eliciting agendas from the communities.[49] By the end of the 1960s, racial-ethnic groups would insist that any alliance be conducted on a basis of absolute respect and equality for all parties.

The AFSC served as an important vehicle for women activists to express their political and social concerns in the postwar world, creating avenues for women to exert leadership in the task of breaking down racial barriers in U.S. society. In AFSC projects ranging from efforts to ease the trauma of relocation for Japanese Americans to those that challenged school integration and community development efforts, women played key roles. Furthermore, gender differences led women to develop a subtly different style from their male colleagues, and the very fact of their sex enabled women to work particularly effectively with the often predominantly female networks of activists in local communities. But most women involved in the AFSC spent little time or energy thinking about their role as women in the organization; rather they focused on common experiences with their male colleagues in creating social change. For them the opportunity to work to create a better society, one based on justice, peace, and respect for human dignity, was a welcome challenge that gave their lives meaning.

4

Women and Peace Activism
in Cold War America

There were few eras in twentieth-century U.S. history when those working to achieve an end to war faced a tougher uphill battle than in the years immediately after World War II. The political landscape was markedly more hostile to peace activism than it had been in the interwar decades. Following World War I, profound disillusionment with the war spread as it became evident that the war had failed to "save the world for democracy" or to produce a permanent peace. Peace activists rode the crest of a wave of widespread revulsion against war during the 1920s and 1930s, organizing the largest peace movement yet witnessed in the United States. In contrast, peace activists after World War II faced a much less hospitable climate of public opinion. Although the advent of the atomic age made the issue of world peace more pressing than ever, political factors militated against peaceful solutions to world problems. As Cold War tensions escalated, U.S. politicians and the press portrayed the world as divided between two mighty armed camps, Communist and capitalist, that diverged not only in economic principles but in moral and spiritual terms as well.

Postwar liberalism fractured over the question of foreign policy. The triumphant side, represented by Americans for Democratic Action and President Truman, advocated military containment of the Soviet Union. In his unsuccessful presidential bid in 1948, Henry Wallace argued for policies of cooperation with the Soviet Union. Liberals withdrew from his campaign in droves when it became clear that he had a number of Communist supporters, and his decisive defeat spelled the end of any serious challenge to the policy of containment. As the United States projected its military power around the globe, commitment to world peace was branded as at best naive, at worst subversive.[1]

The defeat of the secular Left in the postwar period further weakened the forces capable of opposing the creation of a U.S. military-industrial complex, which President Eisenhower warned against. Capitalizing on the opportunities presented by the increased concern with internal subversion, Senator Joseph McCarthy initiated a virulent campaign against domestic Communists and Communist sympathizers, creating a climate of fear and intimidation perhaps unparalleled in U.S. history. As an engulfing tide of anticommunism spread its pall of conformity and fear across life in the United States, many people who were sympathetic to the aims of peace activists were afraid to engage in even the mildest forms of dissent, such as signing petitions or joining organizations that supported peace. So pervasive was this fear that peace activists often had difficulty even in securing public meeting places to hold educational forums on peace. In the face of this political climate, religious pacifists, and to a lesser degree, mainstream liberal internationalists, kept alive the search for peaceful alternatives to war.[2] Each was protected to some degree from red-baiting attacks, religious pacifists in organizations such as the AFSC because of public respect for their Christian principles, and liberal internationalists in groups such as the YWCA because of their air of mainstream respectability.[3]

The obstacles women peace activists faced from the larger political universe were coupled with increasing domination of the peace movement by male leaders, in contrast to the interwar decades, when women's organizations had exerted considerable influence. The leadership of mixed-sex pacifist organizations such as the AFSC consisted largely of men who had served as conscientious objectors (COs) during World Wars I and II. Ironically, just as war privileged men as actors, opposition to war privileged the men who resisted. The pacifist beliefs of COs were tested and hardened and in many cases radicalized by their experiences in Civilian Public Service Camps established for wartime COs, or in federal prison, for those who refused to go to the camps.[4] COs were joined by other men whose wartime experiences facilitated a leadership role, particularly atomic scientists. Many of the scientists who had contributed to the Manhattan Project to develop the atomic bomb worked in a frenzy in the years from 1945 to 1950 to convince the public of the necessity for civilian and international control of atomic energy.[5] This pattern of male domination reflected the larger shape of sexism in U.S. society during the postwar period. Men dominated political and intellectual life, and women suffered the erosion of the separate spheres that had provided a significant power base for them at the turn of the century, without being compensated by genuine sexual integration of major institutions. Ironically, their relative weakness was even more pronounced in the peace movement, where women had provided strong leadership from 1914 through World War II, than in some other areas of social reform, such as the struggle for racial justice.[6]

A sharp gendered division of labor was thus more evident than ever in the peace movement. Its intellectual leaders, those who were the major speakers and writers on issues related to peace, included prominent scientists such as Albert Einstein; Norman Cousins, editor of the *Saturday Review of Literature;* pacifists such as Clarence Pickett, who headed the AFSC, and A. J. Muste—all men. A series of pamphlets published by the AFSC that defined pacifist alternatives to postwar policy were prepared by study groups composed of men. Even a number of women's organizations such as the YWCA, AAUW, and LWV usually relied on male speakers at their educational forums on international relations and peace.

Nevertheless, women activists played a vital role in what survived of the U.S. peace movement during and after World War II, providing much of the grass-roots support for peace activism. Whether women were more widely engaged in peace efforts in the postwar world than men is difficult to ascertain but seems likely. Accounts of the peace movement of the 1920s and 1930s indicate that women's groups constituted a major component of that movement.[7] Survey research suggests the presence of a significant gender gap between men and women in both major political parties in support for the use of military force in international relations from the late 1930s through the 1970s.[8] As this chapter will demonstrate, many liberal women's organizations expressed serious reservations about the increasing militarism of U.S. foreign policy in the postwar world and played a critical role in educating the public about international issues.

Although women continued in the tradition of women's peace activism, they differed from the prewar generation in their justification for their participation. During World War I, when the women's peace movement was formed, women articulated an ideology that suggested that women had a particular connection to peace. Leaders such as Jane Addams and Lillian Wald agreed that women had social experiences (rather than innate biological differences) that led them to articulate different moral priorities from those of men. Key among those was their paramount concern with the preservation of human life. According to this view women were more fervent in their devotion to preserving life than were men because most women bore and nurtured children or cared for the infirm and elderly. Furthermore, women's experience as mothers gave them greater experience in peacefully resolving conflicts. Addams, Wald, and Carrie Chapman Catt, who organized the National Committee on the Cause and Cure of War in 1924, argued that men had developed habits of relying on brute force to get their way, both in terms of dominating women and in asserting their views with other men. Only by ending this reliance on force and including women in the body politic could society become whole; the alternative was a society torn by hostility, inequality, and war.[9]

Arguments based on women's distinctive morality and concern for peace lost both the centrality and the fervor with which they were put forth in the 1910s.[10] In the period after World War II, however, such arguments were heard occasionally within women's organizations as diverse as the YWCA and the WILPF. For example, in her introduction to the Public Affairs Committee report at the 1952 YWCA national convention, Marjorie Reeves Mudge stated that "the desire for peace has always been strong in the hearts of all women, for war brings a special kind of suffering to the mothers, sisters, wives, and sweethearts of men."[11] During that same convention a delegate expressed the view that women must not depend upon military might to solve problems but "must have a higher standard," suggesting that women better understood how to resolve problems peacefully.[12] In her address to the international congress of the Women's International League for Peace and Freedom that met in Copenhagen in 1949, Annalee Steward, president of the U.S. Section, quoted U.S. Senator Margaret Chase Smith, who argued, "In international affairs, women might avoid the seemingly dangerous impasse that men have created."[13] Clearly some women activists continued to believe that women were more committed to peace than men, yet the arguments they drew upon presented no unified explanation for this difference.

If women's organizations at times emphasized the differences between women and men, at other times they stressed the similarities. Women were also urged to work for peace not out of any special propensity, but rather because they should assume equal responsibility with men for running the affairs of the world. This had been a common theme in arguments for suffrage as well as among peace activists such as Carrie Chapman Catt in the 1920s.[14] In 1946 at the Tenth International Congress of WILPF, the Dutch Section argued for disbandment of the organization in order that women and men might work together for peace. Mildred Scott Olmsted, executive secretary of the U.S. Section, countered this suggestion by stressing "the long international experience of the League and the strength of its influence . . . the continued need for women's cooperation in building a world where 'children may grow up safely and happily'; the comprehensive programme of the WILPF for peace, freedom and non-violent change; and the importance of doing nothing that might weaken the peace movement at this crucial moment in world affairs."[15] Only the reference to children suggests anything unique about women's role, and even that reference is not explicit. In her opening speech to the Eleventh International Congress of WILPF in 1949, Marie Lous Mohr, international vice-president, argued that by doing peace work "we women will be able to do our share in the struggle for . . . exterminating war and winning the peace."[16] The YWCA often stressed that women's involvement in the political process was a duty and right of citizenship, seemingly gender-neutral concepts.

Thus no clearly articulated position spelling out women's connections to peace activism is evident in the postwar world, within either women's or mixed-sex organizations. In the former, references were made to that connection, but they suggested no uniform set of ideas about women's motivations to work for peace. Not surprisingly, in a mixed-sex peace organization like the AFSC, no mention was made of any special concern that women might have for peace.

Perhaps the major factor that accounts for the dissipation of gender ideology was the declining influence of feminism generally coupled with the changing ideology underlying feminist efforts in the postwar era. The ideology of women's distinctive relationship to peace was most powerfully articulated at the time of the First World War, nurtured by the surging tide of feminism that had climaxed in the suffrage victory.[17] That ideology emerged from the belief that men and women had different moral priorities, the result of women's distinct social experiences as mothers and nurturers. After the suffrage victory, women activists who had united behind suffrage splintered into groups with competing ideas about political priorities; the notion of "woman" gave way to debates about "women" in all their diversity. Feminist efforts of the 1940s and 1950s attempted to bridge that diversity by calling for equality of opportunity while downplaying gender differences. Women in the peace movement followed a similar trajectory, muting without entirely abandoning ideas about women's pacific qualities.

The Pacifist Alternative to War

Although the postwar peace movement inherited a rich legacy of activism from the prewar movement, it was unalterably transformed by the experience of World War II. During the 1920s and 1930s people of various political persuasions joined forces, first to construct a peaceful world order, and then, faced with the increasing threats of war in Europe and Far East, to prevent the outbreak of war. Pacifists, internationalists, and the radical Left, including Communists and Socialists, all worked together to stave off the coming disaster. Yet the bonds that held these disparate groups together were increasingly strained after 1935 as war loomed ever closer. Pacifists and internationalists divided over the 1935 Neutrality Act, which established an embargo on arms trade with all belligerents. While pacifists supported the legislation, internationalists argued that mandatory arms embargoes prevented any discrimination between aggressors and the victims of aggression; they proposed instead legislation that gave the president discretionary power to decide whether to impose an arms embargo. The eruption of the Spanish civil war brought the issue to a head. During the next three years the unity of the peace movement was shattered by debate over how to respond to the spread of fascism. Pacifists continued to support U.S. neutrality and avoidance of war at all costs, while internationalists embraced the necessity of economic sanctions, selective arms embargoes, and ultimately, the use of armed force to check the aggressive expansion of the Axis powers.[18]

The men and women involved in the AFSC were part of a small group of staunch pacifists, most of them Christian in persuasion, who continued to oppose war even after U.S. entry into the war. During the war male pacifists of draft age entered Civilian Public Service Camps or went to prison. Women pacifists in the AFSC and the WILPF and other organizations supported the rights of conscientious objectors, helped Jewish refugees from Europe in the resettlement process, urged liberalization of immigration laws to allow more Jews to enter the United States, urged the release of Japanese Americans from internment camps, and opposed the possibility of women's conscription. Together, pacifist organizations such as the AFSC, the WILPF, the War Resisters League, and the Fellowship of Reconciliation advocated the application of pacifist ideas to international relations in the postwar world.[19]

Formidable obstacles faced those seeking to apply pacifist ideas during the Cold War. Pacifism directly challenged the underlying assumption that dominated U.S. foreign policy in the postwar era: that the world was sharply divided into two opposing political and economic systems, and that Soviet communism had to be countered in every way possible, particularly through a large American military establishment.[20]

In contrast the religious pacifism of the Society of Friends emphasized the Christian message of the unity of all humankind and invoked Christ's injunction to maintain good will toward all people. The conviction that the entire human race constituted one family and that each individual contained some element of the divine rendered war totally unacceptable to pacifists as a way of dealing with conflict.[21] Further, the AFSC cautioned against simplistic thinking that identified the United States with good and the Soviet Union with evil, arguing that evil was embedded in attitudes prevalent in both countries, particularly through an overemphasis on materialism and the accompanying lust for power. Pacifism suggested that "that which is obtained by love is retained, but what is obtained by hatred proves a burden."[22] Ultimately, then, war could never live up to its promise of solving problems.

Abjuring war as a solution to social problems, religious pacifists believed that the elimination of war required the restructuring of the entire social order. Social problems such as injustice, discrimination, denial of individual rights, and extremes of wealth and poverty would eventually "fester and erupt into war."[23] Only by transforming the social order could the conditions for lasting peace be created.

The AFSC proposed a series of specific steps the United States could undertake to promote peace. These included four specific points: making serious efforts to negotiate with the Soviet Union; strengthening the United Nations in order to make it a genuine forum for resolution of disputes; initiating a large-scale program of aid to improve living standards in developing nations in order to eliminate the devastating poverty that proved a fertile ground for the seeds of war; and negotiating steps toward disarmament.[24] This four-point program formed the basis for much of the peace education work of the AFSC during the late 1940s and 1950s. These ideas had wide currency in the postwar world, not simply in pacifist but in liberal internationalist circles as well. They were discussed in the liberal press and advocated by a variety of groups, including many women's organizations.

By 1955, however, a number of AFSC staff members expressed frustration that these ideas remained confined to the realm of abstract discussions and had made so little impact on public policy. In a pamphlet entitled *Speak Truth to Power*, the AFSC argued that it was inherently contradictory to work toward the creation of a more peaceful world order while simultaneously supporting militarism, as many liberal internationalist organizations did. The pamphlet outlined several reasons for this. First, the arms race contained an inevitable tendency to escalate, which would lead it to absorb most of the financial resources of the United States and the USSR, preventing them from giving significant economic and technical aid to the developing world. Second, preparing for war required the adoption of internal security measures and the centralization of political power, both measures that undermined the democratic tradition. Third, political policies were subordinated to the military containment of communism, pushing the United States to support the "status quo instead of championing the oppressed" in Asia, Africa, and Latin America, and to support German rearmament.[25] Finally, the authors argued, "it is psychologically impossible to be devoted at once to the attitudes that alone make possible the destruction of one's fellow men and to the generous, creative relief of their necessities."[26]

The authors of *Speak Truth to Power* argued that an alternative method of resisting evil had to be developed, and pacifists looked to nonviolent resistance for that alternative. As articulated by Mohandas K. Gandhi in the Indian independence movement, nonviolence was an attempt to counter injustice through the disciplined use of forgiving love. Gandhi hoped to show that resisters could often confuse their oppressors by their willingness to suffer and their refusal to resort to violence. Proponents of nonviolent resistance argued that if large numbers of people engaged in such resistance, even an invading army might conceivably lose its will to conquer.[27]

Speak Truth to Power gained considerable attention in the national press and quickly became the AFSC's best-selling piece of literature. The timing was propitious, for the pamphlet was published in 1955, just as the Cold War began to thaw. With the settlement of the Korean War and the death of Stalin in 1953, followed by the U.S. Senate's censure of McCarthy in 1954, both domestic and international tensions began to ease. As a result the voices of dissent from U.S. Cold War policies began to gain a wider hearing.[28]

The positions the AFSC advanced during the height of the Cold War were remarkably courageous, given the deadening effect of fear and conformity on the intellectual and social climate. The AFSC's forthright pacifist analysis clearly put the organization outside the pale of common political discourse. By calling for dismantling the U.S. military establishment, substituting nonviolent resistance for war, and extending support for social revolutions in developing countries, the AFSC indicated the strength of its vision and the firmness of its conviction that only a total reordering of international affairs could create a sane and just world. Thus the AFSC continued in the centuries-old tradition of the Quaker "peace testimony," presenting a religiously inspired pacifist ideal to a world obsessed with military security. Although many of its specific suggestions for improving international affairs were consistent with wider public opinion, its insistence that specific peacemaking measures would be undermined by support of militarism separated it from liberal internationalist thought in the postwar world.

Liberal Internationalism in the Postwar World

Liberal internationalism seemed to emerge from the war in a very influential position. A major component of the prewar peace movement, the liberal internationalist coalition had worked for disarmament and world organization and, during the 1930s, had urged the United States to assume responsibility for engaging in collective security arrangements. The creation of the United Nations Organization, the major thrust of liberal internationalism, was achieved in 1945, and liberal internationalist approaches seemed triumphant. From 1945 to 1949 there was a flurry of intense interest in the idea of world federalism. World federalists argued that the menace of atomic warfare required nations to give up some degree of national sovereignty and to cooperate in a world government. Others rejected the idea as utopian and called instead for strengthening the United Nations, suggesting that world sovereignty could emerge only from a more gradual process. Liberal internationalists had hopes that their ideas for a new world order, "free trade, national self-determination, freedom of the seas, and constitutional democracy, would become universal principles benefitting all peoples."[29] Central to the internationalists' hopes was strengthening the United Nations so that it would function as a world body capable of mediating disputes and creating the conditions for peace worldwide.

Many women in the prewar peace movement had endorsed liberal internationalist ideas. The National Committee on the Cause and Cure of War (NCCCW), organized by suffrage leader Carrie Chapman Catt in 1925, met annually to discuss a broad range of ideas for creating a peaceful world order. The NCCCW was an umbrella group that pulled together many of the major predominantly white women's groups of the day, including the YWCA, the American Association of University Women (AAUW), the General Federation of Women's Clubs (GFWC), the National Council of Jewish Women (NCJW), the National Federation of Business and Professional Women's Clubs (NFBPW), the League of Women Voters (LWV), and the Women's Trade Union League (WTUL). Liberal internationalist ideas were widely discussed in NCCCW meetings, and endorsed by many of the member groups.

In the face of U.S. entry into war, however, the NCCCW disbanded and most of its constituent groups endorsed war. Following the war a number of these same women's organizations continued to endorse a liberal internationalist perspective. Technically no longer part of a peace movement, for they had endorsed war as a last resort, they nevertheless had a major interest in creating the foundations of a more peaceful world order and worked assiduously for its realization. Prominent in this liberal internationalist coalition after the war were the YWCA, AAUW, BPW, LWV, and WTUL.[30]

Despite the rosy hopes of liberal internationalists immediately after the war, the realities of the Cold War doomed their ideas to defeat. The

United Nations became deadlocked on many issues as the rivalry between the United States and the USSR undermined its peacekeeping potential. Women who endorsed internationalist goals faced a major dilemma. On the one hand, they shared the concern of U.S. political leaders that the Soviet Union posed a real threat, and thus they remained wedded to the fundamental assumption of U.S. foreign policy: that military preparedness was essential for national security. On the other hand, women in the coalition deplored the excessive emphasis on militarism of U.S. foreign policy and urged the government to put more energy and resources into constructive activities that could ease international tensions and create greater economic security throughout the world.

The uneasy tension between these two strains of thought is evident within the YWCA. The YWCA's ambivalence about militarism was a legacy of the Y's position in the interwar period. The organization had ardently supported the cause of peace throughout the interwar decades. The 1922 national convention of the YWCA endorsed the outlawing of war and called for the United States to join the League of Nations. Every YWCA national convention from 1922 through 1938 favored U.S. entrance into both the Permanent Court of International Justice and the League of Nations. The single exception was the YWCA national convention of 1928, which instead endorsed the Kellogg-Briand treaty as an alternative. Throughout the 1920s and early 1930s the YWCA advocated disarmament, and it went on record to oppose the naval building programs of 1928 and 1934.[31]

As Hitler's armies advanced on the helpless nations of Europe and war erupted in the Far East, however, many women in the YWCA began to question pacifism in general and U.S. neutrality in particular. By the late 1930s the YWCA was divided between those who favored armed force to oppose aggression, and those opposed to violence in any situation. Between 1938 and 1942 the question of whether Christians could participate in war was hotly debated within the Student YWCA. The 1940 YWCA national convention split over the question of U.S. military aid to Britain, eventually defeating a proposal that called for U.S. neutrality. When the Lend-Lease program was announced, providing economic support to an embattled Britain, the YWCA National Board endorsed it.[32] When the United States declared war, the YWCA affirmed its support for U.S. participation. In its first meeting after the bombing of Pearl Harbor, the National Board of the YWCA declared, "The forces of aggression must be conquered if the peoples of the world are ever again to be free and secure. . . . We dedicate ourselves to winning the struggle for freedom."[33]

Hopes for peace did not die in the hearts of those women in the YWCA who felt they had no alternative but to support the U.S. war effort. They fervently believed that other ways to reconcile differences between nations had to be developed. In order to create a future without war the YWCA pledged to work "in the great task of building a world order based on law that will promote the common welfare, secure justice and freedom for all peoples, and banish war from the earth."[34]

No dream for a more peaceful world commanded more support from the YWCA than that of making the United Nations an effective organization. During the years immediately after World War II, educating the public about the functions of the UN and organizing support for the new world body was a top priority for the YWCA, as it was for other women's organizations, such as the League of Women Voters and the American Association of University Women.[35] When the United Nations came under attack by right-wing groups in the United States in the early 1950s, the Y responded by sponsoring educational forums to inform people about the work of the United Nations. Support for the UN remained the keystone of official YWCA policy. The YWCA also insisted that inclusion of the People's Republic of China in the UN was essential to the creation of a truly effective world body.[36]

Hopes for the United Nations centered on two different functions it might serve. First, the UN could help resolve international tensions by settling disputes and providing a forum for negotiations over such difficult issues as disarmament. YWCA leaders envisioned that this might lead to a greater degree of international cooperation and eventually, perhaps, to some form of world government. The National Board, in a unanimous resolution passed in 1948, spoke about this hope, declaring, "We hold that national sovereignty should be increasingly limited in order to secure peace" by means of strengthening the United Nations.[37] Second, the UN could provide a channel for long-range efforts to provide aid to developing nations. A YWCA statement declared in 1956, "It is our firm conviction that the spiritual and material strength and the future of the democratic way of life as well as the welfare of the entire world depend to an appreciable degree upon the sharing . . . of skills, wealth and knowledge with the nations that need and want such help."[38] The Y criticized U.S. aid programs for basing decisions about aid on political rather than humanitarian concerns, arguing that the United States should provide aid through the UN and should give aid to neutral countries as generously as to its own allies.[39]

The delicate balancing act between advocating peace and endorsing military defense continued to shape the YWCAs political stance in the postwar world. The YWCA sharply criticized American foreign policy for its overemphasis on military considerations in its pursuit of the Cold War. Although they were in a distinct minority within the YWCA, pacifist women strengthened the YWCA's protest against U.S. militarism. At the 1952 national convention a resolution advocating "strengthening of the free world through mutual aid, economic, military, educational and spiritual," provoked a spirited debate between pacifist and nonpacifist women. A number of delegates opposed inclusion of the word *military* in the resolution, arguing that military methods were not consistent with the Christian purpose of the organization, and that "world peace will never come by military means." The larger nonpacifist majority countered with the argument, "It would be disastrous to us as a nation to work at this time for unilateral disarmament. Our present world situation doesn't . . . make it possible to do that." The nonpacifists won the debate; the word *military* was retained.[40]

Reservations about military policies surfaced in the YWCA's criticism of specific U.S. Cold War policies. In approving U.S. aid to Turkey and Greece, for example, the Y asked, Will the United States "use its predominant power to prevent social changes and thereby sow the seeds of communism or war or both?"[41] Furthermore, when the National Board urged the ratification of NATO, it was careful to note that other concerns, such as faith in the United Nations, the moral responsibility of the United States in the world, and the need to work for economic and social welfare throughout the world, were as important as military security. Even with these reservations, the resolution failed to win the full support of the board; the vote of 23 to 12 in favor indicated that a strong minority opposed the military pact.[42] Five years later the National Public Affairs Committee cautioned, "In the long run the national security will be gained through other than military defenses, through spiritual, social, economic, and psychological strengths which have not yet been fully realized."[43] And again in a statement to the 1958 national convention, the National Board deplored "the primary emphasis which is placed frequently in foreign policy on defense and military preparedness. . . . We plead for a foreign policy in which the creative and constructive genius of the United States is directed toward affecting conditions in the world which will make peace possible."[44]

As an alternative to militarism the YWCA endorsed the far-reaching proposals for peace advanced by the AFSC in *Steps to Peace*. Throughout the 1950s and 1960s the Y's program for international relations stressed the need for negotiation with the Soviet Union, strengthening the United Nations, large-scale economic development programs for the developing world, and disarmament.

Yet because the YWCA assumed that the Soviet Union presented a major threat to U.S. security, it continued to advocate military defense and collective security. Unlike the AFSC and other pacifist organizations that argued that a commitment to military defense doomed positive efforts for peace, the YWCA and other internationalist organizations believed that the two approaches had to be combined. As the National Board cautioned, "We recognize that defense is necessary until progress is made in disarmament."[45] Women in the YWCA hoped that efforts at international cooperation would pave the way for a more peaceful world, and that the UN would become a means of providing collective security. In the interim, military security and international cooperation represented "two types of 'insurance policies.' "[46] By embracing military security the YWCA committed itself to support of the postwar U.S. network of military alliances and the policy of containment. Its position on a number of key issues in the Cold War followed logically from these first premises. For example, the YWCA supported U.S. aid to Turkey and Greece in 1947, endorsed the 1949 NATO pact, and supported the UN intervention in Korea in 1950.[47] Thus the YWCA attempted to find a delicate balance in the postwar world: supporting the basic assumption that the United States had to be prepared to defend its interests through military action, but at the same time suggesting that militarism itself was a limited and ultimately flawed approach to resolving international problems and to promoting world peace.

Strategies for Change:
Peace Education in
the Cold War

During the height of the Cold War, from 1947 to 1955, peace activists faced an extremely hostile climate for their ideas. As a result they tended to embrace only the most cautious of tactics. This was not the time for marches, civil disobedience, or other dramatic tactics, except on the part of a tiny band of radical pacifists who engaged in tax resistance and small militant protest actions.[48] Most peace activists confined themselves to educational activities designed to introduce new audiences to intellectual alternatives to Cold War policies.

Both the YWCA and the AFSC relied heavily on educational techniques, though the formats they employed were somewhat different. International relations was a major part of the YWCA's Public Affairs Program, and local education programs frequently focused on international affairs. Educational activities tended to take the form of evening and weekend forums in which one or more speakers would give a talk, followed by discussion. The YWCA also regularly sponsored certain annual events, such as United Nations Day, which was devoted to publicizing the work of the UN and to urging support for its activities. Other events focused on acquainting women and girls with the variety of cultures around the world, and on increasing international understanding.

The AFSC's peace education program concentrated on in-depth educational activities, ranging from weekend conferences to ten-day seminars and work camps from one week to six weeks in length. In 1947, for example, the AFSC sponsored the following activities: fourteen ten-day Institutes of International Relations, summer conferences in which speakers and discussion groups focused on topics in international relations and pacifist approaches to world problems; 300 one- or two-day conferences; eight high school institutes; ten peace caravans, which consisted of small groups of students, intensively trained in peace education, who traveled to different communities to facilitate discussions about peace and international relations; and seven International Student Service Seminars, which brought students from foreign countries and the United States together to discuss world problems.[49]

Throughout the 1940s and 1950s women continued to be at the heart of peace education activities. In the YWCA women were responsible for initiating, planning, and organizing all programs in peace education, although the association did rely on male speakers at a number of its educational events. In the mixed-sex organization of the AFSC, gendered patterns of hiring are evident. Much of the AFSC's peace work was carried out by the regional offices, with a small staff in the Philadelphia office that coordinated those efforts. Most regional offices employed a peace education secretary, responsible for coordinating peace education among adults. In addition, most offices also employed a college field secretary, who conducted AFSC programs among college students, in which peace education was often a component. The Peace Education Program in the national office was staffed primarily by men, although not exclusively. Most peace education secretaries were male from 1945 to 1960. The position of college secretary, however, was clearly open to women, who constituted half or more of those positions in the same period.[50] Thus the college secretary posts often provided women an opportunity to do peace education work.

Betty Mansfield, for example, directed the AFSC's College Program from 1944 to 1947. The position involved a great deal of traveling, consulting with college peace secretaries throughout the country, delivering speeches, and maintaining links between the regional and national offices. Mansfield also directed training programs for and supervised the Peace Caravans. In 1947 she accepted a position as college secretary for the Midwest Regional Office in Chicago, where her responsibilities included lecturing to college audiences, organizing weekend work camps, arranging scholarships for foreign students, and recruiting students for international service projects. Mansfield found that her work with the AFSC gave her an opportunity to actively pursue the ideal that had inspired her since adolescence—world peace.[51]

Jean Fairfax was also drawn to the AFSC, with which she first became acquainted as an undergraduate in the late 1930s, because of its pacifism. Her interest in the peace issue came out of her own religious upbringing. During her graduate work at Union Theological Seminary during the war years, the issue of pacifism split the student body down the middle. Immediately after the war Fairfax went to Austria with the AFSC to help with rehabilitation efforts there. In Austria she was placed in charge of organizing programs for university students and work camps to help with reconstruction. Her fluent German made her an invaluable addition to the AFSC's Neighborhood Center, which provided recreational, social, educational, and other programs. Her experiences in Europe, working to rebuild a war-torn society, deepened her conviction that war was futile. Returning to the United States, she became college secretary for the AFSC in the New England Region, a position she held from 1949 to 1955. She worked extensively with college students in the area of international relations, setting up and administering international institutes and conducting work camps and work projects.[52]

Although the generation of women active in the 1940s and 1950s played an important role in peace activism, because of the almost exclusive reliance on educational tactics, it is difficult to communicate much of the vitality of the work of peace education. But each organization provided opportunities for women who were deeply committed to the ideal of world peace to bring their knowledge and fervent idealism to a larger audience, hoping to convince them of the necessity of peacemaking. Despite public opposition, women activists worked closely with male allies to keep alive the idea of world peace in a political climate that militated against its survival. Facing tremendous odds these women worked hard to stem the tide of hatred and suspicion that dominated national life, promoting a vision of an alternative means of structuring international relations in order to create a more peaceful world. Furthermore, they demonstrated that women were committed to working actively to realize that vision.

5

Feminism, Domesticity, and Women's Social Reform in Postwar America

The most common picture of the postwar world presented in historical literature suggests that feminism as an explicit ideology was essentially dead. Yet a closer examination attests to feminism's survival, though certainly in a less vital form than during periods of intense feminist activism such as the 1910s or the 1970s. Part of the difficulty here is one of definition. During the 1940s and 1950s the term *feminism* was associated with the National Woman's Party and support for an Equal Rights Amendment. Accompanying that specific organizational connection, the term *feminist* also carried with it a harsh connotation of a woman single-mindedly bent on advancing women's interests at the expense of all other social concerns. Only a tiny minority of women in the United States identified with the term *feminist* and its accompanying connotations during the 1940s and 1950s. Yet if we rely on current definitions, it is hard to escape the conclusion that many more women advocated feminist positions in that period than claimed the label. For purposes of my argument I will rely on Linda Gordon's recent definition: "Feminism is a critique of male supremacy, formed and offered in the light of a will to change it, which in turn assumes a conviction that it is changeable."[1]

The YWCA took a feminist stance on a number of issues in the postwar world, while the AFSC did not. This contrast between the two organizations was largely a result of the fact that the YWCA was a separate women's organization, with a heritage of advancing the cause of women.

In contrast, the AFSC was a mixed-sex organization without an explicit feminist heritage. Historians of women have noted the crucial role that women's separate organizations played in the late nineteenth and early twentieth centuries, providing a strong organizational base from which to develop and pursue feminist politics. Estelle Freedman has argued that the retreat from the principle of separate women's organizations after suffrage seriously weakened the women's movement, for as women turned away from separate women's organizations to enter mixed-sex organizations, they lost a base of power that had reinforced their feminist beliefs and activities. This argument suggests not that all separate women's organizations are feminist, but rather that women with a feminist agenda can sustain and express their views more easily from within women's organizations than from within mixed-sex organizations.[2]

For decades the YWCA had defended the rights of women workers, and it continued to do so in the postwar world. YWCA leaders had little sympathy for the conservative ideology of domesticity that argued that women should confine themselves to the home and eschew participation in the paid labor force. Immediately following the war, when women were urged to abandon their jobs in order to make way for returning veterans, the YWCA supported the principle that all women had the right to work for wages, and that they should have equal opportunities with men in training and employment. In one article that appeared in the *Womans Press* (the YWCA magazine), for example, the author argued that it was unfair to turn women out of their jobs because many women were either self-supporting or providing the sole support for relatives, and because work provided an important sense of social usefulness for women.[3] The Y's 1945 Public Affairs Program explicitly called for equal pay for equal work, and the Y supported equal pay legislation at the state and federal levels. By the mid-1950s YWCA leaders began to refer to equal pay for "comparable," rather than "equal," work, a change that reflected the understanding that men and women rarely held exactly the same jobs.[4] Clearly, then, in the area of women's labor force participation, the YWCA formulated feminist positions that recognized the existence of male supremacy and sought to end it.

The YWCA also addressed questions of gender inequality in the arena of political and civil rights for women in the post–World War II era, much as it had in the earlier decades of the twentieth century. The Y fought to end restrictions aimed specifically at married women, such as state laws that required a husband's consent for a married woman to work or that restricted a wife's legal control of her own wages. In the early 1960s the Y began to address the issue of equity in Social Security legislation as well.[5]

The belief that women faced discrimination, coupled with a determination to fight such discrimination, was commonplace among those women most active in the YWCA during the postwar years. That perspective was evident during discussions held on the convention floor of the 1955 YWCA national convention. One delegate suggested adding the word *sex* to a resolution that read: "We will continue to work for the elimination of segregation and discrimination on the basis of race, creed, and national origin." Her amendment carried without discussion. At a later point in the proceedings, however, another delegate challenged the wording of the amendment, arguing that women did not experience segregation. Others responded that women were, however, subject to discrimination. Only when a delegate pointed out that another section of the Public Affairs Program already called for equal employment opportunities and equal pay for equal work was the amendment to add the word *sex* defeated.[6]

As World War II came to a close, the YWCA's vision of gender equality encompassed far more than equal rights in the economic and legal spheres, however. YWCA leaders also envisioned a partnership between men and women in which women would share responsibility in the construction of a new postwar political and social order. The Y urged women to become well-informed on the great political issues of the day, to develop a sense of social responsibility, and to exercise leadership in economic, educational, political, and religious arenas. Y leaders recognized that women's socialization often prevented them from exercising such leadership, and thus the YWCA explicitly encouraged women to overcome feelings of inferiority and to develop confidence in their ability to function autonomously. As one YWCA pamphlet put it, "Women . . . are seeking freedom to act as individuals in their own right; to form their own opinions as human beings and to act freely in the light of their own convictions."[7] This theme remained a constant one throughout the postwar period, echoing a decade and a half after the war's end in the words of executive secretary of the YWCA Edith Lerrigo: "We are a women's movement . . . this means that the YWCA must help women to see themselves as persons with dignity, integrity, and wholeness: we must show women the great contributions they can make by assuming responsibility and leadership as citizens."[8]

Curiously, the question of whether women had a unique contribution to make to this partnership received little attention in YWCA literature. This is in sharp contrast to earlier generations of women social reformers who hotly debated the question of gender differences and, in some cases, made sweeping proclamations about women's different nature. But occasional references to the particular role of women as mothers and nurturers appeared in YWCA literature, implying, without spelling it out, that women might be more nurturing and cooperative in spirit. In a piece called "Women in 1949" that appeared in the *Womans Press*, Rosalind Cassidy referred to "women's central task of establishing secure homes, and of bearing and nurturing children who are wanted and loved." For those women who did not marry, this nurturing and cherishing role can be extended into aspects of community responsibility—teaching, social welfare, and the like." Cassidy seems to suggest that women have a greater propensity, perhaps inherent, for nurturing activities.[9]

Regardless of what assumptions were made about the results of women's exerting greater leadership, the development of leadership abilities among women was one of the YWCA's central purposes, and that purpose was inherently feminist. Jewel Graham, an African American who rose to a position of prominence in the YWCA during the 1970s and 1980s, reflected that part of the appeal of the YWCA was that is constituted "a place where women made the decisions about what was important." That was significant, in her view, because "one of the most important sources of power . . . is the power to define, the power to name, the power to decide what is important and what isn't important, what's worthy and what's unworthy."[10]

The development of women's leadership began in the Student YWCA. The Student YWCA often worked closely with the Student YMCA on college campuses; frequently the two organizations joined into a single Christian Association on individual campuses. Yet the two clashed over the question of women's leadership. Jean Whittet, who pursued a career in the Student YWCA and eventually became director of public affairs for the YWCA in 1967, recalled such a conflict during the 1940s. Whittet was the adviser to the student YWCA at Cornell University during and after World War II. Women had taken control of the joint association on campus during the war, when most men had entered the armed forces. When the men returned after the war, a contest over leadership erupted. A young woman, "who had great leadership ability" ran for president of the organization against a man with "no qualifications except popularity," in Whittet's view. The male adviser of the group argued that it was important for the prestige of the group for a male to be president; Whittet, of course, disagreed.[11] The Y's effectiveness at developing leadership capabilities among young women is suggested by observing the number of women who got their start in the Student YWCA and later played key roles in other organizations, including the AFSC.[12]

This conflict over whether women would be granted leadership opportunities was at the core of a controversy that erupted over the relationship between the YWCA and the YMCA. In response to the expanding need for recreation facilities and other programs that both the YWCA and the YMCA provided in suburban communities, the YMCA and community funding agencies put pressure on the YWCA to merge with the YMCA in the years following World War II. For more than ten years, beginning in the late 1940s, YWCA leaders debated this issue, and their views provide an important glimpse into their feminist ideology.

In 1954 the YWCA National Board voted unanimously to oppose the idea of merger with the YMCA, arguing that the YWCA had a unique contribution to make as an independent women's organization. Y officials maintained that the YWCA provided opportunities for the development of leadership of women, which a mixed-sex organization would not do. As Myra Smith, a staff member for the National Board, explained:

We should want our rightful place in policy-making bodies . . . not merely token representation as a "bow to the ladies" but genuine full participation. . . . It makes little difference that a man rises to give one of us a seat if, when a woman speaks, he smiles indulgently and pays no more attention than if she had kept silent . . . we shall not be satisfied if only a few women get this enviable status (of leadership), while the rest are pushed into the background.[13]

Furthermore, the National Board was determined that the Y retain its identity in order to preserve its special mission of meeting the distinct needs and concerns of women.

Despite this strong statement by the National Board, the issue of merger continued to be debated throughout the decade of the 1950s. The 1958 national convention directed the National Board to study and evaluate various forms of cooperative experience between the YWCA and the YMCA, to assess whether the YWCA should consider such a merger. The study, published in 1960, strongly endorsed the importance of a separate women's organization, in order to "work for a greater measure of freedom for women."[14] Ida Davidoff, member of the National Board, recalled her fear that women would be "submerged" in a merged organization, relegated to "picking out the curtains and mailing the letters."[15] The principle of a "separate autonomous women's organization" received unanimous endorsement at the 1961 national convention. As one delegate from the floor argued, "Men do not understand the problems of women. They cannot help us solve our problems. If we combine with a man's organization the men will be trying to tell us how to solve our problems."[16]

The Debate about Domesticity

The YWCA participated in a lively debate about the shifting nature of women's roles that swirled through the popular media during the postwar period. For many years historians of women have assumed that the postwar ideology about women uniformly glorified domesticity, the notion that women should devote themselves exclusively to the care of husbands, children, and the home. In fact, the popular discourse of the period presented three distinct points of view about women, and the strident insistence on domesticity that is often associated with the postwar period represented only the most conservative of those positions. The centrists in the debate believed that married women should pursue nondomestic activities such as part-time work and civic and political activism, combining these with their responsibilities as wives and mothers. A third, feminist point of view advocated a full range of choices for women, including that of full-time careers, and argued for an end to gender-based job discrimination.[17]

Individual women active in the YWCA ranged in their views from the dominant centrist position to more explicitly feminist views. These views were expressed in policy statements, convention debates, organizational literature, and personal recollections. Not surprisingly, none advocated the conservative position. YWCA leaders, literature, and publications tended to follow the middle range of discourse on the issue, though occasionally more explicitly feminist positions were expressed. Thus, although the YWCA did suggest some modifications of women's traditional roles, the organization fell far short of issuing a wholesale challenge to such roles, preferring more muted and cautious tones.

As the war drew to a close, Grace Loucks Elliot, YWCA general secretary, declared that for women to exercise their intellectual competence and economic abilities in the postwar world would require "revision of many aspects of the relations between men and women." In her report to the National Board in 1944 Elliot urged a critical look at "patterns of family life so that those patterns may be better fitted to the development of both men and women."[18] The new leadership roles for women that Elliot envisioned would require a modification of the traditional domestic roles and responsibilities of women. This theme received further elaboration during the next few years. The male author of an article that appeared in the *Womans Press* in 1946, for example, argued that "the double standard, of men's field as the world and woman's as the home, is . . . a denial of this basic Christian principle (of equality)."[19] Both these formulations are vague and subject to a variety of interpretations, but they suggest a challenge to the prevailing assumption that women should shoulder the responsibilities of the home single-handed.

The most common view continued to identify home and family as central to women's identity, at the same time endorsing women's activities outside the home. As Grace Loucks Elliot warned in 1948, "Our effectiveness as women outside the home dare not ever be an escape from our responsibilities within it."[20] In a shift of focus from the emphasis on the needs of working women in the prewar era, during the 1950s, the YWCA began to cater to the needs of women who were primarily housewives, establishing "family life" programs. Among the goals of such programs were increased knowledge about marriage and child rearing, the changing roles of men and women, sexuality, and financial management, as well as support for married women active in the work force. The YWCA also discussed the need for child care on the part of working women. Yet the YWCA literature continued to stress that women, whether they were primarily homemakers or not, should take part in community life and be should concerned about national and international problems.[21]

A more explicit, if still somewhat cautious, feminist view was advanced by Fern Babcock, who worked for many years for the Student YWCA. In her 1955 pamphlet entitled "Being a Woman," which was widely distributed to student Y groups, Babcock outlined the major dilemma that faced women considering marriage: how to combine devotion to family with some degree of independence and autonomy. Speaking clearly to the tensions that women experienced when they were expected to subordinate personal goals to those of their husbands and children, Babcock argued that a young woman might worry that "success might jeopardize her matrimonial prospects" and "thwart the development of her feminine qualities." On the other hand, marriage itself might prevent women from expressing their individuality in intellectual, emotional, and creative ways. Caught on the horns of this dilemma, Babcock suggested, most women would want to marry, perhaps alternating years devoted to child rearing with participation in the labor force. She also suggested, however, that some women might never marry, while others might work throughout their married lives. She argued that women had just as much potential for achievement as had men, but that they had been hampered from demonstrating such achievement by their responsibilities for families. Babcock assumed that "the most satisfying life for a man or woman is in a happy marriage," yet was quick to note that a bad marriage was worse than none at all. Cautioning against the tendency of women to stifle their "intellectual and emotional responses" in order to please men, Babcock advocated that women be "honest and free" in their heterosexual relationships. Furthermore, she suggested, women could teach men to "find other values in life than the ego-satisfaction of professional success."[22] She argued that men and women often have different interests and emotional capabilities but was careful to add that it is not clear whether these traits are socially conditioned or inborn.

Although Babcock was cautious in her approach, her nonjudgmental attitude about the range of choices available to women suggests a feminist perspective on the question of how women should deal with the changing relations between the sexes. Another writer for the YWCA criticized in sharper tones the sexism inherent in many marriages, arguing that a partnership with men was possible only when men ceased wanting a "subjected, inferior female."[23]

Interestingly, Babcock herself did not marry until the age of fifty-six. In fact many of the women who worked in top positions of leadership, especially in the Student YWCA, remained single. Dorothy Height, for example, had considered marriage but realized that she was not willing to give up her goals and activities for marriage. She was critical of the dominant pattern of marriage in U.S. society where "the woman has to become sort of the background for the man"; she believed that marriage often "has not given [women] a chance to develop at least some of their own gifts, so they have some autonomous interests."[24] For such women, the YWCA itself served as a family, and they maintained close networks of friendship, love, and support that lasted over the course of their lifetimes. In the early 1980s, for example, a group of former staff members of the Student YWCA and the National Board retired together to a retirement community in Claremont, California. It is likely that some of the close relationships between YWCA activists were lesbian partnerships, but the overwhelming fear of the label of lesbianism that was so prevalent during much of these women's lives made this topic difficult to investigate.

What was notably missing from the debate within the YWCA about women's roles was any forthright challenge to the prevalent belief that women should assume primary responsibility for the care of children and the home. Rather, the position taken most frequently was that women should combine the responsibilities of family care with those of work or volunteer activities. Full-time careers were not precluded, but most women who pursued them remained single, or, if married with children, they either waited until their children were largely grown to assume full-time work or arranged for help with child care. Women were urged to struggle with the contradictions of work and home life on an individual basis rather than through organized campaigns to create social change. The result could be painful. Mildred Persinger, chair of the Public Affairs Committee in the late 1950s and early 1960s, recalled that she felt constantly worried and guilty as she tried to balance her primary responsibility toward her family with her all-consuming career with the YWCA. Only the support of her husband made this conflict somewhat easier to bear.[25]

The focus on equality of opportunity in the realm of education, work, and organizational leadership was the centerpiece of the YWCA's public challenge to male supremacy. Clearly a feminist position that questioned male privilege in the public world, it was nevertheless a fairly tame brand of feminism, hardly one that broke new ground. As historian Nancy Cott has noted, equality of opportunity was a timid compromise in a world where the category of woman encompassed far more diversity than unity. It was a broad goal that would be helpful to most women, and it papered over the ongoing debate over the ERA. It failed, however, to "address the paradoxical realities of women's situation," particularly women's responsibilities for raising children.[26] The failure to confront the division of labor and responsibility within the family was characteristic not simply of the YWCA, but of organized expressions of feminism more generally in the postwar world.

YWCA leaders did understand, however, that the roots of women's oppression could be found not only in their exclusion from the public world, but in their subordinate position in the family. They promoted and participated in a wide-ranging public discussion about women's roles in the years after World War II, particularly within the Student YWCA, where the topic became one of the most commonly discussed questions at YWCA programs and conferences. Although their questions about the private dimensions of women's subordination were far more muted than their challenge to its more public face, the debate over gender roles in the family may have had an even more significant impact in confronting male supremacy than had the fight for equal opportunity in the workplace. That debate raised issues of vital importance to young women as they faced the choices that would determine the nature of their adult lives, and it educated a generation of young women who would soon come of age and find themselves caught up in the women's liberation movement.

Throughout the period, then, the YWCA's nature as a separate women's organization, coupled with its history of commitment to pressing for women's issues, fostered feminist impulses within the organization, providing a language through which women could understand their disabilities and encouraging women to fight against injustices based on gender. The YWCA recognized the uniqueness of women's problems and needs, discussed issues of specific concern to women, and formulated goals that included calls for equal treatment for women in the workplace and in educational institutions.

Exploding Gender Conventions:
Women in the AFSC

The major dilemma of twentieth-century feminism, according to Nancy Cott, is the tension between the desire to "explode gender conventions" and the need to retain "gender consciousness."[27] It is not surprising that women in a woman's organization like the YWCA would emphasize one horn of that dilemma, that of gender consciousness, while those in a mixed-sex organization would emphasize the other, that of exploding gender conventions. A women's organization assumes that gender solidarity has some value and meaning, that working with other women enables the pursuit of goals and work in a way that is not possible in a mixed-sex organization. In contrast, women who hold professional positions in a mixed-sex organization like the AFSC hope or assume that they will be able to function effectively in close interaction with male colleagues and that they will be treated as peers by those colleagues. Women activists in such organizations thus implicitly assume that they have been able to escape the narrow confines of gender conventions, to function smoothly in a predominantly male public world.

Closely connected to that feminist dilemma was the choice faced by women activists in their pursuit of social reform goals throughout the twentieth century: whether to fight for influence within male-dominated organizations or to maintain autonomy by working through separate female institutions. The incentives for allying with or working within male organizations were obvious: access to greater financial resources and more political clout. Yet the liabilities were equally telling, as women who entered mixed-sex organizations quickly learned in the years following the passage of women's suffrage. Women hoped that their political perspectives and personal capabilities would be respected by male colleagues, only to be disappointed as they found themselves relegated to positions of little power. The choice of whether to work in a mixed-sex or single-sex organization was not an either/or choice. Many women, both black and white, chose to work in both types of organizations in the postwar period. For example, black women often joined one or more single-sex organizations such as the YWCA, the National Council of Negro Women, or a black sorority, while at the same time working with the NAACP or the Urban League.

Significant cracks in this pattern of marginalization within mixed-sex organizations first began to occur in mainstream political parties only in the 1970s, with the partial exception of Franklin Roosevelt's New Deal administration. But within mixed-sex social reform and labor organizations, women experienced a growing degree of influence in the period after World War II.[28] Women's power was rarely evident at the highest levels of such organizations. Rather, they achieved positions at the middle ranks of organizational hierarchies and often made their presence felt by working in quieter, less publicly visible ways than did male leaders.

Women's activities in the AFSC clearly illustrate this pattern. The AFSC was a male-dominated organization: the chair of the Board of Directors, the executive secretary of the national office, and all of the executive secretaries of the regional offices, with one exception, were male during the 1940s and 1950s. (Garnet Guild in 1958 was the first woman to be appointed executive secretary of a regional office.) But in the postwar era women began to obtain significant positions as program administrators and on the executive board. Eleanor Stabler Clarke served as associate or assistant executive secretary of the national office from World War II until 1951. Julia Branson served as associate secretary of the Foreign Section (the most important program section of the AFSC at the time) in the late 1940s, and then as secretary from 1950 to 1955. Anna Brinton directed the Institutes of International Relations program in the early 1950s, and during those same years Polly Cuthbertson headed the Institutional Service Program.

By the mid-1950s a number of key leadership roles in the AFSC's community relations programs were filled by women as well. Barbara Moffett, who became associate executive secretary of the Community Relations Division in 1954 and executive secretary in 1956 (a position she continues to hold today), was influential in staffing community relations programs with women. Moffett had very strong convictions about women's capacities for leadership and hired significantly more women than had her predecessors. Among the other women who worked for the Community Relations Division were Thelma Babbitt, who directed the Job Opportunities Program from 1953 to 1957; Tillie Walker, who directed the American Indian Program from 1957 to 1960; Jean Fairfax, who headed the AFSC's civil rights programs from 1957 to 1965; Constance Pennington, who was the field representative for the Farm Labor Program in the early 1960s; and Charlotte Meacham, who headed the Philadelphia Area Housing Opportunities Program from 1960 to 1968.[29]

The influence of women within the AFSC was bolstered by the extensive committee structure. Every program, at both the national and local level, was guided by a committee of volunteers that made policy decisions and in many cases supplemented the work of the staff in carrying out program activities. Women were heavily represented on committees, in part because fewer women than men were employed full-time in this period, and thus women had more available time.[30] Open discussion encouraged women to express their views, and the committee structure allowed women considerable influence in the formulation of policy. Women often served as clerk (chair), a position from which they could wield considerable power and work closely with staff members. For example, Emily Cooper Johnson served as clerk of the Peace Committee in the national office from 1940 through the 1950s and played an important role in that program. Committees functioned in a remarkably democratic manner, owing in part to the use of consensus decision making. "Coming to consensus" was a traditional Quaker practice that involved discussing each issue until all conflict had been resolved and people could arrive at a mutual decision. To practice consensus required great respect for the views of others, as well as patience and good will, and relied heavily on developing techniques of persuasion in the place of debating skills. The effect of the extensive committee structure and of the use of consensus decision making on gender relations in the AFSC was to give greater weight to the voices of women than a typical administrative hierarchy would have afforded.

Other aspects of the organizational milieu of the AFSC also facilitated women's leadership. Women who worked for the AFSC tended to be assertive and confident about their abilities to contribute to social reform activities. The men in the AFSC were also distinct from more typical men in the United States in their behavior and values. Most men involved in the AFSC during the 1940s and 1950s were Quakers, and many had renounced violence and served as conscientious objectors during World War II. These men had been forced by their pacifist convictions to reexamine certain aspects of the conventional male sex role. That reappraisal, coupled with the respect accorded women in Quaker culture, led to significantly more egalitarian relationships between men and women within the AFSC than in the larger society. Many women activists commented on this contrast.

Betty Mansfield, who directed the AFSC's College Program during the mid-1940s, reflected on the differences between her male colleagues in the AFSC and those in her job at a university: "In my work and personal life . . . I was associated with more fine, sensitive men than with insensitive, macho types. The University had more of the latter; the AFSC very few." Patricia Stewart, active in the San Francisco Regional Office for many years, thought of the AFSC as "an oasis compared to the rest of society in terms of women's roles," but she also recalled that she was considered "pushy," a strong appellation for this reserved, quiet-spoken and proper woman.[31]

Below the top level of administration, then, men and women in the AFSC worked as colleagues roughly equal in status; they led projects, administered programs, and worked as community organizers. The task at hand was creating social change, and men and women within the organization assumed that both sexes could contribute to that goal.

A brief look at several progressive labor unions and at the civil rights movement suggests that the AFSC was not the only mixed-sex organization in which women achieved greater influence in the postwar world. The massive influx of women into auto plants during World War II changed the role and status of women in the United Auto Workers (UAW), for example. Women workers organized to exert their collective power after World War II, protesting layoffs of women from the auto industry after the war and fighting to retain seniority rights. Despite their failure to achieve many of their goals, women exerted more power in the UAW than they had during the 1930s.

In civil rights organizations, as well, women moved into increasingly influential positions in the 1940s and 1950s. Thus, for example, Ruby Hurley became youth director of the NAACP in 1943; Daisy Bates was president of the NAACP chapter in Little Rock, Arkansas, using that position to lead the struggle to integrate Central High school; Rosa Parks, secretary of the local NAACP chapter in Montgomery, Alabama, sparked the bus boycott there; Septima Clark directed workshops for civil rights activists at Highlander Folk School in Monteagle, Tennessee, during the 1950s, and developed citizen education programs that became the basis for voter registration drives when she became director of education for the Southern Christian Leadership Conference (SCLC) in

1961. Most influential of all was Ella Baker, who became national director of branches for the NAACP in 1943, coordinator of SCLC's Atlanta office in 1957, and the chief adviser to the Student Nonviolent Coordinating Committee (SNCC) from 1960 to 1964. In Paula Giddings's words, "Ella Baker had become midwife to the two organizations that would have the most far-reaching impact on the civil rights movement: SCLC and SNCC."[32] Yet in all these instances the pressures of sexism were such that women exerted their influence behind the scenes, never achieving the public visibility of male leaders.

In addition to encountering a "glass ceiling" above which they would not be promoted, women in mixed-sex organizations had fewer sources of support for developing or articulating an analysis of discrimination based on gender. During a period when there was no widespread feminist movement, the temptation was either to ignore the effect of sexism or to attempt to overcome it on an individual basis. This tendency is clearly visible if we examine the experience of women activists in the AFSC.

The AFSC never included explicitly feminist demands in its organizational agenda, despite the historical connection of the Religious Society of Friends with feminism. The AFSC's initial organizational purpose did not lend itself to feminist activism; the group had been established as an alternative during World War I for male conscientious objectors to war, offering opportunities for service in reconstruction projects overseas. The AFSC continued reconstruction efforts in Europe during the 1920s, but in the 1930s turned its attention increasingly to peace education and social reform at home. Interestingly, although the AFSC addressed the plight of many disadvantaged groups, including racial-ethnic minorities, prisoners, refugees, and displaced persons, it never focused on problems specific to women. No explicit identification with organized feminism or with feminist issues and concerns appears in organizational literature or programs from the AFSC's establishment in 1917 until the 1960s.

Given the Quaker heritage of the AFSC, this complete silence about feminist issues is somewhat surprising. The Society of Friends had a long history of sexual egalitarianism, and from its origins in the religious ferment of seventeenth-century England women had played a prominent part in the sect. One of the basic tenets of Friends was that men and women were equal in the eyes of God, and that any individual who felt visited by religious insight should speak his or her mind. In place of an ordained ministry, both men and women served as traveling ministers, preachers, and elders. and women were very influential within the sect throughout its history. During the nineteenth and twentieth centuries, Friends Meetings were often dominated by powerful women. Coupled with Friends' longstanding concern for social justice, this heritage led Quaker women to participate in disproportionate numbers in many of the social reform movements of the nineteenth century, including abolition, women's rights, and prison reform. [33]

In the mid-twentieth century, however, despite the tradition of women's activism and respect for female leadership that infused the organizational culture of the AFSC, the organization took no specific position on feminist issues. Several factors help explain this curious absence. First, the organized feminist movement was both relatively quiescent and badly splintered in the period from 1920 to 1960, so that pressure to address questions relating to gender was minimal. Second, as we have noted, the mixed-sex and male-dominated nature of the organization functioned to downplay the significance of feminist concerns. Third, it is possible that the connection between the Religious Society of Friends and feminism weakened over the course of the twentieth century; further research is needed to explore this hypothesis. [34] Finally, Quakerism itself may well have influenced women in the mid–twentieth century in the direction of exploding gender conventions in their own lives rather than that of addressing the systematic discrimination that most women continued to face.

The Quaker tradition provided a greater range of options for women negotiating the demands of the domestic world than women from more conventional backgrounds encountered. Many Quaker women were married to Quaker men; often in such marriages commitment to social reform activities was a mutual goal. Josephine Duveneck and her husband, Frank, worked closely together on a number of projects, in which she remained clearly the leader, he the follower. When their four children were young, much of Josephine's energies were poured into Peninsula School, an experimental school that she helped create and that she headed from 1924 to 1943. Their wealth enabled the Duvenecks to employ a housekeeper to care for their children. Josephine Duveneck's most active years with the AFSC came during the 1940s, 1950s, and 1960s, when her children were grown.

Such husband-wife teams were common among activists in the AFSC. Eleanor Stabler Clarke, who served as associate executive secretary of the AFSC during the war years, viewed her work as an expression of the interests of both herself and her husband. When the Depression had occurred, the two of them agreed that they wanted to devote their attention to the problem of poverty, and because her husband was engaged in supporting the family through his business, they decided that Eleanor would represent them in her work with the AFSC. Polly Cuthbertson was also part of a Quaker husband-wife team, and Barbara Moffett, though not a Quaker, had the full support of her husband for her work. Among the most prominent of such Quaker pairs were William and Hannah Clothier Hull and Howard and Anna Brinton.

Married women activists engaged in a number of strategies to juggle the demands of marriage and motherhood and work activities. Some, like Moffett and Cuthbertson, had no children, greatly lessening the domestic demands on their time. Among those who did have children, a common pattern was to engage in activism before they had children or after their children were partially or fully grown. Madeleine Stephenson, for example, worked for the AFSC's Philadelphia office during World War II, then went to Europe immediately after the war to participate in AFSC reconstruction projects. She married Red Stephenson in 1947, and the two settled in the San Francisco Bay Area, where she became peace education secretary for the AFSC office. During the 1950s, when her children were young, she ceased working full-time but continued to be involved in AFSC committee work, serving as clerk of the Peace Committee and later of the Executive Committee. She remained active in the AFSC until the 1970s, when she and her husband retired. Meanwhile, her husband worked full-time in various positions for the AFSC. Thelma Babbitt, who had been married twice and had one son by her first marriage, became active in AFSC work only after she had raised her son and her second husband had died. Finally, a few women substantially altered the traditional division of labor in the home. Nancy Duryee, for example, directed the AFSC's Latin America work camp program for ten years. She was married and had a stepchild; when her job demanded a heavy traveling schedule, her husband handled child care responsibilities.[35]

There were, as well, women activists in the AFSC who remained single. Barbara Graves is an example; she administered a number of

programs for the AFSC, including the AFSC's central office for reconstruction work in Germany after World War II, and the Voluntary International Service Assignments program from 1962 to 1968. Particularly
for those who matured before the postwar period, recalled Graves, "the
option to be doing other things was socially acceptable." Graves had no
second thoughts about her choice to remain single. She had made a
conscious choice not to marry and was glad. "I don't think of marriage as a
terribly satisfying way to spend your time," she observed. "I think it does
a lot of harmful things and it also does some absolutely wonderful
things. . . . It's been an incredible privilege to be single," she reflected,
since it allowed her so much time and energy to devote to her work with
the AFSC, which was a comfortable home for her.[36]

Irene Osborne, another AFSC staff member who remained single,
was a few years younger than Graves. Perhaps because of that age
difference she was acutely conscious of the pressures on women in the
United States to define themselves in terms of domesticity and feminin-
ity, but rather than acquiesce she struggled to resist those stifling norms.
When a close male political friend needled her about his view that
women should remain feminine, Osborne would "stew about it" but
conclude that "he can't be right." However much she might agonize
over whether she met some narrowly defined ideal of womanhood, she
had far more pressing concerns on her mind—writing the next press
release, planning the next community meeting, or preparing to meet
with school board officials.[37]

The AFSC provided an organizational atmosphere that enabled
women to pursue social reform activities as a major focus of their lives
and to wield a fair degree of influence and be treated with respect by
male peers. Many of those who married had formed unusually egalitarian marriages, although traditional expectations that women would be
the primary caretakers of children tended to be the rule. Nevertheless,
to a large degree, these women's lives were far less restrained by gender
conventions than were those of more typical women in the United
States. To some extent, then, women in the AFSC had succeeded in
"exploding gender conventions." The options for following such a
course were far greater by midcentury than they had been a half century
earlier.

Yet their very success blinded them to systematic sexual discrimination. Women in the AFSC failed to raise their voices individually or

collectively to express grievances based on gender. Because the AFSC ignored feminist concerns, it encouraged women in the organization to coast on their sense of being exceptional women, part of an exceptional organization, or both. As a result, few of these women recognized or confronted the ongoing and systematic discrimination against women that occurred in the larger society.

Barbara Graves's experience in the AFSC perfectly exemplifies this perspective. She recalled that, in her work with the AFSC, "I always had jobs in which my leadership was important and recognized even though there were higher echelons which were males." She was aware of the domination of the AFSC by males, "but that didn't bother me because I had my own arenas." Furthermore, she recalled, "the males in the AFSC were more gentle and respectful of women than the macho types, so it was hard to feel oppressed by them." As a result, "I don't think that the struggles of women ever dawned on me until much later. . . . I had strong respect for the women's movement politically but didn't feel it personally . . . until the early 1970s."[38]

Not surprisingly, one of the women who was most keenly aware of sexism in the AFSC held professional positions in both the AFSC and the YWCA during the 1940s and 1950s; perhaps it was her experience in the latter organization that gave her that perspective. Polly Moss Cuthbertson recalled that there were more opportunities for women to exert leadership in the Y than in the AFSC. Cuthbertson was aware that certain AFSC jobs (personnel director, for example) were male preserves until the late 1950s, and that there were salary discrepancies between male and female employees.[39] In contrast, most of the women reformers in the AFSC would have concurred with Barbara Moffett, secretary for the Community Relations Division of the AFSC, who reflected in the 1980s, "I have no reservations about feminism, but I haven't framed my life experience in those terms."[40] Aware of the problems that most women faced in struggling to shape new identities for themselves, they nevertheless did not develop a feminist consciousness. By focusing so exclusively on exploding gender conventions, they revealed the limitations of that horn of the dilemma of twentieth-century feminism, overlooking the strength and political possibilities inherent in an emphasis on gender solidarity.

The contrast between the YWCA and the AFSC suggests that convictions about gender equality are not sufficient to promote feminist activism. Women in the AFSC tended to assume the existence of such equality, at least in their own lives, while women in the YWCA recognized the systematic discrimination that women faced and made it a priority to reconstruct the gender system through political and personal action. The Y was a feminist organization, at least in terms of the policies and statements of the National Board and the national conventions, which were composed of delegates elected from across the country. Throughout the period the YWCA's commitment to the principle of an autonomous women's organization helped strengthen and sustain feminist impulses within that organization.

Feminism by Other Names

It is clear that many of the women active in the YWCA can be labeled *feminist*, if we apply current definitions of feminism. What is striking, however, is that none of the progressive women in either the YWCA or the AFSC used the term to identify themselves during the decades of the 1940s and 1950s. In fact progressivism and self-identified feminism were largely at odds during the postwar period. The gulf between the two suggests a discrepancy between contemporary definitions of feminism and those current at the time. The discomfort of progressive women with the term *feminism* was the result of shifting historical definitions. The term first came into use in the United States in the 1910s to refer to a social revolution in gender roles that would free women from sexual stereotypes and create egalitarian social and sexual relationships between men and women. In these early years feminism was closely linked with socialist or left-leaning progressive political ideologies. The commonly accepted meaning of the term *feminism* altered radically in the 1920s, however. The National Woman's Party (NWP), proponent of an Equal Rights Amendment, was decisive in altering the public understanding of feminism. As Nancy Cott informs us, "Seizing the term to describe its intent to gain women the same legal rights men had, the party dissipated the emancipatory aura around sexual difference as well as the association of feminism with the socialist left." Furthermore, the NWP insisted that gender was the primary contradiction in women's lives; the net result was to segregate "feminism from other social and political issues that affected women."[41]

Women activists in the 1940s and 1950s were heirs to the particular meanings that feminism had acquired during the 1920s. The issue of the Equal Rights Amendment remained bitterly contested during the 1940s and 1950s. The NWP continued to push for passage of an ERA, arguing that legally mandated equality would have symbolic and practical significance in the struggle for women's advancement. The YWCA and a number of other middle-class women's organizations looked to the Women's Bureau in the Department of Labor to provide leadership in opposition to an ERA.[42] Because of its close identification with the concerns of working-class women, the Women's Bureau coalition opposed an ERA for fear it would undercut protective legislation. At the same time it fought to expand opportunities for women and to end a number of specific economic and legal forms of discrimination against women. In the period after World War II, this coalition sought both to prevent the passage of an ERA and to secure equal pay legislation. The Women's Bureau led the struggle that culminated in the successful passage of the 1963 Equal Pay Act.[43]

In addition to the gulf created by the ERA, women activists in the YWCA and other progressive organizations took issue with other aspects of the NWP's political ideology. In fact the politics of some prominent members of the NWP were abhorrent to progressive women. Alice Paul, leader of the NWP, was known to be openly racist and anti-Semitic in her views. Many women in the NWP were conservative, defending free enterprise against government intrusion of any kind. Further evidence of the inherently conservative bent of ERA supporters lies in the fact that congressional supporters of the ERA were far more likely to be Republicans or conservative Democrats than liberal Democrats. Furthermore, prominent members of the NWP offered support to Senator Joseph McCarthy for his vitriolic anti-Communist campaign, a campaign that was anathema to progressive activists.[44]

Differences in political orientation thus created the chasm that separated the NWP and progressive women's groups. As long as the term *feminism* was associated with the NWP, progressive women would reject the label, even though they too opposed male domination of the social order. Many women on the left end of the political spectrum objected to the narrowness of vision among those who struggled only for women's rights; progressive activists struggled to achieve a better world not only for women, but for all oppressed groups. Augusta Roberts, who held professional positions in the YWCA throughout her life, recalled her own objections to the term. She certainly believed in equal rights for men and women and was aware of discrimination in salaries and other aspects of women's lives. But to her, *feminism* was too limited a term, for women's rights was only one of many issues she was concerned about.[45] Polly Cuthbertson agreed. Strongly committed to women's rights, she was acutely aware of discrimination against women and conscious of the resistance she met as a woman in positions of leadership when she worked with the YMCA and church groups and on college campuses. Yet Cuthbertson did not, and to this day does not, think of herself as a feminist. The term seemed too narrowly focused on only women's issues; her politics included a wide range of issues, of which concern with women's subordination was only one.[46]

Ellen Dubois, in a retrospective on Eleanor Flexner's *Century of Struggle*, has termed this perspective "left feminism," "a perspective which fuses a recognition of the systematic oppression of women with an appreciation of other structures of power underlying American society" and does so with "an understanding that the attainment of genuine equality for women—all women—requires a radical challenge to American society. . . . and fundamental social change."[47] Certainly not all the women in the YWCA or the AFSC thought of themselves as "left," but just as certainly both organizations were on the left-liberal end of the political continuum of postwar U.S. society. It was the right-wing leanings of the NWP, which had successfully claimed the term *feminism* as its own, coupled with the narrowness of vision and single-minded focus that progressive women associated with the term, that led them to reject the label *feminist*.

The Influence of Gender
on Social Reform

Like earlier generations of women activists, women in the YWCA who debated the question of merger with the YMCA were convinced that women held different reform priorities, evident not only in their feminist concerns but also in their commitment to racial justice and other progressive issues. From the perspective of time and distance, how can we assess their claims? An examination of gender difference is necessarily complex and difficult because it operates at a level of such generality. Certainly there were many men who had views every bit as progressive as those of women, and the general postwar shift toward greater concern with racial justice, for example, occurred among both white men and women. Further, the social reform politics of men and women converged to some degree during this period, for unlike the women activists of the Progressive Era, and to some degree those of the interwar years as well, those in the postwar world focused less on the needs of women and children and more on seemingly gender-neutral concerns, such as racial equality. Efforts to counter discrimination based on sex, while still present, were less central to the politics of the era. But differences are nevertheless evident in the social reform politics of men and women. The clearest case for contrasting goals can be made by examining the male counterpart to the YWCA, the YMCA.

The YMCA and the YWCA had emerged from similar historical roots in the mid–nineteenth century, when community YMCAs and YWCAs developed to serve the needs of urban young people. Student YMCAs and YWCAs sprang up as a separate movement in the path of the evangelical fervor that swept college campuses in the last quarter of the nineteenth century. Heavily influenced by the Social Gospel in the first two decades of the twentieth century, student and, to a lesser degree, community YWCAs turned their attention to social and political issues. In 1919 the YMCA adopted the "Social Ideals of the Churches," a statement of Social Gospel principles; the YWCA followed suit at its national convention the following year. During the 1920s and 1930s, black members challenged segregated practices in the two organizations with only meager results outside the Student Divisions. Following the lead of the YWCA, the Student YMCA drew together leaders of black and white student associations in 1933, a decade after the YWCA had taken such action. Finally, after decades of internal struggle, in 1946 both the YWCA and the YMCA pledged themselves to racial integration.[48]

On the surface, then, the two organizations charted parallel courses. Nevertheless, throughout the postwar period the YWCA had a reputation for forthright commitment to social justice, including racial justice, that the YMCA did not. A 1946 survey conducted by the YMCA of city officials, editors, ministers, and educators, black and white, from twenty-four cities across the country, concurred that in most communities the YWCA was far ahead of the YM in race relations. Community

YMCAs rarely worked on interracial activities; in some cities the YMCA had made fewer advances toward integration than all other community agencies surveyed. In contrast, in many of these same communities the YWCA had racially integrated boards of directors and committees and had sponsored interracial projects; the YWCA was often the first agency in town to open its cafeteria or other facilities on an interracial basis. The president of a local branch of the NAACP summed it up by saying, "We're welcome at the YWCA. We know we're not wanted at the YMCA."[49]

A number of blacks interviewed in southern communities in the late 1950s for a study of YM-YW relationships reported that the YWCA often provided their only channel of communication with the white community. Women of the YWCA, according to this study, were more often willing "to make a public confrontation on an issue, and press harder for a program of education on the issues presented," than were the men in the community.[50] The story was similar in the Student YWCA and YMCA. Throughout the period from the 1930s to the 1960s, the two organizations often found it difficult to cooperate because the Student YWCA was far more committed to racial integration. When civil rights organizations planned the March on Washington in 1963, for example, the YWCA was one of the first groups to cosponsor it; the YMCA never did.

The differences between the two organizations are indisputable; the explanations for them are far more elusive, but several factors seem critical. First, although the organizations shared similar religious ideals, those same ideals stimulated greater activism in the YWCA than in the YMCA. Religious idealism has been a potent factor in the lives of U.S. women, and in an earlier century drew thousands of white women into the antislavery struggle. Women have predominated in the congregations of most American religious groups since the early nineteenth century, and today they continue to "manifest greater attachment to religious beliefs and practices than do men," according to survey research.[51] This greater commitment among women to acting out ideals in practice may help account for the "baffling mixture of high purpose and disappointing fulfillments" reported within the YMCA in the early 1960s.[52]

Second, a number of participants have suggested that women in the YWCA had better education, better training, and a more thorough understanding of social and political issues than men in the YMCA.

Here the power of sexism is evident, for men had many opportunities to exert leadership in the United States; for women the opportunities were scarce. As a result, the YWCA may have attracted to leadership a more highly educated, thoughtful, and determined group than did the YMCA. In addition, the YWCA had more in-service training programs and lengthy meetings that allowed women the opportunity to carefully examine important public issues. The YWCA focused on training partly because the development of leadership among women was a key goal of the organization, whereas for the YMCA the provision of programs and activities was more central. In addition, women had more leisure time, which enabled them to take advantage of opportunities for training and discussion, as many were not employed full-time before the 1960s. During the 1950s, for example, members of the National Board of the YWCA often met for a week for their national meetings, a time commitment few men could afford.

Furthermore, the democratic procedures characteristic of the YWCA enabled women to become experts on issues. National conventions of the YWCA involved extensive discussion of the social and political issues of the day, and women often spent considerable time preparing for the conventions in their local associations. In contrast, the YMCA functioned in a more hierarchical manner, with less emphasis on discussion or democratic decision making. These differences in style and mode of operation combined to produce women with a thorough knowledge of the issues and a commitment to social action in areas such as racial justice.[53]

The final critical factor that helps explain the difference between the two organizations concerns the significance of class interests within each organization and the relationship between class and gender. Community YMCAs were dominated by conservative business elements throughout much of the twentieth century. Wealthy women also dominated both the national and local boards of the YWCA before World War II, but during the late 1940s boards began to include increasing numbers of middle-class women. In addition, working-class women played an active role in the YWCA, particularly during the interwar period, and in alliance with middle-class women intensely committed to the Social Gospel they maintained a steady leftward pressure on the association. In contrast, working-class men were less involved in the YMCA, in part because they had greater access to labor unions as an alternative.[54]

Furthermore, women historically have had a more marginal relationship to economic power than have men, for they are usually less active in creating and defending wealth. Women of privilege can and do, in many instances, defend the social order that secures their privilege; yet curiously, and arguably more often than men, they at times fail to do so. For example, in an interesting contrast between the male City Club and the Woman's City Club of Chicago in the Progressive Era (their members were drawn from the upper middle class and often from the same families), Maureen Flanagan found marked differences in the positions the groups took on a number of civic and political issues: the women favored government ownership and operation of municipal services while the men opposed it, and the women displayed much greater sympathy for striking workers than did the men. In another example, wives and sisters of local manufacturers in Durham, North Carolina, took up the cause of white women employed in the textile mills in their state during the 1920s, much to the chagrin of their male relatives. Within the YWCA married women at times took positions on economic and political issues that their prominent husbands disagreed with or, in some cases, felt unwilling to speak up about publicly. Thus women's distinct relationship to economic power led privileged women to side with the powerless more frequently that did men of their class.[55]

Networks of
Women's Communities

Gender differences are less likely to manifest themselves in such sharply defined ways within the context of small, relatively cohesive mixed-sex organizations such as the AFSC. The AFSC brought together men and women of similar political and religious perspectives who were largely in agreement about the social reform goals they wished to pursue. Furthermore, they were employed by the AFSC in parallel positions in a variety of community relations and other programs, and both men and women were viewed as successful organizers of such projects. Nevertheless, some subtle differences existed that were evident in a division of labor and in distinct work styles.

First, although there was no strictly drawn gender division of labor in terms of the programs in which people worked, there were slight differences. For example, women gravitated toward the community relations programs, although men were active here as well, whereas men tended to dominate the peace efforts of the AFSC. There was an even sharper division of labor evident among grass-roots activists. Because many of the efforts AFSC staff undertook focused on school integration or community improvement, they often found themselves working with a predominantly female group of committed local activists. Jean Fairfax noted that men and women played complementary roles in civil rights activity, with black male ministers most visibly out in front in struggles. But in the AFSC's school desegregation work, she noted that "often in rural counties it was this group of very determined tough black women" who provided the sustained efforts to obtain equal educational opportunities for their children. School integration efforts have tended to draw more heavily on the efforts of female activists, both white and black, than of males. During the 1950s, for example, the Women's Division of Christian Service of the Board of Missions of the Methodist Church led a major drive to integrate the schools. When the AFSC sent Thelma Babbitt to Little Rock, Arkansas, during the school integration crisis there, she found that the first whites to protest the closing of the schools had been a group of women who organized the Women's Emergency Committee for Public Schools, although both men and women in the black community were active in the struggle. In Prince Edward County, Virginia, it was largely women who directed and taught in the activity centers. AFSC staff who worked in community organizing efforts, such as North Richmond Neighborhood House or work with California Indians, often found similar patterns.[56]

This emphasis on women's activities should not be taken to minimize the efforts of men. In southern rural communities, fathers of children who pioneered in integrating the schools had to be just as strong and courageous as mothers, for they too were subject to economic and physical reprisals, perhaps in even greater degree. And in Washington, D.C., which had a well-developed middle-class black community, men dominated among the black activists involved in school integration, while the whites involved were more evenly divided between men and women.[57] In this case leadership patterns may have varied between middle-class black communities in urban areas and poorer black communities in rural areas. But, in general, women predominated in the work on school integration.

Historically, women's concern with children had led them to be particularly involved in school issues, serving on school boards and running PTAs. The issue of quality schooling for children may have been nearer the hearts of mothers; certainly in cases where schools were closed it was they who bore the immediate burden of increased child-care responsibilities. Community organizing efforts, too, may appeal more to women because they are often more directly involved in daily activities of local communities. In a study of black women's organizational efforts in postwar Wisconsin, Marie Laberge found confirmation of such an issue-based division of labor within the NAACP: men focused on employment and legal redress issues and women on housing and community work.[58] The predominance of women in efforts for school desegregation and community organizing was replicated in the civil rights movement. Historians have noted that women provided the backbone of that movement, although men remained in the limelight as leaders. "The movement of the fifties and sixties was carried largely by women, since it came out of the church groups," according to Ella Baker.[59]

Women's grass-roots activism can be explained by a variety of factors. For white and, to a lesser degree, black middle-class women during the postwar period, the lower number of women employed full-time gave them more time to devote to community efforts. In rural southern black communities, women may have believed they were less vulnerable to violence than their men, and thus were able to be more public in their protests. In a study of civil rights activism in the Mississippi Delta, Charles Payne has suggested two reasons to explain the greater numbers of adult black women involved: their greater propensity for strong religious faith, and their closer connections to a network of kinship and friends who were likely to draw them into the movement. These gendered patterns characterize women from diverse racial-ethnic groups.[60]

Finally, female organizers and grass-roots activists employed a female ethic in their efforts at community organization. Women staff members were effective because of their ability to draw on and help sustain female networks of community activists, calling upon female patterns of socialization that emphasized the need to remain embedded in interpersonal networks.[61] Women staff also faced fewer social barriers in making connections with the preponderance of grass-roots activists who were women than did male organizers. At an institutional level the AFSC gave little explicit attention to the importance of cultivating personal relationships as a means to building communities of activists. Yet many participants and observers credited the willingness of women to nurture relationships with other activists as a major source of their effectiveness as community organizers.

Barbara Graves, who administered several of the AFSC's overseas programs in the postwar period, reflected on the subtle gender differences within the organization, recalling, "Certain attitudes bothered me—patterns of refusing to acknowledge that anybody needed any help or any supervision . . . this strong sense of the individual and *his* light being what guided us in this institution. I struggled a lot to develop better personnel policies and some understanding of the suffering that men and women went through overseas with loneliness, a sense of failure, and a lack of support. I attributed a lot of that to the male ethic that dominated our institutional patterns."[62] Despite that male ethic, which emphasized the importance of the individual rather than the connections between individuals, women activists in the AFSC worked to ensure the incorporation of a female ethic in the ongoing daily work of AFSC projects.

During a period of social and political conservatism women in the YWCA and AFSC helped sustain a progressive critique of the nation's social order and, explicitly in the case of the YWCA and implicitly in the case of the AFSC, of women's place in that order. Women in the YWCA focused on the need to set their own priorities as women and to develop women's leadership in order to pursue their social reform goals, which included feminist demands for greater inclusion in the public world. Women in the AFSC quietly demonstrated their competence and assumed their ability to function in positions of equality with men, yet they incorporated gendered patterns in their work. Pursuing different strategies, the two groups of women shared a common vision of a world based on gender equality. Yet they never separated that ideal from a broader vision of social justice and peace for all humanity. If, as Joan Scott argues, gender is one axis for social domination, and gender language and imagery permeate and help justify other such relationships, then dismantling hierarchies based on gender will necessarily contribute to dismantling those based on race and class as well.[63] From this perspective, the elite women who pursued legal rights for women while defending a social and economic order grounded in class and racial privilege followed a fundamentally flawed strategy. For women social reformers in the YWCA and the AFSC, women's liberation could only be achieved as part of a larger movement that demanded social justice for all humankind.

6

New Sprouts from Old Roots: The Development of the Protest Movements of the 1960s

In the opening months of 1960, the sit-in movement spread like wildfire across the face of the South, signifying a fresh and restless spirit of change at work in the United States and marking the beginning of a decade of social protest. Yet, although 1960 represented a break with the past, the roots of the tumultuous protests that followed were firmly planted in the 1950s. The real point when political quiescence first began to shift toward social protest occurred during the mid-1950s. Cold War tensions, both domestic and international, eased after Soviet Premier Stalin died in 1953 and the U. S. Senate censured Senator Joseph McCarthy in 1954. As the intense climate of suspicion and fear that characterized the McCarthy period began to loosen its grip, new political possibilities emerged. In 1955, more than a year after *Brown v. Board of Education*, the bus boycott in Montgomery, Alabama, initiated techniques of nonviolent direct action that were to become the hallmark of the civil rights movement. That movement blended Christian religious idealism and the Gandhian philosophy of nonviolence into a powerful social force for change. The peace movement also emerged from its moribund state in the late 1950s, responding to a sudden intense burst of concern about the dangers of radioactive fallout to demand an atmospheric test ban treaty. When Students for a Democratic Society (SDS) was formed in 1960, the fledgling organization looked less to the "old Left" of the Communist party for inspiration than to that broad stream of progressive thought and action represented by such diverse influences as the civil rights movement, pacifism, and dissident cultural and intellectual voices such as those of C. Wright Mills, Paul Goodman, and the beats.[1] Although young people in the civil rights movement and the northern student movement quickly outstripped their elders in the brashness of their tactics, they maintained an ambivalent stance toward the older generation of activists, looking to them for support at the same time that they often challenged their leadership. An examination of this complex intergenerational relationship reveals elements of both continuity and discontinuity.

To fully comprehend the emergence of social protest in the 1960s we must also examine the participation of women. Many accounts of the decade focus on the activities of male leaders, marginalizing the role of women. Men dominated the leadership of the protest movements of that decade, with the exception of the women's movement. Whether we look to student and youth groups, such as the Student Nonviolent Coordinating Committee (SNCC), Students for a Democratic Society (SDS), and the draft resistance movement, or to the more mature leaders of civil rights and peace groups, men held the most visible positions of leadership. But at the grass-roots level, women participated at least in equal numbers, at times far outnumbering men. Furthermore, although they were never accorded as much attention as men, women held influential positions in organizations concerned with social change. Thus an examination of how women came into the movement, and of what activities they engaged in, will expand our partial understanding of the social protest movements of this era.

Two generations of women took part in the social movements of the 1960s. Mature adults, with a history of activism stretching back into earlier decades, helped direct the activities of organizations that served to sustain and support civil rights and peace activities. For example, after a decade as an AFSC college secretary, Garnet Guild in 1959 became the first woman executive secretary of an AFSC regional office. For the next decade, Guild directed the South Central Regional Office, located first in Austin, Texas, and, after 1962, in Houston. She supervised Thelma Babbitt in her work in Little Rock, oversaw the efforts of Merit in Employment Projects in Baton Rouge, Louisiana, and in Dallas and Houston, and closely followed AFSC efforts to promote school integration in Houston.[2] Similarly, Jean Whittet was one of many women in managerial positions in the YWCA whose liberal politics helped shape the organization's response to the civil rights movement. As associate for program development in the College and University Division of the YWCA (the Student YWCA) from 1956 to 1965, and as director of public affairs for the National Board from 1967 to 1976, Whittet focused on civil rights as a major priority. She prepared publications that discussed civil rights concerns, organized workshops, and worked to create alliances with churches and civil rights organizations. Older activists also attended civil rights marches and participated in demonstrations, picket lines, and vigils against the Vietnam War. They wrote letters to elected representatives, passed out leaflets about a variety of issues, and donated money to organizations involved in direct action activities.

The younger generation of women, those just reaching adulthood, were often swept into the movement with the force of religious conversion, as the movement became the central focus of their lives. These women marched in demonstrations, got arrested and went to jail, and took summers or even years away from school to become full-time organizers and participants in what they fervently hoped and imagined would be a social revolution that would shake their society to its roots and set it on a course more consistent with its professed ideals. Younger women tended to participate more actively on the front lines of direct action than did the older generation; the latter supplied leadership, as well as quieter forms of support.

The YWCA and the
Civil Rights Movement

The YWCA provides an interesting window into the relationship between generations of women activists, for the Y included large numbers of women of all ages. Like many other student organizations, the Student YWCA was transformed by the electrifying impact of the civil rights movement. In spring of 1960 the local YWCA student association at Trinity University joined sit-ins in San Antonio, Texas. The arrest of Java Mae Thompson, chair of the Southern Regional Council of the Student YWCA, along with other students at Southern University in Baton Rouge, Louisiana, at a sit-in in December 1961 further galvanized the YWCA into action. A month earlier the National Student Council of the YWCA had established a special fund to provide financial aid for bail to freedom riders and others involved in direct action; some of those funds were sent to the students from Southern University.[3] Soon hundreds of members of the Student YWCA sought ways to become involved in civil rights activity.

The National Student Council of the YMCA and YWCA (NSC) sought to meet this need by sponsoring a variety of projects. They conducted workshops on race relations to train students for future campus and community civil rights work. The 1963 national summer workshop brought together such major figures as Kenneth B. Clark, noted author and psychologist; Ella Baker, one of the major architects of the southern civil rights movement; and Constance Baker Motley of the NAACP Legal Defense and Education Fund to speak and to meet with students.[4] The NSC also called on students to work for passage of civil rights legislation and fair housing programs. By the summer of 1964, regional reports from student YWCAs indicated that "the major program and action concern in all regions during the past year has been civil rights."[5] After the passage of the 1964 Civil Rights Act and the 1965 Voting Rights Act, the NSC urged campus groups to undertake educational campaigns about the legislation and to participate in economic boycotts, picketing, and demonstrations to pressure local businesses to comply with the new laws.

The Student YWCA sponsored voter registration projects, literacy classes, tutoring projects, and conferences on the problems of the inner city in communities where Student YWCA chapters were located. Larger voter registration projects were held during Easter breaks and summers, recruiting hundreds of northern and southern students, black and white, to work in both southern and northern cities. Often the projects were cosponsored by the NAACP Legal Defense and Education Fund.[6] In addition, the Student YWCA urged students to work to insure the total desegregation of all aspects of campus life. Local student Y members met with sororities and fraternities to discuss the need to open membership to all races and visited college officials to urge them to open up admissions, campus housing, and scholarship grants to all races.[7] Thus the Student YWCA served as a conduit for civil rights activity.

While the Student YWCA participated in student civil rights activity, the National Board of the YWCA, along with many community YWCAs, offered other forms of support to the civil rights movement. When the sit-ins first began, the National Board endorsed the "objectives of nonviolent demonstrations of students," and the Public Affairs Committee immediately responded by offering funds and legal aid for arrested student YWCA members. The president of the YWCA wrote letters urging large department store chains with southern branches to end segregation at lunch counters and endorsed the 1963 March on Washington.[8] The YWCA participated in the National Women's Committee for Civil Rights, a coalition of women's groups called together by President John Kennedy in July 1963 to discuss the role such groups could play in the civil rights struggle.[9]

As the momentum of the civil rights movement built, the YWCA intensified its longstanding efforts to bring local associations into line with national policies about racial integration, concentrating its efforts on southern associations. In June 1963 only 13 percent of YWCA associations in southern states were desegregated; by May 1965 60 percent of them were. National leaders endorsed a National Action Program, in which national leaders met directly with local leaders in workshops and meetings, urging them to open their services to all racial groups in order to comply with national policy.[10] Slowly, as a result of the changing political climate and in response to discussions with staff of the National Board, southern YWCAs moved to desegregate. Furthermore, through a constant process of self-evaluation, YWCAs in all parts of the country examined their patterns of leadership, striving to improve the degree of racial inclusiveness in their associations.

In 1965 the National Board of the YWCA created the Office of Racial Justice in order "to accelerate the work of the National Board in going beyond token integration to full racial integration in the YWCA and the Community." Its job was to monitor the progress of the National Board, to keep abreast of the civil rights movement and of community efforts to change, and to suggest activities for local associations to pursue. Dorothy Height was appointed director.

In May of the following year Height proposed an ambitious agenda for the YWCA entitled "YWCA Project Equality." First, she suggested, the Y should work to assure equal opportunities to racial minorities in staff and volunteer positions. At that time 25 percent of 326 people on the staff of the National Board were from minority groups, including 19 percent of executive and office management staff, and 10.4 percent of total professional staff. Second, she urged, the Y must undertake a series of "member dialogue groups" to be held prior to the White House Conference on Civil Rights entitled "To Fulfill These Rights." One hundred seven such groups were held. A third focus was for the YWCA to establish a policy to support businesses with equal employment practices through the awarding of contracts for the purchase of supplies, goods, and services. Height also proposed that the YWCA should intensify its work in the South on voter education and registration and on facilitating school desegregation.

The following year the National Board endorsed a major push to become involved in open housing efforts, suggesting a pilot project in four cities to try to achieve open housing.[11] Under Height's leadership the National Board engaged in an in-depth educational process, devoting weekends to meetings in which members discussed the problems of institutional racism in the housing market, the justice system, and other areas.

Throughout the early 1960s the National Board of the YWCA met frequently with leaders of the major civil rights organizations in order to keep abreast of developments and to determine what actions the Y could take that would be most supportive of the movement. Dorothy Height provided a direct link to other civil rights leader. For eighteen years she had served as director of training for the National Board, and after 1965 she directed the Office of Racial Justice. Since 1957 Height had also been president of the National Council of Negro Women, which was actively involved in civil rights activity in the South during the 1960s. In that capacity she sat on the Council for United Civil Rights Leadership. Her dual role with NCNW and the YWCA provided close linkage between the Y and the major civil rights organizations.[12]

The issue of racism assumed center stage at the YWCA's national convention in 1970. Following standard procedure the National Board brought a series of resolutions, stated as "imperatives," to the convention for approval. But African-American women, under the leadership of Dorothy Height, met in caucus before the convention and insisted that the Y focus on a single imperative, the elimination of racism. The convention was stormy and tense, with rumors circulating of a threatened walkout on the part of black women. Presiding was Helen Wilkins Claytor, who had coauthored the study of interracial practices in the early 1940s, had been a member of the National Board since 1946 and had been elected as the first black woman to serve as president of the YWCA, a position she held from 1967 to 1973. Claytor was extremely skillful at maintaining a degree of harmony in the tense climate. After much debate the convention passed the "one imperative," which stated in part:" Racism in our institutional structures and patterns of behavior is all pervasive in our society. No other single factor has such profound implications for our nation's achievement of its own goals of equality, freedom, and justice. Therefore, we determine . . . to thrust our collective power toward the Elimination of Racism wherever it exists by any means necessary."[13]

At the same convention a major effort was made to expand the racial inclusiveness of the National Board; a number of white women stepped aside to make places available to women of color, providing entry for a number of African-American women who moved into top leadership positions in the YWCA in the next decades. Jewel Graham was one of the African-Americans who joined the National Board at that time, marking her reentry into active participation in the Y. She had first joined the Y as a young girl in Springfield, Ohio, during the 1930s. She had directed the teenage program for the YWCA in Grand Rapids, Michigan, in the years following World War II. There she met Helen Wilkins Claytor, who had moved to Grand Rapids after her second marriage; the two became lifetime friends. Graham received a master of arts degree in social service administration from Case Reserve in 1950, worked for the Detroit YWCA during the early 1950s, then married and moved to Yellow Springs, Ohio, with her husband. There she raised two children, joined the faculty of Antioch College, and got involved in a number of volunteer activities, including work with the YWCA in Springfield, Ohio. One of the major reasons she remained in the YWCA was its commitment to racial justice.

Not until 1970 did the YWCA once again become central to Graham's life, however. A friend asked her to run for the National Board that year, convincing her that the YWCA was committed to getting more women of color on the board. She was elected and served for eighteen years, becoming President of the National Board from 1979 to

1985, and president of the World YWCA from 1987 to 1991. In the latter capacity she traveled throughout the world, conducting workshops and talking with women about pressing issues in their lives, such as the status of women, education, environmental problems, and peace. Graham found a real sisterhood in the YWCA, which consisted of "lifelong relationships with women, characterized by warmth and shared values and common interests."[14]

Like Graham, much of the black leadership on the National Board during the 1970s and 1980s had begun work with the YWCA in segregated black branches just before and after World War II. There they developed leadership skills, and as the YWCA increasingly opened up leadership to women of color they moved up through the ranks in the national organization. From its initial commitment in 1946 to the Interracial Charter, through the "one imperative" of eliminating racism in 1970, and further, the YWCA had moved through several stages in its interracial relationships.

During the 1940s and 1950s the emphasis was on creating an interracial organization. Because the YWCA had a black branch structure, African-American women were able to exert a greater degree of influence from within the organization than would have been possible without that separatist base. Nevertheless, during those decades integration occurred primarily in terms of black women and other women of color being assimilated into a predominantly white organization. During the 1960s the YWCA was transformed by its commitment to the fight for racial justice, and black women struggled within the organization to exert more power in determining the direction of the organization. By the 1970s women of color had become empowered within the organization. As they increased in numbers and influence to the point where they no longer functioned as tokens, women of color exercised strong leadership within a racially mixed organization and insisted on a process of integration that involved cultural reciprocity rather than adaptation to a white norm.

Following the lead of African-American women, during the 1970s and 1980s other women of color joined the ranks of the YWCA in increasing numbers, transmuting it into one of the most fully integrated organizations in the country, with African-American and other women of color gaining significant positions of leadership in an organization that was increasingly diverse in its racial-ethnic composition.

Mentoring in the YWCA

Throughout the crescendo of civil rights activity from the mid-1950s through the 1960s, the YWCA focused the energies of women of widely diverse ages on the struggle for racial justice. Yet tensions existed between various groups within the Y. The Student YWCA had a reputation for being more radical on the issue of racial justice, as well as other issues, than the community YWCAs, which served as a source of frustration for the students, who often put pressure on their parent body. On the other hand, the staff of the National Board was, by and large, just as forthright in their commitment to racial justice as were the students and provided clear and decisive leadership in that arena. Despite differences and tensions between these two generations, older women often played crucial roles as mentors and role models for younger members. Particularly as adult advisers to college chapters of the Student YWCA, older women initiated intellectual experiences that sharpened the political understanding of the students, taught them the ropes of political organizing, and provided models of how to fashion a personal identity and manage the conflicting demands on their time in an era when gender roles were undergoing rapid transformation.

As a woman's organization with both a student and an adult division, the YWCA provided particularly fertile ground for the development of intergenerational links. The Y was significant for generations of young women who came of age in the late 1950s and early 1960s because it combined a long history of commitment to racial justice with a major focus on the development of women's leadership. For young women, then, the YWCA encouraged not only the development of a politics based on social justice, but the personal skills, confidence, and determination that allowed women to function as leaders in movements for social change. This was particularly crucial in a time when most other organizations offered little room for the development of women's leadership. If women were first able to exert leadership in an all-female organization, they were more likely to be able to hold their own in a mixed-sex setting at a later date. The development of leadership occurred both as a result of specific training in leadership skills, and because the adult advisers to the student YWCAs were often inspirational women who provided models of assertive womanhood.

The rich blend of politics and mentoring provided by the Student

YWCA is evident in the personal histories of young activists. One of these was Charlotte Bunch, who became a major activist, organizer, and theorist in the feminist movement in the late 1960s and 1970s. Bunch grew up in New Mexico, daughter of Methodist parents imbued with liberal moral and church-based values. "When I left home for college," recalled Bunch, "I was bright, optimistic, adventuresome, civic-minded, experienced in organizations, with a strong moral sense, but essentially apolitical and naive."[15]

Bunch attended Duke University in 1962, where she was immediately attracted to the Methodist Student Movement (MSM) and the YWCA, which worked closely together on campus. The YWCA, Bunch recalled, molded the familiar into a new form, for it included "values of liberal church progressive thought" that Bunch had been reared on but translated those values into a more political form. At the separate women's college that Duke maintained, Bunch and her friends were given an exciting intellectual and political education by the YWCA program. When Duke began token desegregation of its undergraduate student body in the fall of 1963, young white women who were active in the YWCA undertook to create a supportive environment for the brave black students who attended Duke. Slowly, through her involvement with the YWCA, Bunch became involved in off-campus civil rights actions, first attending a pray-in at a local church, and then joining demonstrations led by students at North Carolina College, a local black school. Partly in response to her YWCA experience Bunch "moved gradually but inexorably from morally opposing the unfairness of racism in the South to an understanding of such oppression as political."[16] By the time she left college, Bunch's primary political identity was as part of the civil rights movement.

Bunch's leadership abilities were carefully nurtured by the student YWCA, which explicitly endorsed the need for women to take responsibility for public affairs. Bobbie Benedict, the YWCA student adviser at Duke, was an inspiration to Bunch, attending demonstrations and evidencing no reticence about speaking up on controversial topics and exerting her point of view. Bunch recalled that the most important aspect of the YWCA for her was that it encouraged a woman "to become a person with a public persona." That training clearly took with Bunch. In her senior year she was elected co-president of her local YWCA, when she and her friend Sara Evans insisted on sharing the job rather than running against each other in an election. She also was elected to the National Council of the MSM. In the latter capacity she attended the civil rights march in Selma, Alabama, helping to arrange housing for the marchers. The year after her college graduation Bunch served as the first president of the University Christian Movement, a coalition that included the student movements of the major Protestant denominations and the YWCA.[17]

Sandra Cason (more widely known as Casey Hayden after her marriage to Tom Hayden) was also deeply influenced by the YWCA. A young white woman who arrived at the University of Texas in 1955, Hayden honed her liberal sentiments into a more sharply political vision during her college years, in part as a result of her involvement with the Student YWCA. As a national officer in the Student Y, she attended national meetings where she chaired workshops on "world peace and disarmament, race relations, meaning in work, and the changing roles of men and women." Her mentor, Rosalie Oakes, was the director of the Student YWCA at the University of Texas and was a tremendous influence in her life. Hayden remembered her as a quiet-spoken but solid and courageous woman, the first woman Hayden had met with a social conscience.[18] Through the Y Hayden met black students and learned from them directly the cost of the nation's racial caste system. She met several students who had been involved in sit-ins, and when the sit-in movement hit Austin, she was quick to join.

After graduation she was hired by the YWCA for a brief stint as campus program director for the student YWCA at the University of Illinois, and then to conduct a "human relations project" in the South. For this job she traveled to southern campuses ostensibly to talk about academic freedom, but in reality to broach the much more controversial subject of racial integration. The YWCA set up workshops on "race relations," bringing together black and white students to talk about segregation. In her spare time Hayden worked with SNCC, and shortly after she left the Y project, she joined their staff. She remained an active member of SNCC until the organization embraced black nationalism and pushed whites out after 1965.

Mary King, too, found the YWCA instrumental in her development as a civil rights activist. King had grown up in a liberal southern white family that had relocated to New York, where her father was a minister in the tradition of the radical social gospel. As a student at Ohio Wesleyan in the early 1960s, she took a trip south in 1962 and was powerfully drawn to the young SNCC activists whom she met there. Later that year, after she graduated, she was asked by Rosetta Gardner, director of the YWCA's College Division in the southern region, to take Casey Hayden's place on the YWCA's human relations project.

King and her co-worker, Roberta Yancy, who was black, had as advisers and adult supervisors two remarkable black women, Gardner and Ella Baker, who was an adviser to the YWCA program. From Gardner, King learned to prepare in advance for unseen contingencies, such as giving extemporaneous speeches. Ella Baker, one of the major influences on the development of the southern civil rights movement, transformed and shaped King's understanding of social change. Baker constantly urged King and Yancy to articulate the purpose of their activities and to examine their strategies in light of that purpose. Baker also imparted the understanding that no single strategy could encompass the work of social change; she urged King to avoid doctrinaire positions and to remain flexible.[19] Like Hayden, King volunteered her extra time to work with SNCC, and she joined their staff when funding for her position with the YWCA ended in June 1963.

Perhaps no story more perfectly illustrates the interconnection of generations of women within the YWCA than that of Margarita Mendoza de Sugiyama. Born in Yakima, Washington, in 1948, Margarita Mendoza was from a Mexican-American family that made a living through migratory farm work, supplemented later by her father's career in the military. Growing up in Yakima, Margarita Mendoza was convinced that the YWCA was "never a place for us," because of both her Catholic religion and her race. As the second oldest of eleven children, she worked at a job in order to help support her family throughout high school, getting passing grades but nurturing no aspirations about going to college.

Mendoza's goals changed dramatically when, in the summer between her junior and senior years in high school, she attended an Upward Bound program. Upward Bound was part of President Johnson's poverty program, designed to encourage children living in poverty to attend college. For the first time ever she "entertained the idea that education was an option" in her life, as she discovered that she enjoyed intellectual activity. The program also politicized her, for the staff of Upward Bound were leftists in their politics and introduced the students to ideas about the systematic impact of racism in U.S. society. She returned to high school with a new determination, enrolled in all college preparatory classes, and completed the year with a 3.85 grade point average. The reaction of her white teachers to her newfound academic success shocked and embittered her, however; they were angry that she had "wasted their time" the previous year.

In 1967 Margarita Mendoza married Masao Sugiyama, whose family had been confined to a concentration camp at Heart Mountain, Wyoming, during the internment of Japanese during World War II. By the time the two of them went to Washington State University (WSU) in Pullman, Washington, in 1969, Margarita Mendoza de Sugiyama was firmly convinced that all white people were racists. "I had no room in my heart or my life for anybody who even remotely looked like they were somehow part of this [racist system]. I was very intolerant," she reflected.[20]

She immediately founded and became spokesperson for a chapter of Movemiento Estudiante Chicano de Atzlan (MECHA) on campus. The group worked on a number of issues, chief among them support for the United Farmworkers' boycott of grapes and lettuce. Much to her surprise, she found that many of the other people working on the boycott were white women from the Student YWCA. Slowly, her idea that all whites were racists began to break down, she reflected, "because there were too many exceptions and they were people with faces and good hearts and feelings and I cared about them. All of a sudden there were individuals, not just white people. . . . After you are out there picketing and people are flipping you the bird and calling you names and trying to run you over, you develop a bond with folks."[21]

Mendoza de Sugiyama was still reluctant, however, when a white friend of hers "dragged her" to meet the director of the Student YWCA at WSU, Elaine Zakarison. Zakarison was white, and to make matters worse from Mendoza de Sugiyama's point of view, she was married to a farmer. Zakarison talked to Mendoza de Sugiyama about MECHA, inquiring how the Y could support MECHA in its activities, and asking Mendoza de Sugiyama to join the cabinet of the Student YWCA, the decision-making body for the organization. "I was hostile," Margarita recalled laughingly of that first meeting. "I swore and was disagreeable," stating that "I didn't want to belong to a white racist organization." Unperturbed, Zakarison "accepted me, accepted the anger and the expletives," and continued to request her participation on the student council. Finally, a reluctant Mendoza de Sugiyama agreed, but she demanded a vote, despite her refusal to join the organization. To her amazement the YWCA agreed.[22]

Zakarison was to have a transforming effect on Mendoza de Sugiyama's life, becoming both mentor and friend. Through their association Mendoza de Sugiyama gradually overcame her hatred for whites. Zakarison was "so unpretentious, so caring, so sincere about what she does . . . so centered in who she is." Mendoza de Sugiyama was impressed by her ability to "establish rapport," which she credited to her respect for people, her lack of righteousness, her "open, non-threatening, caring attitude and presence." "It took having a relationship with one [white person, Zakarison] and developing a relationship with many around issues to get beyond the race barrier and the cultural barrier." Zakarison "has probably radicalized more women, created more feminists, sent more of us into the civil rights arena than any woman I know," reflected Mendoza de Sugiyama.[23]

When the 1970 YWCA national convention adopted the one imperative of the elimination of racism, it came "like a revelation" to Mendoza de Sugiyama. She had to admit that she was absolutely wrong in her characterization of the YWCA as racist, and she immediately decided to join the organization. That was the beginning of a lifelong passionate commitment to the YWCA. The following year the Student YWCA sponsored a number of conferences across the country on "The Web of Racism," a reference to institutional racism. Each examined a specific topic, such as the justice system, higher education, or the health system, analyzing each in terms of institutional racism. Mendoza de Sugiyama attended as many as she could and was startled by the degree of fighting and disagreement that occurred but also impressed at the "openness and acceptance of diversity" displayed.

In the summer of 1971 Mendoza de Sugiyama attended the national convention of the National Student Association of the YWCA. Zakarison had urged her to run for national office, and once there, she found herself drafted by the women of color caucus. One white woman, a previous officer, spoke from the floor of the convention in tears, warning that the organization would be torn apart if Mendoza de Sugiyama was elected. For Mendoza de Sugiyama was outspoken, confronting people about racism wherever she saw it, and she spoke roughly, not in the polite language to which most of the middle-class white students were accustomed. Nevertheless, she was elected, and she served two terms as national chair of the Student YWCA.

In her position as national chair, Mendoza de Sugiyama was an ex-officio member of the National Board, and in 1971 she attended her first National Board meeting dressed in hiking boots, jeans, a blue work shirt, a red bandanna, and a *huelga* necklace, an emblem of the United Farm Workers. She found attending the board meeting was "like walking into a Fellini flick." Suddenly she was in the midst of "all these grey-haired women" dressed in suits, some with gloves and hats, in an atmosphere "so proper" and so different from her own cultural experience. But she was immediately struck by their treatment of her "like someone they loved." She also felt honored to be in the company of "the giants" of the YWCA, women who were distinguished in their professional lives yet who had made "a lifelong commitment to bringing equity into the world . . . freedom, justice, dignity for all people."[24]

There were moments of both hilarity and tension in that first meeting. As the board members sat around the table discussing a number of issues, Margarita Mendoza de Sugiyama noted the status differences inherent in the practice of older women addressing her by her first name, while she was expected to address them by a title such as Mrs., Miss, or Dr. She scanned their nametags for first names, but found that married women's tags referred to them by their husbands' first names. Undaunted, Mendoza de Sugiyama began addressing them as "Robert," or "Calvin." The older women quickly pointed out that the name on their tag was their husband's name, not their own. Playing dumb, Sugiyama said, "I'm sorry, I couldn't tell." Soon nametags were torn apart, and the women wrote their own first names on the tags. Not long after, the directory of the National Board began to list board members by their own first names, rather than by those of their husbands.

After two terms as national chair of the Student YWCA, Mendoza de Sugiyama was elected to a six-year term on the National Board, the first Chicana to sit on the board. Following her years on the National Board, Mendoza de Sugiyama decided to devote her efforts to the local level, becoming very active first in the YWCA in Boise, Idaho, and later in Olympia, Washington. Throughout her involvement in the Y, she saw herself as part of an intergenerational chain, mentored and nurtured by Elaine Zakarison and others. She in her turn nurtured younger women, such as Maya Bellon, a Native American. She had known Bellon since her birth, for Bellon's parents were friends of hers. In the late 1980s, when Mendoza de Sugiyama worked as special assistant to the president on affirmative action at Evergreen State College in Olympia, Maya Bellon worked for her as a student assistant. When Mendoza de Sugiyama started a Student YWCA chapter on campus, she involved Maya Bellon. Bellon was elected national chair of the Student YWCA in 1990. Mendoza de Sugiyama remains impressed by the YWCA, which has brought together "women of such diverse world views, interests, investments, and concerns . . . and created something that was inclusive."[25]

For each of these women as well as for thousands of others, the YWCA provided support to empower themselves, individually and collectively. That support came partly from the institutional setting and environment of the YWCA and partly from the inspirational examples and mentoring that older women provided to younger. In many ways the torch that younger women carried during the 1960s and in later decades had been passed on to them by that older generation of women activists.

AFSC and Civil Rights

Like the YWCA, the AFSC responded immediately to the intensified pace of civil rights activity in 1960. When the first sit-ins occurred in 1960, the South Central and Southeast Regional Offices issued statements of support, convened workshops on nonviolent action, arranged conferences for lawyers and others on legal issues, and played a supportive role in negotiations carried out by mayors and civic groups in a number of southern cities.[26] The AFSC sponsored projects for young people that included such activities as voter registration, citizenship education, and tutoring.[27] Most of the civil rights work of the AFSC, however, continued to focus on three major areas already defined: in the south, employment and school desegregation; in the north, employment and housing. Each of these areas deserves extensive study in itself. For example, the AFSC, made a significant pioneering contribution to the development of the fair housing movement in northern and western cities in the 1950s and 1960s. But what connected the AFSC most visibly to the larger civil rights movement was its continuing work on school desegregation.

The AFSC continued its work in Prince Edward County, Virginia, where the public schools remained closed from 1959 to 1964. Helen Baker directed the AFSC's Emergency Placement Program, established to send students to the north for school. Baker believed the program had a very positive effect on the students, broadening their vocational interests and inspiring many to attend college. When the first of the students returned from their first year in the north, Baker commented that, "they are a self-assured lot. . . . One thing is certain, they have come back to Farmville with some new visions of what can be. . . . The first student to return from this year's school experience was Joseph Wiley. . . . In all my life I had never seen such a metamorphosis . . . he talked with ease and confidence and clearness such as I had not met in months."[28]

While many students managed to receive an education outside the county, hundreds remained without any educational opportunities. To meet that need the AFSC established activity centers for the black students; although not designed to be schools, these did provide some educational activities. Baker supplemented her work with students with programs in the adult black community, stressing leadership development and citizenship education.[29] In 1963 federal officials in the Kennedy administration raised private funds and established the Free Schools, which most black students in the county attended during the 1963–1964 school year. Finally, in 1964, the Supreme Court resolved the legal issues by declaring that Prince Edward County must reopen the public schools on a nondiscriminatory basis. In the fall of 1964 the public schools reopened enrolling an almost entirely black student body.[30]

By 1964 the legal situation in the South had changed dramatically, as a number of school districts were under court order to desegregate. The AFSC decided to focus its efforts in areas where massive resistance was not anticipated, hoping to facilitate peaceful integration. In the spring of 1964 the AFSC sent two staff members to Jackson, Mississippi, to begin work in Jackson, Biloxi, and Leake counties, all of which were under court order to produce desegregation plans by 15 July, 1964. In each of the three counties, the school boards submitted plans for integrating the schools one grade at a time. As in the past, the AFSC planned to reach out to both blacks and whites, providing encouragement and advice to black parents willing to initiate school desegregation, as well as organizing sympathetic whites to support the process.[31]

Jean Fairfax, longtime employee of the AFSC and national representative of southern programs since 1957, assumed the task of working in the black community. Fairfax sought out parents in the community to inform them about the school board's plans for desegregation. Parents "had to maneuver a maze of regulations" to gain access to integrated schools, Fairfax recalled. Her job entailed contacting families to locate children who would enter first grade, and offering information, encouragement, and support to enable parents to pursue integrated schooling for their children.[32] Fairfax visited 300 black families in Jackson and persuaded forty-four families who had children entering the first grade to register their children in the integrated public school. All were accepted, and thirty-nine of the children actually entered and integrated public school that fall.

The courage required of black parents and their children was enormous in the tense summer and fall of 1964, when three civil rights workers disappeared in Mississippi. After a massive search, their bodies were discovered just weeks before school opened in the fall. Black children who attended integrated schools faced threatening situations, and apprehension ran high in the black community. Yet school desegregation proceeded relatively smoothly in Jackson. In rural Leake County, where Fairfax met blacks who had been working for civil rights for a generation, things proved more difficult. Here, eight of nine families who had enrolled their children in formerly white schools lost their jobs or were subject to other forms of intimidation and harassment.[33] The AFSC was soon to address this problem through the development of a Family Aid Program for civil rights workers who faced economic intimidation.

Fairfax was joined by Connie Curry, a young white activist hired by the AFSC. Her first assignment was to work with sympathetic whites to prevent the collapse of public school systems in Mississippi. Curry, daughter of Irish immigrants, had grown up in North Carolina but did not identify with the southern white tradition. Instead, her parents had taught her "to have my own mind, and to be able to feel pretty secure being and doing what I thought was right."[34] And she was absolutely clear that racial equality was right.

From 1951 to 1955 Curry attended Agnes Scott College in Atlanta,

Georgia. Gregarious, eager to be involved in virtually every campus activity, Curry became a delegate to the National Student Association congress (NSA) at age eighteen. There she met with 800 to 900 students from across the country and was "awestruck" to find so many students interested in something other than sorority and fraternity life, to be part of stimulating intellectual debates about the eighteen-year-old vote, international issues, or racial integration. During her junior year she was elected chair of the Great Southern Region for NSA, an area that covered the Deep South but included only four college chapters. Curry never forgot an incident that occurred at a meeting of NSA delegates from the Great Southern Region in Atlanta. Among the delegates was a young black woman from Xavier College in New Orleans with whom Curry had become close friends. When the delegates broke for lunch, black and white students had to part ways, for no place would serve them together. It was a moment of pain and clarity for Curry when she realized that "I couldn't eat with one of the people I really loved." That moment "jelled what [had been] my instincts and my politics from as long as I can remember."[35]

In 1957 Curry was offered a job as field secretary for the Collegiate Council of the United Nations. Based in New York for the next two years, she traveled to colleges across the country to start model United Nations, establishing contacts with students through the Student YWCA or international relations clubs. Then, in 1959, NSA asked her to direct the Southern Student Human Relations Project, funded by the Field Foundation. For two years NSA had been running human relations seminars, drawing students from black and white colleges in the south to ten-day race relations seminars held on midwestern campuses, cites of the annual NSA congress. These seminars gave historical, political, and social background on the South and urged participants to return to the South to set up other interracial meetings. Curry was instructed to recruit students for the summer seminars, and to set up interracial student meetings in the South to discuss a variety of political issues, as a means of breaking down racial fears and creating interracial alliances. Curry moved to Atlanta to start the project in December 1959.

It was but two short months before sit-ins in Greensboro, North Carolina, ignited the most intense phase of the civil rights movement. Immediately, Curry was drawn into the orbit of the young activists who would soon form SNCC. She was asked to become one of two adult advisers to SNCC, along with Ella Baker. Curry herself was only a few years older than most of the students, but she had valuable organizing experience, contacts all over the country, and access to funds, some of which, with the Field Foundation's blessing, she was able to divert to pay SNCC's phone bills and other expenses. From 1960 to 1964 Curry recruited students from southern campuses for NSA summer seminars, meeting in the process such people as Casey Hayden, Chuck McDew, and Bob Zellner (all of whom attended the NSA seminars and all of whom became leaders in SNCC). Her position required that she not participate in direct actions such as sit-ins, but she provided publicity and attended advisory committee meetings of SNCC, where questions of strategy and tactics were debated. Through her involvement in the Southern Interagency Conference she met Jean Fairfax, who hired her to join the AFSC staff in the spring of 1964.

When Curry moved to Jackson, Mississippi, in May 1964, she met Winifred Green Falls and several other white women whom Fairfax had contacted. They were eager to work to "keep Jackson peaceful," a carefully coded phrase that cloaked their support for school integration. It was a strange summer for Curry, because her closest friends were working on the SNCC Freedom Summer project across town, yet she couldn't have contact with them. Because the label of "outside agitator" was the death knell for any organizer, Curry was unable to mention her identification even with the AFSC, let alone SNCC; instead, she was introduced as an old college friend of Winifred Falls's. "One time I had to hide in a closet," Curry recalled, to keep from having her identity revealed by a woman who knew she was on the AFSC staff and was planning to attend a meeting.[36]

Winifred Falls was a sixth-generation Mississippian who grew up in a conventional southern white family. As a teenager she was active in the Episcopal church's youth group, and in 1952 she was elected a delegate to the General Convention of Young Churchmen, which met that year in Boston. There she met black Episcopalians and made lifelong friends. When she returned home, however, she kept this crossing of the race barrier to herself. In 1959 she married her high school sweetheart, and in 1963 she completed college. That year the Mississippi legislature began to discuss closing the schools in order to avoid court desegregation order. Falls met Pat Derian, wife of a physician, and their group quickly expanded to five, two Jews and three Protestants, who met to discuss the need to maintain the schools. "We were very unsophisticated, and had never done *anything*," Falls recalled, so they approached Jane Scutt of Church Women United for help in organizing a group. She introduced them to Jean Fairfax, who met with them and encouraged them. Falls recalled that Fairfax was poised and confident; she assured them that they were capable of organizing a group to support the schools, and she offered her assistance. [37]

Curry and Falls set to work organizing Mississippians for Public Education (MPE), a statewide group of white women who supported the public schools. Technically, MPE took no position on segregation but instead focused on the need to obey the law and to prevent the disruption that had occurred in Little Rock. Members met in homes in small groups and avoided big public meetings. Curry and Falls traveled to many communities throughout Mississippi, establishing contacts with sympathetic women, holding meetings, and researching and writing educational materials for the group. The women in MPE quickly educated themselves about proposed tuition grant programs and worked to defeat pending legislation that would have established such a program for the state of Mississippi. During that summer they sponsored billboard signs and spot announcements on TV urging support for public schools, issued press releases, and held approximately seventy-five coffee klatch meetings in women's homes to talk to white parents, encouraging them to send their children to public schools. [38] When the schools opened in the fall, school desegregation proceeded smoothly. For Winifred Falls, life would never be the same. She left her marriage and threw herself into civil rights activity, joining the staff of the AFSC in 1965.

The passage of the Civil Rights Act in July 1964 presented new opportunities for civil rights work. Because Title VI of that act barred discrimination in any federally funded program, it empowered the federal government to insist on school desegregation and to withdraw federal funds from school districts that refused to comply. Barbara Moffett, secretary of community relations and a key actor in responding to the changing legal climate, had no illusions that the law by itself would create substantial change; rather, she believed that there had to be an interplay between grass-roots movements and public policy. [39]

In 1965 the AFSC teamed up with the NAACP Legal Defense and Education Fund (LDEF) to send a School Desegregation Task Force into seven southern states to facilitate the school desegregation process. For the next two years the project monitored the implementation of the Civil Rights Act in some 200 school districts. The project combined the skills of community organizers hired by the AFSC with those of lawyers supplied by the LDEF. Together the two organizations educated African-American parents about their rights and encouraged them to be pioneers in the school desegregation process. At the same time they applied steady pressure on the federal government to insure adequate enforcement of Title VI.[40]

Connie Curry was appointed director of the School Desegregation Task Force for the AFSC, which prepared and distributed materials explaining to parents their rights. AFSC staff and other organizations sponsored statewide leadership training workshops on desegregation. Curry hired several staff to aid her, including Winifred Green (who dropped her married name, Falls, after her divorce) and Hayes Mizell. Curry, Green, and Mizell visited hundreds of local communities, primarily in Georgia, Alabama, Mississippi, and South Carolina. In the cities they met with supportive whites occasionally, but in rural communities they worked exclusively with blacks. They talked to groups of parents to encourage them to send their children to integrated schools, attended mass meetings, escorted students into schools, worked with harassed families, and gleaned information from local communities about violations of desegregation plans. Organizers like Green and Curry worked long hours with few breaks, but as Green recalled, "It wasn't work, it was life," offering an opportunity to "integrate life and work . . . and the excitement of the possibility of change" that proved to be "a terrifically energizing force." The work involved exercising leadership, encouraging local people to believe they could do something, supporting what they did, and thus enabling others to develop leadership.[41]

In addition to paid staff, the AFSC also recruited a number of program associates from local activists in black communities, who received some financial assistance from the AFSC to pay for child care and transportation, and in some cases a small stipend to support their work.[42] At times the AFSC had as many as 200 people working as volunteers or paid associates in southern black communities, informing people of their rights, recruiting parents to send their children to integrated schools, forming local groups to put pressure on school boards to insure successful integration, and informing the Department of Health, Education, and Welfare (HEW) when violations of desegregation plans occurred. The program associates constituted a virtually all-female work force, based on strong black women already trying to make school systems work for their children. Although most of the paid volunteers were women, many of the families who pioneered school desegregation efforts included strong black fathers who participated actively in the struggle as well.

The School Desegregation Task Force played part gadfly, part ally to the federal government. On the one hand, it applied constant pressure on federal agencies responsible for enforcing the law, particularly HEW and the Justice Department. On the other hand, federal officials at times solicited information and aid from the AFSC in order to perform their enforcement function more effectively.[43] The civil rights bill was signed into law in July 1964, but no guidelines for school desegregation appeared until April 1965. The AFSC was sharply critical of the federal government in that first year, arguing that little information was forthcoming from the government about school desegregation, that local school officials failed to cooperate, that complaints were investigated very slowly, and that in no school district had federal funds been terminated.[44] When guidelines were finally issued, AFSC staff felt some satisfaction that their critical report had made some impact.[45]

The AFSC did a thorough job of collecting information from local communities.[46] This work was a team effort, from program associates at work in local communities, to Curry and Green and other staff who stayed in close contact with local activists, to Moffett and Fairfax, who compiled the information and presented it in "a way that Washington would listen to."[47] The AFSC's success resulted from a variety of factors. One was its style of work, which began at the community level, listening to people and organizing them. Thus the AFSC "earned the right to speak at the national level because of deep involvement at the community level," according to Jean Fairfax.[48] A second factor was the ability of the agency to meticulously document what was happening at the local level. Barbara Moffett, who was trained as a journalist, insisted that her staff write comprehensive reports of all their activities. Furthermore, when Fairfax and Moffett went to Washington to testify before congressional committees or to consult with agency officials, they offered not just information but a host of specific recommendations about how to improve enforcement efforts. At times the AFSC would bring local black activists to Washington to testify, providing a direct channel of communication between such activists and the government.

When the School Desegregation Task Force ended in 1967, the AFSC continued its work in southern black communities. After 1966 the work continued under the name Southeastern Public Education Program. Winifred Green became director of the project in 1968, a position she held for a decade. Over time, as the urgency of the initial process of school desegregation faded, other issues came to the fore. AFSC staff worked with parents, encouraging them to get involved in the schools to help plan programs to aid African-American students. These newly involved parents put pressure on the schools to examine all of their policies in light of the more diverse student body, developing new curriculum, reviewing policies of discipline, and encouraging the election of school board members to represent the black community.[49]

Black parents often paid a high price for their activism, losing jobs, facing eviction, or enduring threats of physical violence. The AFSC began to grant aid to families who suffered such reprisals. Following the murder of Reverend James Reeb during the 1965 march to Selma, Alabama, contributions flowed in from all over the country to the SCLC, the AFSC, and the Unitarian Universalist Association. The money was used to establish the James Reeb Memorial Fund, to provide assistance to individuals or families suffering because of their involvement in the civil rights movement. The AFSC's Family Aid Fund Program evolved out of this, and by the fall of 1965 the fund was deluged with requests from black families in crisis who had enrolled their children in desegregated schools. Connie Curry assumed responsibility for administering the fund in 1966. In March 1967, as money began to run low, a grant from the Ford Foundation extended the fund's life. From 1965 to 1975 aid was granted to a number of families to allow them to successfully resist reprisals and to stay in their communities to work for change. By 1969, as economic reprisals began to taper off, the fund expanded its purpose and supported a number of experiments in economic development in southern rural black communities, including a pallet factory, a cooperative supermarket, farming, and housing cooperatives.[50]

For almost two decades, the AFSC worked to facilitate the integration of public schools in the South. Yet the strategies employed by the organization shifted over time. By the mid-1960s earlier attempts to persuade public officials to initiate and support school desegregation were regarded as largely futile. Recognizing that power relationships were sharply etched in the South and could be transformed only by empowering those without power, Barbara Moffett believed that the AFSC had to "stand with those members of the black community who wanted to exercise their rights."[51] Fairfax echoed her sentiment: "The idea was to enable those who were powerless to understand and use their power to initiate and demand change."[52]

The AFSC played a significant role in civil rights efforts in the South. Unlike other civil rights groups, the AFSC did not have to depend on the vagaries of shifting funding priorities. Most civil rights organizations suffered major cutbacks in funds in 1966, when advocates of black power emerged to dominate SNCC and CORE, and public sympathy on the part of northern whites declined precipitously. Because its funding sources were more stable, the AFSC could make a long-term commitment to school desegregation efforts. It was one of the few organizations that could provide well-trained professional staff over the long term. As a result the AFSC was able to mount "a remarkable professional work of high professional quality" compared to other organizations, which operated on a shoestring, in Fairfax's estimation.[53]

The results of school desegregation in the South have fallen far short of the hopes of many, for many white students fled to private academies, and public schools became largely black. Nevertheless, the South was permanently changed by the experience. For once, African Americans were given choices, empowered to act on their own behalf, and afforded the dignity of knowing they had rights as individuals. Without the backing of federal law and some willingness to enforce it, however spotty, the change could not have come. But organizations such as the AFSC and LDEF were critical actors in the process by which black communities gained access to nominally integrated public schooling.

Mentoring in the AFSC

The AFSC played such a significant role in sustaining civil rights activism in the 1960s that one scholar of the civil rights movement has referred to it as a "halfway house" for the movement, providing "social change resources such as skilled activists, tactical knowledge, media contacts, workshops, knowledge of past movements, and a vision of a future society."[54] Yet as a far smaller organization than the YWCA, and with less extensive outreach to students, the AFSC probably had less impact on young people who became activists in the 1960s. But networks of activists worked together in the AFSC, playing distinct roles and learning from and supporting each other. Throughout the course of the AFSC's school desegregation work, for example, four women worked closely together: Connie Curry and Winifred Green on the front line in the South, doing the daily work of organizing; and Jean Fairfax and Barbara Moffett working out of the national office. Fairfax supervised Curry when she was first hired by the AFSC. When Fairfax left the AFSC to work for the NAACP Legal Defense and Education Fund in 1965, the two continued to work closely as colleagues on the School Desegregation Task Force. Green was one of Curry's staff, as well as a close colleague and friend. And Barbara Moffett was simultaneously boss and friend to all.

It is hard to characterize the relationships among these four women as ones of mentoring, but the four certainly provided a great deal of support to one another. Fairfax and Moffett were approximately a decade older than Curry and Green, and each had decades of experience in organizational work. Yet Curry brought extensive organizational experience to her work with the AFSC as well. Curry and Fairfax functioned as colleagues during the time they worked for AFSC and LDEF respectively.

Curry and Green certainly looked to Moffett and Fairfax for kinds of support that enabled them to sustain morale under difficult circumstances. For example, Curry recalled a hot Saturday afternoon in a small Georgia town when she and Green had been terrified by a local sheriff and a crowd of hostile residents who gathered to threaten them. "See Benji over there," one of the locals drawled, pointing to a large man who appeared to be mentally retarded. "He hates nigger lovers, and when we tell him what ya'll been doing we can't tell what will happen." The sheriff escorted them to the county line and warned them never to set foot in the county again. Terrified, they fled to the next county, where they checked into a motel. They called Jean Fairfax, who immediately got on the phone to the Justice Department. An official from the Justice Department called them shortly afterwards to check on their safety. Teasing, Curry and Green threatened to resign that day. Sustaining the difficult work was made easier because they knew that they could call

Moffett or Fairfax at any time of the day or night if frightened or discouraged. At the same time, from Curry and Green's intense work partnership evolved a very close lifelong friendship.

Curry had the strong sense that the staff were all in the struggle together. "Jean was an inspiration," Curry recalled, because she was "so single-minded." A dedicated and exacting worker, she pushed herself hard and expected others to display as much commitment. Both Moffet and Fairfax had "great faith in and appreciation of me," recalled Curry. She counted both of them as close friends. From her position in the national office, Moffett was always supportive, sympathetic, and compassionate, according to staff who worked for her.[55]

Fairfax and Moffett together taught Green important lessons, chief among them "not to give up; if one thing doesn't work figure out another way to approach the problem." From Jean she learned the importance of attention to detail, and the need for total respect for the people you worked with. "I learned to admire and emulate the real joy she had in her work," recalled Green, "a sense that what I was doing was important," and I learned also to "have fun." For all these women, the lines of authority were blurred by strong ties of friendship and community. Curry recalled that one of the most precious things about working for the AFSC was the existence of "a group of like-minded people who loved you and cared about you."[56]

Mentoring did occur within the AFSC, and in a mixed-sex organization, older women activists at times served as models for young men as well as for young women. Barbara Graves recalled, for example, that during the years in the 1960s when she directed the AFSC's Voluntary International Service program, young people, both men and women, "tended to idealize the lady from Philadelphia who didn't look her age." The chain of activism continued into later decades as well, connecting Charlotte Meacham and Ho'oipo De Cambra in a close bond of friendship. Charlotte Meacham had worked for the AFSC's Community Relations Division in the Philadelphia office in the late 1950s and the 1960s, focusing her efforts for a number of years on fair housing efforts in the Philadelphia area. At the end of the 1960s she shifted to work on the AFSC's prison program. In 1971 she and her husband, Stewart Meacham, who had directed the Peace Education Program for the Philadelphia office, went to Southeast Asia to direct the AFSC's program of Quaker seminars in Southeast Asia. In 1977 the two retired to Hawaii.

There, they met Ho'oipo De Cambra, a native Hawaiian. "Charlotte and Stewart were the first Quakers I ever met in my life," recalled De Cambra. They were "older people that I could admire and identify with . . . and become very close to over the next decade." Through them she learned to appreciate Quakerism, finding herself "challenged by Quakers . . . to see the light in everyone, even our opponents." Married, with children, she had been doing volunteer work but lacked much confidence in her abilities to work with an organization. Laughingly, De Cambra recalled how Charlotte Meacham had "plotted" to get her involved in the AFSC, urging her to apply for a job with the organization. Reluctantly, she applied and got the job and went to work in 1981, focusing her efforts on organizing native women around issues of concern to them. A powerful bond of love and delight in one another's company was evident between this oddly matched pair of women when I interviewed them; De Cambra a large native Hawaiian in her midforties, Meacham a tiny, frail, wheelchair-bound white woman in her midseventies.[57] Thus the older generation continued to influence the younger, providing models of activism it could build on.

Resurgence of Peace Activism

The history of the peace movement, like that of the civil rights movement, illustrates elements of continuity and discontinuity in progressive social reform from World War II through the 1960s. The peace movement had survived, if just barely, during the bleak first years of the Cold War and McCarthyism, maintained by such pacifist organizations as the AFSC and the Fellowship of Reconciliation (FOR). It blossomed again in the thaw of the late 1950s, when growing public concern with the dangers of radioactive fallout led to the resurgence of peace activity. That activity drew in both traditional pacifist groups and liberal internationalists. Most important among the pacifist groups were the AFSC, the FOR, the War Resisters League, and the Catholic Worker Movement. Of these, the AFSC and FOR were central, for they managed to combine under the same roof traditional pacifists, who believed in individual refusal to participate in war, and radical pacifists, who were committed to organized social resistance.

In 1957 two umbrella organizations were created to pull together the diverse groups working for peace and to capitalize on increasing public concern about radioactive fallout. The AFSC played a critical role in organizing these new organizations, with Lawrence Scott and Robert Gilmore, peace education secretaries in the Chicago and New York AFSC regional offices, urging both radical pacifists and peace liberals to combine forces in a new effort.[58] The first result was the Committee for a Sane Nuclear Policy (SANE), chaired by Clarence Pickett, former executive secretary of the AFSC, and Norman Cousins, editor of the *Saturday Review*, and organized to protest nuclear testing through educational activities such as conferences, newspaper advertisements, and petition and letter-writing campaigns. The second was the Committee for Non-Violent Action (CNVA), a direct-action group that applied Gandhian techniques of nonviolent resistance to peace work, engaging in civil disobedience at a series of sites in the late 1950s.[59] The primary objective for peace activists from 1957 to 1963 was finally achieved in 1963, when an atmospheric test ban treaty was signed. Yet the larger goals of the peace movement, such as disarmament and the end to the Cold War, seemed as elusive as ever.

The coalition that had formed around the test ban issue lost focus and drifted after 1963. But in 1965, when the war in Vietnam heated up, the peace movement quickly turned its attention to protesting the war. The movement was in a strong position to provide information, critiques of U.S. foreign policy, and personnel for the budding antiwar movement. The movement consisted largely of adults, but it had also served to politicize a number of students in the late 1950s and early 1960s, many of whom joined Students for a Democratic Society (SDS), the major organization of the New Left in the early 1960s.[60] Thus as least some of the young activists who would help organize the antiwar movement were politicized by their elders in the peace movement.

But, by 1965, many of those younger activists rejected significant aspects of the politics of their elders. Matters came to a head when SDS planned its first antiwar march, scheduled for Washington, D.C., in April 1965. The platform, tactics, and refusal to exclude the far Left all were destined to antagonize traditional adult peace groups. First, SDS unilaterally announced a call for the march, insisting on sole sponsorship, a move that stepped on the toes of older organizations accustomed to carefully negotiating coalitions to sponsor marches. Furthermore, the march was scheduled for the same time as the traditional disarmament marches held by the peace movement, thus undercutting those activities. More critical, however, was SDS's decision to allow any group to join the march, including Communists. This infuriated a number of older peace activists who believed SDS was blind to the dangers of Communist infiltration. The debate over inclusivity did not follow strictly generational lines, but most younger activists were on the side of inclusivity, finding the older generation's fear of working with groups on the far Left incomprehensible.[61]

Differences in analysis further complicated the picture, for the New Left (joined by radical pacifists) embraced a leftist interpretation of the war, arguing that U.S. policy in Vietnam was but one example of U.S. imperialist domination of the third world. In contrast, liberal peace activists sympathized with the U.S. government's concern to prevent Communist domination of South Vietnam but opposed the war as an instrument of that policy, pushing for negotiations and UN supervision of a peace settlement. After the dramatic success of the SDS-sponsored march, which drew 20,000 people to Washington, the liberal and radical arms of the peace movement had an increasingly difficult time cooperating.[62]

Yet even then the two halves of the peace movement relied on one another. The AFSC continued to play a prominent role in peace activity. It ran a full-page ad in the *New York Times* in October 1965 calling for an end to bombing, a cease-fire, and negotiations with the goal of self-determination. The following year the AFSC published a major pamphlet, *Peace in Vietnam*, which explained the role of nationalism and socioeconomic change in Southeast Asia, traced the history of U.S. involvement in Vietnam, and called for U.S. withdrawal and recognition of self-determination for the Vietnamese.[63] When draft resistance mushroomed in 1966–1967, the AFSC and other traditional pacifist groups cooperated with student activists in draft counseling activities. In 1967 some regional offices of the AFSC cooperated with the 15 April Mobilization Against the War in Vietnam and participated in Vietnam Summer, an attempt by peace activists to educate people about the war through door-to-door campaigns.[64] Throughout the course of the war the AFSC continued to participate in coalitions such as the 1969 New Mobilization Committee to End the War in Vietnam, and to sponsor marches, vigils, lobbying efforts, and other antiwar actions.

The AFSC's antiwar activities were dominated by men, but women participated actively as well. Most of the peace education secretaries in the AFSC's national and the regional offices were men. Yet even though they were often denied positions of leadership, women held positions as college or high school secretaries, served on and chaired peace committees, and found myriad ways to contribute to the AFSC's antiwar actions.

As a liberal internationalist organization, the YWCA also continued to work to achieve a more peaceful world throughout the 1960s and 1970s. The Public Affairs Program of the YWCA outlined a strategy to achieve peace that changed little during the 1960s: disarmament through negotiation, the control of nuclear power for peaceful purposes, the maintenance of the international police force, and the improvement of standards of living in the developing nations, all through the auspices of the United Nations. The YWCA also marshalled its resources to support the nuclear test ban treaty in the early 1960s.[65]

Although the YWCA was never in the forefront of the peace movement, by 1966–1967 the organization put its full weight behind the call for an end to the war. In 1966, for example, the National Student Council of the YWCA passed a resolution urging an end to the war through negotiation with the National Liberation Front. That same year the National Board urged the United States to work through the United Nations to find a peaceful solution to the situation in Vietnam, including ensuring free elections.[66] Certainly throughout the second half of the 1960s, the war in Vietnam was a key issue discussed by both students and adults in the YWCA, and opposition to the war was widespread in the organization. Many of the members of the organization sent letters to Congress and participated in the large-scale marches and demonstrations.

The YWCA took a stronger antimilitarist position in 1970, when the tone and some of the substance of the Public Affairs Program shifted. For the first time the Y called for an end to all weapons of mass destruction—nuclear, chemical, and biological. It also argued for a "de-emphasis on bilateral military alliances and spheres of influence in favor of strengthening the international peacekeeping role of the UN" and an end to the sale of arms to developing nations. In 1973 the YWCA endorsed the "elimination of world poverty" by contributions of industrialized nations of 1 percent of their GNP to world social and economic development.[67] Although the YWCA was not one of the more prominent groups in the antiwar coalition, throughout the 1960s and 1970s it took consistent positions in opposition to the war in Vietnam and in favor of a more peaceful world, providing an arena for women of all ages to discuss the issue and take a stand against war.

Roots of the
Women's Movement

Just as the YWCA was more sympathetic to feminist issues than was the AFSC during the 1940s and 1950s, so the YWCA connected more easily to the revival of the women's movement in the late 1960s and 1970s. Most women activists in the AFSC in the years following World War II were convinced that men and women were equal, yet they tended to view such equality as an established fact. They had lived exceptional lives and were "oriented to the positive goal that women should go out and do whatever they wanted." For some, discrimination against women had always been evident, but for others it remained largely invisible. In any case, feminists were often viewed as "unattractive mannish" people, or simply as too single-minded in their focus.[68] Barbara Graves recalled the pattern well: "I thought I was liberated all my life. I had very few difficulties achieving in whatever I was doing." Thus, when the feminist movement came along, it took women like Graves "a long time to recognize my own oppression." She believed in the goal of equality, was aware of discrimination against women, but did not identify with that oppression herself. When the women's movement emerged, she was very sympathetic, but it never became her major focus.[69]

Nevertheless, because women in the AFSC were strong, capable women, exerting leadership in a variety of activities, they served as role models for younger women, demonstrating the possibilities for women's activism. Not feminist in itself, such modeling nevertheless may have encouraged the development of feminism among women whose lives had been influenced by this older generation of activists.

The YWCA contributed more directly to the first stirrings of the new feminist movement that emerged in the 1960s. Young women activists often credited the Student YWCA with awakening their consciousness about women's issues. Casey Hayden recalled being exposed to "women as a social issue" in the late 1950s through the YWCA. In the fall of 1965 she and Mary King joined forces to write a memo about women's experiences of subordination in the New Left. It was this memo that sparked debate within SDS that year, crystallizing the discontent that many women activists felt with their treatment in movement circles. Several years later the growing debate in SDS and elsewhere led a number of women to break with the New Left to found the women's liberation movement.[70]

Discussions of what later would be termed sexism continued to percolate in Student YWCA circles in the early 1960s. The Student YWCA sponsored a special seminar in the summer of 1963 on the changing roles of women for student advisers in the YWCA, and the 1963 National Student Association Convention of YMCAs and YWCAs also took up the topic. Charlotte Bunch was first exposed to Betty Friedan's *Feminine Mystique* in 1963 when her Student YWCA adviser urged her campus chapter to read the book just months after it was published. In it Friedan described the boredom and frustration experienced by college-educated women of her generation who had married, had children, and focused their lives on their families, finding little outlet for intellectual and creative interests. The book had an electrifying impact on Bunch, who recalled thinking, "Yes, that's it, that's what happened to my mother, that's what happened to that generation, and it will never happen to me." The group of young women in Bunch's Y chapter were gripped by debate and discussion of the issues posed by Friedan. Out of that group emerged at least three strong feminists: Bunch herself; Sara Evans, who was involved in organizing the women's movement in Chicago and who later wrote *Personal Politics: The Roots of the Women's Liberation in the Civil Rights Movement and the New Left;* and Caryn McTighe, past director of the National Women's Studies Association.

The YWCA's practice of fostering women's leadership was critical to Bunch's development. When she moved to Washington, D.C., where she worked for the Institute for Policy Studies and organized for the New Left, she was confronted with sexism on the Left, a sharp contrast to her experience in the Y. For the first time, she recalled, she had the classic female experience of sitting in a room full of men, making a statement that was ignored, and five minutes later, watching the group respond enthusiastically to a man who said essentially the same thing. Past president of the University Christian Movement, Bunch "wasn't prepared for invisibility." In 1968 she joined one of the first women's groups organized by women fleeing the New Left, and she quickly decided to devote her energies to the budding women's movement. She became a key organizer for the movement, and a theorist and editor of the important feminist journal *Quest*.[71]

The National Board and community YWCAs also participated in what many scholars have identified as the older branch of the women's movement, one that crystallized with President Kennedy's Commission on the Status of Women, which brought widespread public attention to the problems of sex discrimination.[72] The YWCA was one of a number of women's organizations that contributed to the work of the committee and were further stimulated by it. Several prominent members of the Y served on the commission: Dorothy Height, president of the National Council of Negro Women and prominent staff member on the National Board of the YWCA, was a member of the commission itself; Mildred Persinger, chair of the National Public Affairs Committee of the YWCA, sat on the Committee on Social Insurance and Taxes; and Mildred Jones, vice-president of the National Board of the Y sat on the Committee on Protective Labor Legislation.

The YWCA's sensitivity to the problems that Betty Friedan exposed in *The Feminine Mystique* is evident in the Vistas for Women project developed in 1963. Several pilot projects, conducted from 1963 to 1965 in four cities around the country, were designed to help middle-aged women, usually married with older children, to return to work. The projects established career counseling services and job placement services and steered women into business and technical schools, or college and university programs.[73]

Despite its legacy of many decades of commitment to advancing women's status, the YWCA's response to the feminist movement was at first ambivalent. That ambivalence was shaped in part by the long-standing divide in the community of organized women over the Equal Rights Amendment. The YWCA had opposed the ERA for four decades, concerned about its potential impact on working-class women. Thus the Y was cautious about the women's movement when the National Organization for Women (NOW) endorsed the ERA in 1967. Not until 1973 did the YWCA take a stand in favor of the ERA.

A second source of the Y's ambivalence toward the feminist movement was the common perception that the movement was one of white middle-class women. The 1970 convention, with its endorsement of the elimination of racism as the YWCA's major focus, began a period of tremendous ferment and a process of consciousness-raising on the part of the board about issues of racism, with African-American women leading the way. At that time the YWCA National Board was a multiracial board that gave priority to the elimination of racism. Although the board was far from hostile to women's issues, they were not a major focus. As a result community YWCAs were often more deeply engrossed in the women's movement than was the National Board, for community Ys established women's shelters and worked on a variety of women's issues. Some members of the National Board expressed uneasiness that a new focus on middle-class women's concerns might drain energy from the Y's commitment to eliminate racism.[74]

Personal attitudes also informed the Y's ambivalence toward the new feminist movement. Many older women were somewhat resentful of the burst of enthusiasm for women's rights they witnessed among younger women. Augusta Roberts recalled that she was both "amused and distressed" when the women's movement arose, because young women seemed unaware that they were building on a tradition. "Did they believe they were inventing the wheel?" she and her colleagues in the YWCA asked. The emphasis on the needs of middle-class educated women also annoyed some women in the YWCA, who were more accustomed to directing their energies towards disadvantaged women. Jean Whittet recalled that some women in the YWCA "were contemptuous of the feminist movement at first," viewing these women as "Johnny-come-latelies." "We had been out in the trenches working for low-income women and minority women for decades," she recalled, and she and her colleagues tended to view poverty and racism as the major problems faced by women. Whittet had been acutely aware, as a staff member for the Student YWCA, of the discrimination that women faced. Nevertheless, she found it hard to validate the problems faced by white middle-class women compared to those faced by women disadvantaged by race or class.[75]

Gradually, women in the YWCA came to ally themselves more firmly with the women's movement. That transformation took place in the early years of the 1970s. The 1970 Public Affairs Program noted the "cultural and institutional forces . . . which deny women decision-making power in proportion to their numbers and abilities," as well as "traditional patterns of self-limitation which limit the variety and potential of who women are, and what they can do in both public and private life."[76] Included in their priorities for action were items that the Y had worked for during the 1940s and 1950s, such as equal access to education, to job training, and to employment. In addition, however, certain changes that the Y called for clearly reflected the development of the women's movement, such as "an extensive network of adequate child care services," family planning and maternal and child health services, "repeal of all laws restricting or prohibiting abortions" performed by a physician, and greater involvement of women in elective and appointive government positions.[77] By 1973 the YWCA ended its historic opposition to the ERA, endorsing it for the first time. Furthermore, the language the Y used had altered, clearly indicating its alignment with the women's movement, for it called for the "empowerment of women" through efforts to "eradicate sexism."[78]

The YWCA had a complex relationship to the revival of feminism during the 1960s and 1970s. It had fostered feminist sentiments during the 1940s and 1950s at a time when widespread public support for such ideas was lacking. It had nurtured the young women who would provide some of the leadership for the new movement. When it came, however, the YWCA was caught off guard and did not immediately assume leadership on the new set of issues advanced by that younger generation of women activists. Fairly quickly, nevertheless, the YWCA followed the lead of younger women and became a staunch advocate of many of the ideas advanced by that movement.

The social protest movements of the 1960s appear on the surface to be distinct from anything that preceded them. The ferocity of the protests unleashed during the decade, the challenge they presented to the nation's social order, one that threatened at times to tear the social fabric apart, were a far cry from the tenor and tone of the preceding two decades. Yet if we examine the underlying values that first led to protest, the idealism that fired that younger generation, we realize they were not anomalies. Instead, they were a legacy from earlier generations of social reformers, those who had envisioned a society built on economic justice, world peace, racial justice, and an equal partnership between the sexes. Furthermore, women played a critical role in that intergenerational chain of activism, nurturing a younger generation of women and some young men as well. Given women's propensity to value connections with others more than many men do, women may have bonded more easily across generational lines than did their male colleagues. Older women schooled younger women in the progressive values they embraced and opened their eyes to new possibilities for women's lives. Together these progressive women activists, whatever their generation, dared to dream and work for a better world, a world free from war, with dignity, justice, and equality for all.

Conclusion

Following in the footsteps of earlier generations, women progressive activists continued to seek social and political change in the postwar world. The efforts of women in the 1940s and 1950s provided an important bridge between earlier generations of women activists and those involved in social movements of the 1960s. During this transitional period a consensus began to develop about the need to eliminate racial segregation and discrimination from U.S. society, and many women activists moved far beyond the tentative attempts made to create interracial dialogue in the interwar period. A new sense of urgency about racial injustice informed the efforts of progressive women activists after 1945. A number of white women's organizations opened their membership to the participation of African-American women, and some women worked actively to transform the nation's racist attitudes and practices. In the 1960s the struggle for civil rights took center stage on the nation's agenda of social and political reform, and women in the YWCA and the AFSC intensified their efforts to achieve racial justice.

By the end of the 1960s and into the 1970s, the tentative interracial alliances formed in earlier decades began to shift from a model of integration based on assimilation of women of color into the dominant white culture, toward a more genuine pluralism based on mutual respect and fundamental learning about differences between women from varied racial-ethnic backgrounds. In the process African-American women and other women of color often served as the conscience for white women, educating the latter and deepening their understanding of the pervasiveness of racism in the United States.

Women's peace activism also underwent a profound transformation in the postwar years, while remaining a critical component of progressive activism. As male conscientious objectors took leadership positions in peace organizations, women experienced a more subordinate status within the larger peace movement than they had in interwar decades or would again in the antinuclear campaigns of the 1980s. Yet women in large numbers continued to enter the ranks of activists committed to the dream of a more peaceful world. They educated the public on international issues, supported the fledgling United Nations, and urged negotiation and disarmament. The peace movement shifted its focus from the need to challenge the polarized thinking of the Cold War during the late 1940s and early 1950s, to the campaign for a nuclear test ban treaty in the late 1950s, and to the struggle to end the U.S. war in Vietnam in the 1960s.

Progressive women activists also maintained a heritage of feminist activism, although few named it that at the time. Some attempted to ignore many of the traditional conventions of gender, combining work, family, and social reform in new ways. Others went farther, noting that they suffered subordination and exclusion from the centers of power, and insisting that they be allowed to participate more fully in public life. They thus kept alive a feminist critique during a period when the word *feminist* was largely discredited in public discourse, providing both an intellectual tradition and personal examples that inspired younger women who created the revitalized women's movement of the 1960s and 1970s.

The strategies and tactics employed by women activists to achieve their goals drew on the heritage of the past, yet transformed women's progressive politics. Traditional methods of pressure-group politics, developed by women's voluntary groups in earlier decades, remained a significant focus for the YWCA, which relied on its large and influential membership to apply pressure in favor of civil rights and other progressive legislation. The AFSC also sought to put pressure on government and private individuals deemed sufficiently powerful to bring about change, thus working through established channels of influence even when not directly engaged in lobbying activities.

Newer techniques that presaged the "personal politics" of the civil rights and feminist movements of the 1960s were also evident during the 1940s and 1950s. Women in both the YWCA and the AFSC employed a female ethic in their organizing efforts, one that relied on building interpersonal networks both to raise consciousness and to sustain the daily tasks of organization. The YWCA's efforts to conduct antiracist education as an important first step in challenging racist institutions was markedly similar to the later attempt of the women's movement to transform consciousness about gender relations as a means of transforming those relations. At an institutional level the AFSC gave less explicit attention to individual needs and relationships. Yet in the context of organizing that relied heavily on networks of women activists in local communities, women in the AFSC maintained a female ethic in their daily organizing activities. Furthermore, by the 1950s, as men and women worked together within the AFSC to mobilize larger groups in the community to demand change, they moved away from an emphasis on applying moral suasion in one-on-one encounters with powerful individuals and embraced the techniques of community organizing. The civil rights organizations took the next step, staging massive nonviolent demonstrations that became the hallmark of the movement.

Though women in the post–World War II era married more often and had children in greater numbers than in the previous generation, they did not abandon social activism. Rather, women activists, such as those in the YWCA and AFSC, played critical roles in sustaining a progressive critique of politics and social relations in the United States during precisely those decades when so much effort was made to mute female voices. They endorsed racial integration within women's voluntary groups, lobbied for civil rights legislation, and worked in communities to open schools, housing, and employment opportunities to all Americans. They persisted in their efforts to educate the public about international issues and to inspire others with their hopes for a new world order based on cooperation, negotiation, and a more equitable distribution of world resources. They continued to advocate a world in which women would receive equal treatment in education and employment, and in the formulation of public policy. Women made an important difference in both single-sex and mixed-sex organizations, bringing a female ethic to the work they did in communities and organizations.

The story of this generation of women political activists dramatizes for us the importance of sustaining women's social reform efforts during conservative eras like our own, in order to maintain a legacy for younger generations. Just as important is the example these women provide of linking different forms of oppression and inequality. For progressive women activists, women's liberation could only be achieved as part of a larger movement that demanded social justice for all.

List of Interviews

The following in-person interviews were conducted by the author:

Rosalyn Abernathy, 2 February 1989, telephone.

Thelma Babbitt, 23 September 1987, telephone.

Daisy Bates, 16 March 1989, telephone.

Charlotte Bunch, 2 April 1991, New Brunswick, New Jersey.

Eleanor Stabler Clarke, 7 March 1984, Kennett Square, Pennsylvania.

Helen Jackson Wilkins Claytor, 4 January 1992, telephone.

Emelita Cohen, 29 November 1983, Oakland, California.

Irene Samuel Cook, 15 February 1989, telephone.

Constance Curry, 13 April 1991, Louisville, Kentucky.

Mary Moss (Polly) Cuthbertson, 2 March 1984, Philadelphia, Pennsylvania, and 20 February 1988, telephone.

M. Ho'oipo DeCambra, 14 July 1989, Santa Rosa, California.

Ida Davidoff, 10 November 1991, telephone.

Nancy R. Duryee, 2 March 1984, Philadelphia, Pennsylvania.

Frank Duveneck, 7 August 1983, Los Altos Hills, California.

Jean Fairfax, 4 March 1984, Philadelphia, Pennsylvania, and 6 July 1990, telephone.

Jewel Graham, 7 November and 12 December 1990, Yellow Springs, Ohio.

Helen M. Grant, 27 October 1983, Oakland, California.

Barbara Graves, 11 November 1983, San Francisco, California, and 9 December 1987, telephone.

Winifred Green (Falls), 17 September 1991, telephone.

Garnet Guild, 7 July 1990, telephone.

Alvessie Hackshaw, 20 September 1984, Oakland, California.

Virginia Heck, 24 January 1984, Santa Rosa, California.

Dorothy Irene Height, 3 April 1984, New York; 28 November 1988, telephone; and 13 June 1990, Washington, D.C.

Verneta E. Hill, 11 November 1984, San Francisco, California.

Pat House, 23 April 1989, telephone.

Wesley Huss, 9 October 1984, Oakland, California.

Gerda Isenberg, 14 December 1983, Woodside, California.

Mary Hoxie Jones, 3 March 1984, Kennett Square, Pennsylvania.

Mary L. Jorgensen, 25 January 1984, Santa Rosa, California.

Russell F. Jorgensen, 25 January 1984, Santa Rosa, California.

Edith M. Lerrigo, 5 December 1984, Claremont, California.

Charlotte C. Meacham, 14 July 1989, Santa Rosa, California.

Margarita Mendoza de Sugiyama, 10 July 1991, Olympia, Washington.

Barbara W. Moffett, 8 March 1984 and 24 May 1989, Philadelphia, Pennsylvania.

Irene Osborne, 5 March 1984 and 23 May 1989, Phildelphia, Pennsylvania.

Helen Perkins, 25 January 1984, Santa Rosa, California.

Mildred E. Persinger, 3 April 1984 and 6 May 1989, New York, New York.

Dorothy M. Pete, 3 May 1984, Oakland, California.

Frank Quinn, 15 November 1984, telephone.

Robert Rankin, 5 December 1984, Claremont, California.

Augusta Roberts, 6 December 1984, Claremont, California, and 6 March 1988, telephone.

Alma Surlock, 17 June 1989, telephone.

Ben Seaver, 14 November 1983, San Francisco, California.

Madge T. Seaver, 14 November 1983, San Francisco, California.

Marjorie A. Smith, 25 October 1989, Dayton, Ohio.

Madeleine Stephenson, 25 January 1984, Santa Rosa, California.

Red Stephenson, 25 January 1984, Santa Rosa, California.

Patricia Stewart, 27 October 1983, Berkeley, California.

Stephen H. Theirmann, 8 March 1984, Philadelphia, Pennsylvania.

Mary Tusher, 10 May 1984, Oakland, California.

Tillie Walker, 4 July 1991, telephone.

Jean M. Whittet, 6 December 1984, Claremont, California.

Lamitsoi Williamson, 27 June 1984, Oakland, California.

Jimmie Woodward, 5 December 1984, Claremont, California.

Mildred B. Young, 5 March 1984, Philadelphia, Pennsylvania.

The following material was provided by respondents to my questions:

Thelma W. Babbitt, material taped in response to author's questions, September 1984.

Elizabeth Mansfield, manuscript prepared in response to author's questions, September 1984.

Notes

Introduction

1. "Toward the Elimination of Segregation in the Nation's Capital; A Report of an AFSC Community Relations Project with Public Schools and Recreation Areas, 1951–1955" (AFSC, Philadelphia, 1955).
2. Irene Osborne, interview with author, 5 March 1984, Philadelphia; Alma Scurlock, telephone interview with author, 17 June 1989.
3. The AAUW did, however, endorse racial integration of its own organization after World War II. See Jan Leone, "Integrating the American Association of University Women," *Historian*, May 1989. Other organizations in the progressive coalition included, among others, the Congress of Racial Equality, the Fellowship of Reconciliation, the War Resisters League, the Federal Council of Churches, the Anti-Defamation League of B'nai B'rith, the Catholic Worker Movement, and Church Women United. The progressive coalition also included a strong working-class component, represented by the AFL-CIO, and a number of progressive unions such as the United Auto Workers.
4. Leila Rupp and Verta Taylor, *Survival in the Doldrums: The American Women's Rights Movement, 1945 to the 1960s* (New York: Oxford University Press, 1987); Cynthia Harrison, *On Account of Sex: The Politics of Women's Issues, 1945–1968* (Berkeley: University of California Press, 1988).
5. Paula Baker, "The Domestication of Politics: Women and American Political Society, 1780–1920," *American Historical Review* 89 (1984): 620–647; Kathryn Kish Sklar, "Florence Kelley and the Integration of 'Women's Sphere' into American Politics, 1890–1921" (Paper presented at the Organization of American Historians, New York City, April 1986); Nancy F. Cott, *The Grounding of Modern Feminism* (New Haven, Conn.: Yale University Press, 1987).
6. Carol Gilligan, *In a Different Voice: Psychological Theory and Women's Development* (Cambridge, Mass.:Harvard University Press, 1982); Mary Field Belenky, Blythe McVicker Clinchy, Nancy Rule Goldberger, and Jill Mattuck Tarule, *Women's Ways of Knowing: The Development of Self, Voice, and Mind* (New York: Basic Books, 1986); Nancy Chodorow, *The Reproduction of Mothering: Psychoanalysis and the Sociology of Gender* (Berkeley: University of California Press, 1978). Gilligan and Chodorow have been criticized because their studies are based on white middle-class women. Yet

black scholars have also noted the centrality of networks of extended family and friends in the lives of black women; see Patricia Hill Collins, "The Social Construction of Black Feminist Thought," *Signs* 14 (1989): 745–773; Elsa Barkley Brown, "Mothers of Mind," *Sage: A Scholarly Journal on Black Women* 6 (1989): 4–11.

7.   Kathryn Kish Sklar, "Hull House in the 1890s: A Community of Women Reformers," *Signs* 10 (1985): 658–677.

8.   Sara Evans, *Personal Politics: The Roots of Women's Liberation in the Civil Rights Movement and the New Left* (New York: Vintage Books, 1980).

9.   Seth Koven and Sonya Michel, "Womanly Duties: Maternalist Politics and the Origins of Welfare States in France, Germany, Great Britain, and the United States, 1880–1920," *American Historical Review* 95 (1990): 1076–1108. The shift from maternalism toward interracialism occurred somewhat earlier among black women and a few of their white allies, for during the interwar years black women began to demand racial integration in groups like the YWCA.

10.   Cott, *The Grounding of Modern Feminism*, 87–89; Alice Kessler-Harris, *Out to Work: A History of Wage-Earning Women in the United States* (New York: Oxford University Press, 1982), 305–306.

11.   Mary Frederickson, "Citizens for Democracy: The Industrial Programs of the YWCA," in *Sisterhood and Solidarity: Workers' Education for Women, 1914–1984.* Joyce L. Kornbluh and Mary Frederickson, ed. (Philadelphia: Temple University Press, 1984), 77–106.

12.   By 1947 membership in the YWCA's Industrial Department dropped to 11,000. On the end of the Industrial Department, see Karen Sue Mittelman, " 'A Spirit That Touches the Problems of Today': Women and Social Reform in the Philadelphia Young Women's Christian Association, 1920–1945" (Ph.D. diss., University of Pennsylvania, 1987), 242–267. On women's activism in the CIO, see Ruth Milkman, *Gender at Work: The Dynamics of Job Segregation by Sex During World War II* (Urbana: University of Illinois Press, 1987); Nancy Gabin, *Feminism in the Labor Movement: Women in the United Auto Workers, 1935–1975* (Ithaca, N.Y.: Cornell University Press, 1990).

13.   Thomas R. Brooks, *The Walls Come Tumbling Down: A History of the Civil Rights Movement, 1940–1970* (Englewood Cliffs, N.J.: Prentice-Hall, 1974): Richard M. Dalfiume, "The 'Forgotten Years' of the Negro Revolution," *Journal of American History* 55 (1968): 90–106. Harvard Sitkoff, "Racial Militancy and Interracial Violence in the Second World War," *Journal of American History* 51 (1971): 661–81.

14.   Rosalyn Terborg-Penn, "Discontented Black Feminists: Prelude and Postscript to the Passage of the Nineteenth Amendment, in *Decades of Discontent: The Women's Movement, 1920–1940*, Lois Scharf and Joan M. Jensen, eds. (Westport, Conn.: Greenwood, 1983), 261–278; Angela Y. Davis, *Women, Race and Class* (New York: Vintage Books, 1981); on the Communist party, see Robin D. G. Kelley, *Hammer and Hoe: Alabama Communists During the Great Depression* (Chapel Hill: University of North Carolina Press, 1990); James Weinstein, *Ambiguous Legacy: The Left in American Politics* (New York: New Viewpoints, 1975); Robert L. Allen, with collaboration of Pamela P. Allen, *Reluctant Reformers: Racism and Social Reform Movements in the United States* (Washington, D.C.: Howard University Press, 1974).

15.   Estelle Freedman, "Separatism as Strategy: Female Institution Building and American Feminism, 1870–1930," *Feminist Studies* 5 (1979): 512–529.

16.   Betty Friedan, *The Feminine Mystique* (New York: Norton, 1963). Joanne Meyerowitz presented an important reinterpretation of this literature in "Beyond

'The Feminine Mystique': The Discourse on American Women, 1945–1950" (Paper presented at the 8th Annual Berkshire Conference on the History of Women, Douglass College, 8–10 June 1990). For a useful overview of the literature on domesticity in post-World War II America, see, for example, Rupp and Taylor, *Survival in the Doldrums.*

17. On patterns of marriage and child rearing, see Ethel Klein, *Gender Politics: From Consciousness to Mass Politics* (Cambridge, Mass.: Harvard University Press, 1984), 47–81. On the significance of civic activism within the League of Women Voters during the 1950s, see Susan Ware, "American Women in the 1950s: Nonpartisan Politics and Women's Politicization," in *Women, Politics, and Change,* Louise Tilly and Patricia Gurin, eds. (New York: Sage, 1990); on WSP, see Amy Swerdlow, "Ladies' Day at the Capitol: Women Strike for Peace versus HUAC," *Feminist Studies* 8 (1982) 493–520.

18. Paula Giddings, *When and Where I Enter: The Impact of Black Women on Race and Sex in America* (New York: Morrow, 1984), 243–46; Terborg-Penn, "Discontented Black Feminists," 274; Jacqueline Ann Rouse, *Eugenia Burns Hope: Black Southern Reformer* (Athens: University of Georgia Press, 1989); Cynthia Neverdon-Morton, *Afro-American Women of the South and the Advancement of the Race, 1895–1925* (Knoxville, Tenn.: University of Tennessee Press, 1989); Anne Firor Scott, "Most Invisible of All: Black Women's Voluntary Organizations," *Journal of Southern History* 56 (1990): 3–22; Eileen Boris, "The Power of Motherhood: Black and White Activist Women Redefine the 'Political'," *Yale Journal of Law and Feminism* 2 (1989): 25–49; Stephanie Shaw, "Black Women in White Collars: A Social History of Lower-Level Professional Black Women Workers, 1870–1940" (Ph.D. diss., Ohio State University, 1986).

19. These questions about white working-class women are beginning to be addressed by scholars. See Dorothy Sue Cobble, "Reassessing the Doldrum Years: Working-Class Feminism in the 1940s" (Paper presented at the 8th Annual Berkshire Conference on the History of Women, Douglass College, June 8–10, 1990); Meyerowitz, " 'Beyond the Feminine Mystique'." Susan Levine has explored the question of working-class women's relationship to conventional gender roles in "Workers' Wives: Gender, Class and Consumerism in the 1920s United States," *Gender and History* 3 (1991), 45–64.

1 *"The Changer and the Changed"*

"The Changer and the Changed" is the title of a record album by Chris Williamson (Olivia Records, 1975).

1. Dorothy Height, interview with author, 3 April 1984, New York City; Dorothy Height, telephone interview with author, 28 November 1988.

2. Ruth Edmonds Hill, ed., *The Black Women Oral History Project: from the Arthur and Elizabeth Schlesinger Library on the History of Woman in America, Radcliffe College* (Westport, Conn.: Meckler), 1991, 5:94.

3. See List of Interviews.

4. William M. King, "The Radical Political Reorientation of the Social Gospel" (Paper delivered at the Annual Convention of the Organization of American Historians, Louisville, Kentucky, 11–14 April 1991.

5. Walter Rauschenbusch, *Christianity and the Social Crisis* (New York: Macmillan,

1907; New York: Harper and Row, 1964), 247; Rauschenbusch, *Christianity and the Social Order* (New York: Macmillan, 1919), 397.

6.   Eileen Eagan, *Class, Culture, and the Classroom: The Student Peace Movement of the 1930s* (Philadelphia: Temple University Press, 1981), 154–155; World YWCA, *Christian Basis for a New Society*, n.d., YWCA, National Board Archives, New York. On the Social Gospel, see Paul A. Carter, *The Decline and Revival of the Social Gospel: Social and Political Liberalism in American Protestant Churches, 1920–1940* (Ithaca, N.Y.: Cornell University Press, 1954); Robert T. Handy, "The American Religious Depression, 1925–1935," *Church History* 29 (1960): 3–16; Donald B. Meyer, *The Protestant Search for Political Realism, 1919–1941* (Westport, Conn.: Greenwood Press, 1973); Robert Moats Miller, *American Protestantism and Social Issues, 1919–1939* (Chapel Hill: University of North Carolina Press, 1958); Ferenc Szasz Morton, *The Divided Mind of Protestant America* (Tuscaloosa: University of Alabama Press, 1982).

7.   Charles Chatfield, *For Peace and Justice: Pacifism in America, 1914–1941* (Knoxville: University of Tennessee Press, 1971); Charles De Benedetti, *The Peace Reform in American History* (Bloomington: Indiana University Press, 1980); C. Roland Marchand, *The American Peace Movement and Social Reform, 1898–1918* (Princeton: Princeton University Press 1973.)

8.   Rufus Jones, *A Service of Love in Wartime: American Friends Relief Work: Europe, 1917–1919* (New York: Macmillan, 1921), 8–9.

9.   Norman Thomas, *The Challenge of War: An Economic Interpretation* (New York: League of Industrial Democracy, 1924), 12; Lawrence S. Wittner, *Rebels Against War: The American Peace Movement, 1933–1983* (Philadelphia: Temple University Press, 1984).

10.   Conference on the Churches and World Peace of the Federal Council of Churches, 1929; quoted from Wittner, *Rebels Against War*, 5.

11.   Wittner, *Rebels Against War*, 6.

12.   Eagan, *Class, Culture, and the Classroom*, 120; Chatfield, *For Peace and Justice*, 260. Wittner's figures are more modest than those of Chatfield or Eagan, suggesting that 60,000 students participated (*Rebels Against War*, 7).

13.   Robin D. G. Kelley, *Hammer and Hoe: Alabama Communists During the Great Depression* (Chapel Hill: University of North Carolina Press, 1990); Weinstein, *Ambiguous Legacy;* Robert L. Allen, with collaboration of Pamela P. Allen, *Reluctant Reformers: Racism and Social Reform Movements in the United States* (Washington, D.C.: Howard University Press, 1974).

14.   Frances Taylor, " 'On the Edge of Tomorrow': Southern Women, the Student YWCA, and Race, 1920–1944" (Ph.D. diss., Stanford University, 1984); David M. Reimers, *The White Protestant and the Negro* (New York: Oxford University Press, 1965); Jacquelyn Dowd Hall, *Revolt Against Chivalry: Jessie Daniel Ames and the Women's Campaign Against Lynching* (New York: Columbia University Press, 1979); John B. Kirby, *Black Americans in the Roosevelt Era: Liberalism and Race* (Knoxville: University of Tennessee Press, 1980).

15.   The Foreign Division and the United Service Organization, in the relevant years during and after World War II, were parallel organizational jurisdictions within the YWCA.

16.   The discussion of social movements in this chapter draws on recent developments in the theory of social movements. In particular I have employed the contributions of resource mobilization theory, supplemented by the able critique of that theory offered by Aldon Morris. In contrast to the classical collective behavior

model, resource mobilization theory has avoided an emphasis on psychological motivations of movement participants to stress instead the political nature of social
movement participation. Resource mobilization theory further emphasizes the ratio-
nality of movement participants, the significance of the resources available to unorga-
nized groups who seek changes in the political system in explaining their success or
failure, and the significance of organizational groups as a vehicle for the movement.

Doug McAdam has presented an alternate model that stresses the reluctance of
elite groups to provide resources to promote social change and has emphasized
instead the importance of the mass base of social movements. According to his
political process model, social insurgency is generated as a result of three factors:
"The first is the level of organization within the aggrieved population; the second,
the collective assessment of the prospects for successful insurgency within that same
population; and the third, the political alignment of the group within the larger
political environment, . . . or the structure of political opportunities" (Doug Mc-
Adam, *Political Process and the Development of Black Insurgency, 1930–1970* [Chicago:
University of Chicago Press, 1982], 40). For the 1920s and 1930s, I have emphasized
the political opportunities presented by the results of world war and depression, the
significance of a transformation in consciousness for participation in the movement,
and the organizational resources provided to the social movement by established
organizations in terms of communications networks, leaders, potential followers,
and financial backing. I have also found the collective behavior model useful at times
as well, however, because resource mobilization theory discounts the influence of
ideology and moral fervor more than necessary.

On resource mobilization theory, see, for example, John D. McCarthy and
Mayer N. Zald, *The Trend of Social Movements in America: Professionalization and
Resource Mobilization* (Morristown, N.J.: General Learning Press, 1973); Anthony
Oberschall, *Social Conflict and Social Movements* (Englewood Cliffs, N.J.: Prentice-
Hall, 1973); William A. Gamson, *The Strategy of Social Protest* (Homewood, Ill.:
Dorsey, 1975); Mayer N. Zald and John D. McCarthy, *The Dynamics of Social
Movements: Resource Mobilization, Social Control and Tactics* (Cambridge, Mass.: Win-
throp, 1979). For the collective behavior perspective, see Ralph H. Turner and
Lewis M. Killian, eds., *Collective Behavior*, 3d ed. (Englewood Cliffs, N.J.:
Prentice-Hall, 1987); Ralph H. Turner, "Collective Behavior and Resource Mobili-
zation as Approaches to Social Movements: Issues and Continuities," in *Research in
Social Movements, Conflicts, and Change: A Research Annual*, Louis Kriesberg, ed.,
Vol. 4 (Greenwich, Conn.: JAI Press, 1981).

17.   Thomas D. Hamm, *The Transformation of American Quakerism: Orthodox Friends,
1800–1907* (Bloomington: Indiana University Press, 1988), 147–151.

18.   Rufus M. Jones, "The Philosophy of Quaker Service," 1940, AFSC Archives,
Philadelphia; Statement Prepared by AFSC Community Relations Program, Washington, D.C., 10 May 1952, AFSC Archives, Philadelphia.

19.   Chatfield, *For Peace and Justice*, 136–138.

20.   John Wilson, *Introduction to Social Movements* (New York: Basic Books, 1973);
Turner and Killian, *Collective Behavior.*

21.   Historians differ widely in their interpretations of the degree of political involvement of mainstream black churches in the twentieth century; some argue that
the churches have emphasized spiritual concerns, while others claim that the
churches have been an important source of political activism. Those who contend
that the black churches have played a political role point to urbanization and the

increased education of northern blacks as trends that challenged the conservative, other-worldly aspects of religion, and they suggest that the churches had to respond to the economic problems of black communities during the depression. Much of the political commitment black churches have expressed has centered on the struggle for racial justice. See John Brown Childs, *The Political Black Minister: A Study in Afro-American Politics and Religion* (Boston: Hall, 1980), 9–15, for a useful summary of the historiography on the role of the black churches.

22.   On the Quaker social reform tradition, see Ira De A. Reid, "Race Relations," in *The Quaker Approach to Contemporary Problems*, John Davanaugh, ed. (New York: Putnam, 1953); Margaret Hope Bacon, *The Quiet Rebels: The Story of Quakers in America* (Philadelphia: New Society, 1985).

23.   Madge Seaver, interview with author, 14 November 1983, San Francisco.

24.   Anne Firor Scott, "Education and the Contemporary Woman," in *Making the Invisible Woman Visible*, Scott, ed. (Chicago: University of Illinois Press, 1984), 394.

25.   The Student Christian Movement was formally organized in regional groups in New England, the Middle Atlantic states, and New York in the mid-1930s. Outside those areas, the term was widely used to refer to student Christian activism, although there was no formal organization outside of the Student YWCA and YMCA. Fern Babcock Grant, "The Student Christian Movement in the USA, 1921–1955," unpublished manuscript in possession of author. See also Eagan, *Class, Culture and the Classroom.*

26.   *YWCA of the USA* (New York: YWCA, 1940), 14.

27.   Mary Moss Cuthbertson, interview with author, 2 March 1984, Philadelphia.

28.   The words are those of his biographer, Richard Wightman Fox, in *Reinhold Niebuhr: A Biography* (New York: Pantheon, 1985), 140.

29.   Garnet Guild, telephone interview with author, 7 July 1990.

30.   Taylor, " 'On the Edge of Tomorrow,' " 138.

31.   Cuthbertson interview, 2 March 1984.

32.   Verneta Hill, interview with author, 11 November 1984, San Francisco.

33.   Hill interview, 11 November 1984.

34.   Bernard K. Johnpoll, *Pacifists's Progress: Norman Thomas and the Decline of American Socialism* (Chicago: Quadrangle, 1970); W. A. Swanberg, *Norman Thomas: The Last Idealist* (New York: Scribner's, 1976).

35.   Elizabeth Mansfield, manuscript sent in response to author's questions, September 1984.

36.   Mansfield manuscript, September 1984.

37.   Barbara Graves, interview with author, 11 November 1983. San Francisco.

38.   Elizabeth Anne Payne, *Labor, Reform and Feminism: Margaret Dreier Robins and the Women's Trade Union League* (Urbana: University of Illinois Press, 1988), 183.

2   Children of One Father

1.   Alvessie Hackshaw, interview with author, 20 September 1984, Oakland, California.

2.   I follow Evelyn Nakano Glenn here in using the term *racial ethnic* to denote groups that are simultaneously racial and ethnic minorities. See Glenn, "Racial Ethnic Women's Labor: The Intersection of Race, Gender and Class Oppression," *Review of Radical Political Economics* 17 (1985); 86–108.

3.   Juliet O. Bell and Helen J. Willkins, *Interracial Practices in Community YWCAs: A Study Under the Auspices of the Commission to Gather Interracial Experience as Requested by the 16th National Convention of the YWCAs of the USA* (New York: National Board of the YWCA, 1944).

4.   "Integration of Minority Groups in the Total Life of the Country: The Concern and Activities of the YWCA" (Presentation by Myrna Smith, Executive of the Department of Data and Trends, National Board of the YWCA, to National Social Work Council Meeting, 6 October 1944). YWCA of the U.S.A., National Board Archives, New York, Records Files Collection (hereafter cited as RFC).

5.   *Figures Talk Back: From the Annual Statistical Reports of Community YWCAs for the Year 1940* (New York: National Board of the YWCA, Department of Data and Trends, 1940): see also the publication under the same name for the years 1941–1960.

6.   Rouse, *Eugeneia Burns Hope; Reformer* Adrienne Lash Jones, "Struggle Among Saints: Black Women in the YWCA, 1860–1920" (Paper presented at the Organization of American Historians, Louisville, Kentucky, 12 April 1991); Gerda Lerner, *Black Women in White America: A Documentary History* (new York: Vintage, 1972), 477–497; Hall, *Revolt Against Chivaalry*, 86–106.

7.   Frances Taylor, " 'On the Edge of Tomorrow': Southern Women, the Student YWCA, and Race, 1920–1944" (Ph.D. diss., Stanford University, 1984); Gladys Gilkey Calkins, "The Negro in the Young Women's Christian Association: A Study of the Development of YWCA Interracial Policies and Practices in this Historical Setting" (Master's thesis, George Washington University, 1960). Clarence P. Shedd, *Two Centuries of Student Christian Movements: Their Origin and Intercollegiate Life* (New York: Association Press, 1934); "Moving into A New Century: An Historical Outline of the National Student YWCA, 1873 to the Present," 1974, YWCA, NBA.

8.   Untitled memo, YWCA of the U.S.A., National Board Archives, New York, Record Files Collection, Sophia Smith Collection, Smith College, Northampton, Mass. (hereafter Smith Collection); Young Women's Christian Associations of the U.S.A., 14th Biennial Convention, 1936, *Proceedings*, 95.

9.   Untitled short history of Oakland YWCA Race Relations, found in records of Oakland, California, YWCA; Hackshaw, interview, 20 September 1984; Emelita Cohen, interview with author, 29 November 1983, Oakland, California.

10.   Sharlene Voogd Cochrane, " 'And the Pressure Never Let Up': Black Women, White Women, and the Boston YWCA, 1918–1948," in *Women and the Civil Rights Movement: Trailblazers and Torchbearers, 1941–1965*, Vicki L. Crawford, Jacqueline Anne Rouse, and Barbara Woods, eds. (New York: Carlson, 1990), 259–269.

11.   Visitation Report, St. Louis, Missouri, from Winifred Wygal, 15–22 March 1939, Western Historical Manuscripts Collections, University of Missouri, St. Louis.

12.   St. Louis Metropolitan YWCA Records, Western Historical Manuscripts Collections, University of Missouri, St. Louis.

13.   National Board of the YWCA, *The Interracial Charter and Related Policy*, 1955.

14.   Bell and Wilkins, *Interracial Practices in Community YWCAs*.

15.   Height interview, 3 April 1984.

16.   Young Women's Christian Associations of the U.S.A., 17th Triennial Convention, 1946, *Proceedings*, 85–90 (Mrs. C. D. Atkins's given name was not noted); memo from Genevieve Lowry, Executive, Division of Community YWCAs, to Mrs. J. Ross Tuttle, 24 May 1946, Smith Collection.

17. Benjamin E. Mays, "The High Road to Freedom" (Address presented to the 17th National Convention of the YWCA, 2–8 March 1946, Atlantic City, N.J., RFC.

18. Dorothy Sabiston and Margaret Hiller, *Toward Better Race Relations* (New York: Woman's Press, 1949), 2–3: Helen Grant, interview with author, 27 October 1983, Oakland, California.

19. Sabiston and Hiller, *Toward Better Race Relations*, 21.

20. Hackshaw interview, 20 September 1984.

21. Mildred Persinger, interview with author, 3 April 1984, New York City; Jewel Graham, interview with author, 7 November 1990, Yellow Springs, Ohio; Height interview, 3 April 1984.

22. Hill interview, 11 November 1984.

23. Grant interview, 27 October 1983.

24. Augusta Roberts, interview with author, 6 December 1984, Claremont, California.

25. Bell and Wilkins, *Interracial Practices in Community YWCAs*, 47, 104–105; "Response to Questionnaire by National Association of Employed Officers," 1944, RFC; Gladys Jarrett, "Facing Facts," *Womans Press*, February 1944, 71–72.

26. "Findings of the Workshop on Interracial Practices," Vassar Alumnae House, Poughkeepsie, New York, November 30–December 4, 1948, RFC.

27. Grant interview, 27 October 1983; Hackshaw interview, 20 September 1984.

28. By comparing the data from this study with those of the 1944 study of interracial practices, it is clear that real advances in achieving integration had been made. Greater numbers of associations were interracial in programs, services, and facilities than had been true in the 1940s. In the 1944 study, only 36 out of a total of 148 associations reporting, or 24 percent, had black members on boards of directors, while in 1957 165 out of a total of 225 associations, or 73 percent, had interracial boards. Of those associations that maintained camping programs 72 percent had some type of interracial camping in 1957, compared to only 19 percent in 1944. Integrated residential accommodations had increased from 1 percent of all residences to 53 percent of permanent residences and 70 percent of transient residences; 81 percent of YWCA cafeterias were operated on an interracial basis by 1957, as well as 74 percent of the swimming pools. National Board of the YWCA, *The Extent of Certain Practices Relating to Racial Inclusiveness in Community YWCAs*, 1957, 3–4, RFC.

29. *National Board Report: Progress Toward Racial Inclusiveness, 1946–1958*. New York: National Board of the YWCA of the U.S.A., 1958.

30. For example, in 1961 in the Southern Region racial integration was practiced in only 4 of 37 community YWCA pools, 5 of 53 transient residences, 1 of 56 permanent residences, and 1 of 18 camps. In the late 1950s a number of YWCAs in the South were still segregated, with no black members. Bell and Wilkins, *Interracial Practices in Community YWCAs;* National Board, *Extent of Certain Practices;* "Evaluation of Membership and Administrative Practices in Community YWCAs by Size of Community and Existence of Branches," February 1961, RFC; "Interracial Notes," 1957, RFC.

31. Address by Mrs. Henry Ingraham, member of National Board, to 22nd National Convention of the YWCA, 10 May 1961, unpublished proceedings, 253–257, RFC.

32. Membership is a somewhat confusing category within the YWCA, since the

definition of membership changed a number of times and is not consistent across time. The figures from 1946 include electoral members and associate members. From *Figures Talk Back: From the Annual Statistical Reports of Community YWCAs for the Year 1946*. New York: National Board of the YWCA, 1946. The figure of 3 million participants appears in Dorothy I. Height, ed., *Interracial Policies of the Young Women's Christian Associations of the U.S.A.* (New York: Woman's Press, 1948), 7, and in *The Interracial Charter and Related Policy* (New York: National Board of the YWCA, 1955), 5.

33. Edith Lerrigo, Augusta Roberts, Jimmie Woodward, Helen Grant, Mary Moss Cuthbertson, and Elizabeth Mansfield all reported similar experiences; see Edith Lerrigo, interview with author, 5 December 1984, Claremont, California; Roberts interview, 6 December 1984; Jimmie Woodward, interview with author, 5 December 1984, Claremont, California; Grant interview, 27 October 1983. For typical examples of YWCA literature on race relations, see Sabiston and Hiller, *Toward Better Race Relations*, 75–77.

34. In 1942, for example, the participants in the West Virginia Negro Leadership Conference, which had met for many years, decided that they no longer wanted to meet in a segregated body. That same year, the Southern Area Conference of Business and Professional Girls, a section of the Community Division, decided to open all further conferences to all racial groups. In 1944, as we have noted, the Southern Regional Council of the Student YWCA decided to withdraw official southern support from any function that was not fully interracial. "Comments on Negro Leadership Conference, West Virginia, 1942," Smith Collection; "Supplementary Report on History of Interracial Experiment at the Southern Business and Professional Girls Conference at Sapphire, North Carolina," Smith Collection.

35. "Response to Questionnaire by National Association of Employed Officers," 1944, RFC; Bell and Wilkins, *Interracial Practices in Community YWCAs*, 80–83.

36. "Methods of Combatting Discrimination: Descriptive Record Submitted to World YWCA by YWCA of USA, 1954," RFC.

37. Letter to "Anne," 24 June 1944, from Business and Professional Summer Conference, Summer Area, 13–19 June 1944, Hendersonville, North Carolina, Smith Collection.

38. "Methods of Combatting Discrimination"; "A Study of the Effect of the Interracial Aspect of the Program of Six Y-Teen Summer Conferences in the Southern Region on Girls Who Attended from 1958 through 1962," reported by Lillian H. Jackson, Field Consultant, Southern Region, RFC.

39. Gunnar Myrdal, *An American Dilemma: The Negro Problem and Modern Democracy* (New York: Harper Bros., 1944); Oliver Cromwell Cox, *Caste, Class, and Race: A Study in Social Dynamics* (New York: Monthly Review, 1959); Leo P. Crespi, "Is Gunnary Myrdal on the Right Track?" *Public Opinion Quarterly* 9 (1945): 201–12.

40. "Integration of Minority Groups."

41. Hill interview, 11 November 1984; Grant interview, 27 October 1983.

42. Persinger interview, 3 April 1984.

43. "Short Summary of Legislative Work and Public Action in the Realm of Race Relations," National Board of the YWCA, November 1944, RFC.

44. Minutes of the National Board, 3 March and 7 July 1943, RFC.

45. "The West Coast Evacuation in Relation to the Struggle for Freedom," *Public Affairs News Services* 6 (12 May 1942): 8; F.I. to Miss Ingels, 10 February 1943, Smith Collection.

46.   Young Women's Christian Associations of the U.S.A., 18th Triennial Convention, 1949, *Proceedings*.

47.   "Summary of Report on Project Responsibilities, 1956–57," Grace T. Hamilton to Edith Lerrigo, 28 August 1957, RFC; "Report of Projects Undertaken in the Area of Racial Inclusiveness during the Current Triennium, 1955–1958," RFC.

48.   Statement of the National Board of YWCAs of the U.S.A. in support of civil rights legislation, 8 July 1958, RFC; minutes of the National Board, 6 May 1959, RFC.

49.   Susan M. Hartmann, *The Home Front and Beyond: American Women in the 1940s* (Boston: Twayne, 1982), 148.

50.   *American Association of University Women Convention Daily*, 18 April 1947, 2; Reel #9, II-A-23, Reel 116, 595, AAUW Archives, Stanford University; the "National Legislative Program" for the years 1954 to 1960, reported in the *AAUW Journal*, never mentioned the Supreme Court decision. Although an article appeared in the *AAUW Journal* about *Brown*, it contained a vaguely worded suggestion about the need to accept change without damaging the social fabric but did not forthrightly endorse the Supreme Court's decision. See Ira Corinne Brown, "We, the People," *AAUW Journal*, March 1955, 85. On racial integration within the AAUW, see Leone, "Integrating the American Association of University Women," 423–445.

51.   Calkins, "Negro in the YWCA," 82. Dorothy Height, Helen Grant, and Lucy Mitchell, among others, refer to the importance of this YWCA purpose. Height interview, 3 April 1984; Grant interview, 27 October 1983; "Black Women Oral History Project: Lucy Miller Mitchell," 1977, Schlesinger Library, Radcliffe College.

3   Speaking Truth to Power

1.   "The Japanese Evacuation," 1942, AFSC Archives, Philadelphia (hereafter AFSC Archives).

2.   Grace Nichols Pearson to Raymond Booth, 1 May 1942, Grace Nichols Pearson Papers, Hoover Library, Stanford, California.

3.   Josephine Whitney Duveneck, *Life on Two Levels: An Autobiography* (Los Altos, Calif.: Kaufmann, 1978), 240.; see also minutes of the Committee on Japanese American Relocation, 21 February, 22 August, and 20 November 1945, AFSC San Francisco Regional Office Files (hereafter SF Files).

4.   Lincoln Kanai to Grace Nichols Pearson, 3 July 1943, Pearson Papers.

5.   Gilligan, *In a Different Voice*; Belenky et al., *Women's Ways of Knowing*; Chodorow, *Reproduction of Mothering*; See chap. 1, n. 6, for comment on criticisms of these studies.

6.   Minutes of the Race Relations Committee of the Philadelphia Yearly Meeting of the Religious Society of Friends, 9 January 1940, AFSC Archives, Philadelphia; "History and Problems of the Race Relations Committee of the AFSC, 1944–49," prepared by G. James FLeming, Secretary of Race Relations Committee, AFSC Archives.

7.   1950 American Friends Service Committee Staff Directory, AFSC Archives, Philadelphia; *In the House of Friends: A Social Science View of a Quaker Program in Race Relations* (Philadelphia: Community Relations Program, AFSC, 1955), 62.

8. American Friends Service Committee, *Speak Truth to Power: A Quaker Search for an Alternative to Violence* (Philadelphia, 1955), iv.

9. Clarence E. Pickett, *For More Than Bread: An Autobiographical Account of Twenty-Two Years' Work with the American Friends Service Committee* (Boston: Little, Brown, 1953), 378; "AFSC Race Relations Committee Program," 1948, AFSC Archives; "Characteristics of an AFSC Program," Notes on Colin Bell's recent visit to San Francisco Regional Office, 20 November 1959, SF Files.

10. On *racial-ethnic*, see Glenn, "Racial Ethnic Women's Labor; 86.

11. Taped material provided by Thelma Babbitt in response to questions by author, September 1984.

12. "Summary of Testimony Prepared for the Sub-Committee on Civil Rights, Committee on Labor and Public Welfare, U.S. Senate, Regarding S.692, A Bill to Prohibit Discrimination in Employment," by Thelma Babbitt, Job Opportunities Program, AFSC, 24 February 1954, AFSC Archives.

13. Guild interview, 7 July 1990.

14. Harvard Sitkoff, *The Struggle for Black Equality, 1954–1980* (New York: Hill and Wang, 1981), 19.

15. Osborne interview, 23 May 1989.

16. Osborne interview, 5 March 1984; "Toward the Elimination of Segregation in the Nation's Capital"; Alma Scurlock, telephone interview with author, 17 June 1989; Michael S. Mayer, "The Eisenhower Administration and the Desegregation of Washington, D.C.," *Journal of Policy History* 3 (1990); 24–41.

17. Barbara Moffett, interview with author, 8 March 1984, Philadelphia.

18. Jean Fairfax, interview with author, 4 March 1984, Philadelphia; Gerald Jonas, *On Doing Good: The Quaker Experiment* (New York: Scribner, 1971), 161.

19. Robert J. Rossborough, Friends Relief Service, to Clarence E. Pickett, Executive Secretary, AFSC, 12 October 1946, AFSC Archives.

20. Clarence Pickett to John Judkin, 1 October 1946, AFSC Archives; G. James Fleming to Cornelius Kruse, Secretary of Foreign Service Section, AFSC, 20 September 1946, AFSC Archives; Fairfax interview, 4 March 1984.

21. "A Report on Little Rock Community Relations Program," September 1959 to December 1960, by Thelma W. Babbitt, Director, AFSC Archives; Babbitt tape, September 1984; Thelma Babbitt, telephone interview with author, 23 September 1987; Daisy Bates, *The Long Shadow of Little Rock: A Memoir* (New York: McKay, 1962); telephone interviews with women activists in Little Rock, Arkansas: Daisy Bates, 16 March 1989; Rosalyn Abernathy, 2 February 1989; Irene Samuel Cook, 15 February 1989; and Pat House, 23 April 1989.

22. Minutes of the Community Relations Committee, 20 September, 1960 AFSC Archives.

23. Guild interview, 7 July 1990; Fairfax interview, 6 July 1990.

24. Minutes of the Community Relations Roundup, 28 February–4 March 1960, AFSC Archives; "Public Schools and Token Desegregation in North Carolina," Resource Paper for 1960 Community Relations Roundup, Bill Bagwell, Director, North Carolina School Desegregation Program, AFSC Archives; Community Relations Round-Up, 7–12 April 1957, AFSC Archives; Max Hierich, "Summary Evaluation of AFSC Workshop on Nonviolence," 2 April 1960, AFSC Archives; visit to Southeast Regional Office, 31 August to 2 September 1959, Jean Fairfax; memo to Subcommittee on Southern Programs from Jean Fairfax, 8 November 1960, AFSC

Archives; David J. Garrow, ed., *The Montgomery Bus Boycott and the Women Who Started It: The Memoir of Jo Ann Gibson Robinson* (Knoxville: University of Tennessee Press, 1987).
25. Aldon D. Morris, *The Origins of the Civil Rights Movement: Black Communities Organizing for Change* (New York: Free Press, 1984), 141.
26. P. David Finks, *The Radical Vision of Saul Alinsky* (New York: Paulist, 1984); Harry C. Boyte, *Commonwealth: A Return to Citizen Politics* (New York: Free Press, 1989).
27. Fred Ross, who worked off and on for Alinsky in the 1940s and 1950s, provided a link between Alinsky and the AFSC, for Ross also worked for the AFSC San Francisco office. Ross had been employed in 1946–1947 by the American Council on Race Relations (ACRR), which had been funded by the AFSC and the Rosenwald Fund to set up research and education programs in racially troubled communities. In his work with ACRR Ross had begun organizing Mexican-American communities in Southern California. When the ACCR disbanded in 1947, Alinsky hired Ross to organize chapters of the Community Service Organization (CSO), a Mexican-American organization aimed at solving the problems faced by Mexican-American communities. Alinsky soon found himself unable to support Ross, at which point the San Francisco office of the AFSC hired Ross to organize a CSO chapter in San Jose, California. It was there that Ross found and trained Cesar Chavez. Josephine Duveneck attended closely to the San Jose efforts and came to know both Ross and Chavez. See Finks, *Radical Vision of Saul Alinsky.*
28. Duveneck, *Life on Two Levels.*
29. Paul Seaver to author, June 1985, in author's possession.
30. Stephen H. Thiermann, *Welcome to the World: Discoveries with the American Friends Service Committee on the Frontiers of Social Change* (San Francisco: AFSC, 1968), 17; Stephen H. Theirmann, interview with author, 8 March 1984, Philadelphia.
31. Thiermann, *Welcome to the World,* 67–70.
32. Interview with Frank Duveneck, 7 August 1983, Los Altos Hills, California.
33. Minutes of the Executive Committee, 19 October 1946, 15 February and 15 November 1947, 11 September 1948, SF Files; minutes of the Social-Industrial Committee, 21 April 1949, SF Files.
34. Minutes of the Executive Committee, 12 February 1949, SF Files; minutes of the Social-Industrial Committee, 12 October 1949, SF Files.
35. Minutes of the Social-Industrial Committee, 9 November 1950, SF Files.
36. Ibid., 12 February 1953; "One Big Home Would Help," AFSC *Bulletin,* June 1952, 11; Thiermann, *Welcome to the World,* 71–76.
37. "Memo to Round-Up Attenders," from Barbara Moffett, 17 February 1960, AFSC Archives; "Bases of Friends Social Concerns," a talk by Josephine Duveneck to the Palo Alto Meeting of the Religious Society of Friends, March 1964, reported in Theirmann interview, 8 March 1984.
38. Minutes of the Social-Industrial Committee, 30 September 1954, 7 June 1955, SF Files; "E. P. (Red) Stephenson, Transition: White Man in a Black Town, 1950–1967" (Transcript, Bay Area Foundation History Series, Vol. 5, Bancroft Library, University of California, Berkeley), 54.
39. The Dawes Severalty Act controlled federal policy toward Indians from its enactment in 1887 until the New Deal.
40. Larry W. Burt, *Tribalism in Crisis: Federal Indian Policy, 1953–1961* (Albuquerque: University of New Mexico Press, 1982).

41. *The Spirit They Live In: A Report on Problems Confronting American Indians, Their Fellow Citizens and their Government* (Philadelphia: AFSC, 1956), 19.
42. Minutes of the Social-Industrial Committee, 12 November 1953, SF Files.
43. Burt, *Tribalism in Crisis*, 113; Annual Report to the American Section Executive Committee from the Community Relations Program, 31 October 1957, AFSC Archives; Frank Quinn, telephone interview with author, 15 November 1984, San Francisco.
44. Duveneck, *Life on Two Levels*, 272–274. Sandy Turner, telephone interview with author, 15 November 1984; Quinn interview, 15 November 1984.
45. Paul Seaver, comments on draft of chapter, June 1985.
46. Minutes of the Social-Industrial Committee, 7 June 1955, SF Files; "Intertribal Friendship House," a report by Joan Adams and Wesley Huss, 1958, AFSC San Francisco Regional Office Files; Steve Theirmann, *Welcome to the World*; Wes Huss, interview with author, 9 October 1984, Oakland, California.
47. Duveneck, *Life on Two Levels*, 64.
48. Guild interview, 7 July 1990.
49. Clayborne Carson, *In Struggle: SNCC and the Black Awakening of the 1960s* (Cambridge, Mass.: Harvard University Press, 1981).

4 Women and Peace Activism

1. Wittner, *Rebels Against War*, 151–239; DeBenedetti, *Peace Reform in American History*, chap. 7.
2. DeBenedetti, *Peace Reform in American History*; Charles DeBenedetti, "American Peace Activism, 1945–1985," in *Peace Movements and Political Cultures*, Charles Chatfield and Peter Van Den Dungen, eds., (Knoxville: University of Tennessee Press, 1988), 222–229.
3. The YWCA did face some red-baiting attacks. In 1948 Joseph P. Kamp of the Constitutional Educational League charged in a pamphlet, "Behind the Lace Curtains of the YWCA," that leaders of the National Board were affiliated with the Communist party or Communist front organizations.
4. Carole Stoneburner, "Introduction: Drawing a Profile of American Female Public Friends as Shapers of Human Space," in *The Influence of Quaker Women on American History: Biographical Studies*, Carol and John Stoneburner, eds. (Lewiston, N.Y.: The Edwin Mellen Press, 1986), p. 35.
5. Paul Boyer, *By the Bomb's Early Light: American Thought and Culture at the Dawn of the Atomic Age* (New York: Pantheon, 1985), chap. 3.
6. Freedman, "Separatism as Strategy," 512–529.
7. Chatfield, *For Peace and Justice*; Linda Kay Schott, "Women Against War: Pacifism, Feminism, and Social Justice in the United States, 1915–1941" (Ph.D. diss., Stanford University, 1986); Joan Jensen, "All Pink Sisters: The War Department and the Feminist Movement in the 1920s," in *Decades of Discontent: The Women's Movement, 1920–1940*, Lois Scharf and Joan M. Jensen, eds. (Westport, Conn.: Greenwood, 1983), 199–222; Barbara Miller Solomon, "Dilemmas of Pacifist Women, Quakers and Others, in World Wars I and II," in *Witnesses for Change: Quaker Women Over Three Centuries*, Elisabeth Potts Brown and Susan Mosher Stuard, eds. (New Brunswick, N.J.: Rutgers University Press, 1989), 123–148; Margaret Hope Bacon, *Mothers of*

Feminism: The Story of Quaker Women in America (San Francisco: Harper & Row, 1986), chap. 13; DeBenedetti, *Peace Reform in American History.*

8.   M. Kent Jennings, "Women in Party Politics," in *Women, Politics, and Change,* Louise A. Tilly and Patricia Gurin, eds. (New York: Sage, 1990), 238; Tom W. Smith, "The Polls: Gender And Attitudes Toward Violence," *Public Opinion Quarterly* 48 (1984): 384–396.

9.   Schott, "Women Against War," chap. 2 and 121–127; Barbara Steinson, " 'The Mother Half of Humanity': American Women in the Peace and Preparedness Movements in World War I," in *Women, War, and Revolution,* Carol R. Berkin and Clara M. Lovett, eds. (New York: Holmes and Meier, 1980); Jensen, "All Pink Sisters," 199–222.

10.   Joan Jensen makes this point about the Women's International League for Peace and Freedom in the 1920s; see "All Pink Sisters," 202.

11.   Young Women's Christian Associations of the U.S.A., 19th Triennial Convention, 1952, *Proceedings*, 88–89.

12.   Ibid., 201

13.   Address of Annalee Stewart, president, U.S. Section, 11 August 1949, 11th International WILPF Congress, Copenhagen, Papers of the Women's International League for Peace and Freedom, 1919–1959, Rutgers University Libraries.

14.   Aileen Kraditor, *The Ideas of the Woman Suffrage Movement, 1890–1920* (New York: Columbia University Press, 1965).

15.   Gertrude Bussey and Margaret Tims, *Pioneers for Peace: The Women's International League for Peace and Freedom, 1915–1965* (Oxford: Alden, 1980), 188.

16.   Marie Lous Mohr, Norway, opening speech to 11th International WILPF Congress, Copenhagen, 11–15 August 1949, Papers of the Women's International League for Peace and Freedom, 1915–1959.

17.   Kraditor, *Woman's Suffrage Movement*; Schott, "Women Against War."

18.   Even an organization like the WILPF faced internal dissension over this issue. Some members argued that avoidance of war required strict neutrality, while others argued for economic sanctions of aggressor nations. At the annual meeting in 1939, 75 percent of the membership voted to support the position of mandatory neutrality. Some of the prominent leaders who supported the more internationalist position, such as Emily Greene Balch and Mildred Scott Olmsted, remained in the organization. But WILPF also lost members over this issue. Anne Marie Pois, "The Politics of Organizing for Change: the United States Section of the Women's International League for Peace and Freedom, 1919–1939" (Ph.D. diss., University of Colorado, 1988), 464–465. See also Solomon, "Dilemmas of Pacifist Women," 137–139.

19.   WILPF was led by a number of women from Quaker backgrounds, and some individuals worked for both organizations. WILPF, like the AFSC, opposed the integration of western Germany into the Western alliance, arguing instead for a demilitarized and neutral Germany. WILPF opposed both the NATO alliance and U.S. participation in the Korean War. During the 1950s WILPF forwarded a proposal for a world truce, in which nations would pledge to cease the use and production of all arms, to be followed by a disarmament conference. Throughout this period, WILPF argued that nations and individuals should experiment with nonviolent techniques as an alternative to militarism.

20.   *Speak Truth to Power: A Quaker Search for an Alternative to Violence* (Philadelphia: AFSC, 1955), 16, 22.

21. Margaret E. Hirst, *The Quakers in Peace and War: An Account of Their Peace Principles and Practice* (London: Swarthmore, 1972).

22. *Speak Truth to Power*, iv.

23. "Highacres Statement," August 1942, AFSC Archives.

24. *Steps to Peace: A Quaker View of U.S. Foreign Policy* (Philadelphia: AFSC, 1951).

25. *Speak Truth to Power*, 21.

26. *Speak Truth to Power*, 7–8.

27. Cecil E. Hinshaw, *An Adequate and Moral National Defense*, (Philadelphia, AFSC, n.d.).

28. In 1955 an international group of scientists, headed by Bertrand Russell and Albert Einstein, attracted considerable international attention by issuing an appeal to governments around the world to end the threat of nuclear war. See Wittner, *Rebels Against War*, 235–239.

29. Harold Josephson, "The Search for Lasting Peace: Internationalism and American Foreign Policy, 1920–1950," in *Peace Movements and Political Cultures*, Chatfield and Van Den Dungen, eds., 209.

30. "Attitudes of Women's Groups Toward International Issues," 12 February 1951, Department of State, Division of Public Studies, Office of Public Affairs, Ruth Frances Woodsmall Papers, 1906–1963, Smith Collection.

31. Mary S. Sims, *The Natural History of a Social Institution: The Young Woman's Christian Association* (New York: Woman's Press, 1936), 82; "Summary of National Convention Actions on Peace and International Relations of the YWCAS of the U.S.A.," RFC.

32. Fern Babcock, "New Program Book for Student Christian Associations," National Intercollegiate Christian Council (New York: Woman's Press, 1943); Young Women's Christian Associations of the U.S.A., 16th Biennial Convention, 1940, *Proceedings*, 163–196; Mary S. Sims, *The YWCA—An Unfolding Purpose*, (New York: Woman's Press, 1950), 82.

33. Minutes of the National Board of the YWCA, 7 January 1942, RFC.

34. Statement of the National Board of the YWCA, 7 January 1942, RFC; "Summary of National Convention Actions on Peace."

35. Louise M. Young, *In the Public Interest: The League of Women Voters, 1920–1970* (Westport, Conn.: Greenwood, 1989).

36. Minutes of the Public Affairs Committee, 20 May 1952, 19 April 1955, RFC; minutes of the National Board of the YWCA, 7 June 1950, RFC.

37. Statement adopted by National Board of the YWCA, 21 June 1941, RFC.

38. Statement on Foreign Economic Aid, Revised Draft, 30 January 1956, RFC.

39. "Filling the World's Market Basket," *Public Affairs News Service*, 10, 2: Statement by YWCA National Board, 2 February 1956, RFC.

40. Young Women's Christian Associations of the U.S.A., 19th Triennial Convention, 1952, *Proceedings*, 106–111.

41. YWCA Public Affairs Newsletter, 7 April 1947.

42. Minutes of the National Board of the YWCA, 1 June 1949, RFC.

43. "UMT," Report of the National Public Affairs Committee, March 1955, RFC.

44. Young Women's Christian Associations of the U.S.A., 21st Triennial Convention, 1958, *Proceedings*, 169.

45. Ibid.

46.   Dorothy Groeling, "The YWCA and the United Nations: Education, Activities, and Action for World Understanding," *Public Affairs News Service* 13, 2 (May 1949): 21.

47.   Young Women's Christian Associations of the U.S.A., 18th Triennial Convention, 1949, *Proceedings*, xxvii.

48.   DeBenedetti, *Peace Reform in American History*, 152–153.

49.   "A Survey of the Peace Section of the AFSC," AFSC Archives.

50.   Wanneta Chance was the one woman employed regularly by the Peace Education Program in the Philadelphia office, where she headed the program for Mexico. Several other women worked for the program, but most program heads were male. Personnel Files, AFSC Archives.

51.   Mansfield manuscript, September 1984.

52.   Fairfax interview, 4 March 1984.

5   *Women's Social Reform*

1.   Meyerowitz, "Beyond 'The Feminine Mystique'; Linda Gordon, "What's New in Women's History," in *Feminist Studies/Critical Studies*, Teresa De Lauretis, ed. (Bloomington: Indiana University Press, 1986), 29.

2.   Freedman, "Separatism as Strategy"; Sklar, "Hull House in the 1890s," 658–677.

3.   Kathleen MacArthur, "Shibboleths or Security," *Womans Press*, April 1945, 11–13; see also Young Women's Christian Associations of the U.S.A., 16th Biennial Convention, 1940, *Proceedings*, 200.

4.   Letter from Mrs. Henry A. Ingraham to Senator James E. Murray, 29 October 1945, RFC; letter from Mrs. Paul McClellan Jones, Chair, and Mrs. Esther Cole Franklin, Director of National Public Affairs Committee, to all Executive Directors and Public Affairs Chairmen, December 1955, RFC.

5.   "YWCA Serves the Working Woman: YWCA in Action, 1958–59" (New York: YWCA, 1959).

6.   Young Women's Christian Associations of the U.S.A., 20th Triennial Convention, 1955, *Proceedings*, 232–236.

7.   Edith Clysdale Magruder, *Basic Issues of the War and Peace: Under God a New Birth of Freedom in This World* (New York: National Student Council of the YWCA, 1943), 37; see also Linda Taylor, "Woman's Part in Reconstruction," *Womans Press*, December 1944, 547–548.

8.   Edith Lerrigo, "The Edge of a New Chapter," *YWCA Magazine* (October 1961), 7.

9.   Rosalind Cassidy, "Women in 1949," *Womans Press*, April 1949, 22–23.

10.   Graham interview, 12 December 1990.

11.   Jean Whittet, interview with author, 6 December 1984, Claremont, California.

12.   Ella Baker, who was active in the NAACP and a key figure in SCLC and in SNCC, was also active in the YWCA as a young woman. Garnet Guild, Jean Fairfax, Polly Cuthbertson, and Betty Mansfield, all active in the AFSC, were involved in the YWCA in their earlier years as well.

13.   Young Women's Christian Associations of the U.S.A., 18th Triennial Convention, 1949, *Proceedings*, 107–108.

14.   Dan W. Dodson, *The Role of the YWCA in a Changing Era: The YWCA Study of*

YMCA-YWCA Cooperative Experiences (New York: National Board of the YWCA of the U.S.A., 1960), 84.

15. Telephone interview with Ida Davidoff, 10 November 1991.

16. Young Women's Christian Associations of the U.S.A., 22nd Triennial Convention, 1961, *Proceedings*, 178, 182.

17. Meyerowitz, "Beyond 'The Feminine Mystique'."

18. Grace Loucks Elliott, "Our Struggle Is But Begun," *Womans Press*, October 1944, 421; minutes of the National Board, January 1944, Report of the General Secretary, RFC.

19. Harold Colvin, "What We Have Learned from the Women," *Womans Press*, February 1946, 24–38.

20. Report of the General Secretary to the National Board, 4 May 1948, RFC.

21. "Progress Report of the Family Life Cluster," 14 September 1956, RFC; "YWCA Home Women's Groups—A Study by the Department of Data and Trends," prepared by Naomi S. Hanks, Edna H. Porter, National Board of the YWCA, 1948; Grace Loucks Elliott, "The Nature of Women," *YWCA Magazine*, November 1957, 3, 31.

22. Fern Babcock, *Being a Woman: The Role of College-Trained Women in America* (New York: National Student Council of the YMCA and YWCA, 1955), 10, 33, 47.

23. Rosaline Cassidy, "Women in 1949," *Womans Press*, April 1949, 22–23.

24. Hills, *Black Woman Oral History Project*, 5:93.

25. Persinger interview, 3 April 1984.

26. Cott, *The Grounding of Modern Feminism*, 276.

27. Ibid., 239.

28. Susan Ware, *Beyond Suffrage: Women in the New Deal* (Cambridge, Mass.: Harvard University Press, 1981); Susan Ware, *Partner and I: Molly Dewson, Feminism, and New Deal Politics* (New Haven, Conn.: Yale University Press, 1987).

29. During the 1940s and 1950s approximately one-third of the members of the AFSC Executive Board were women, and usually one of the three vice-chairs was a woman.

30. Guild interview, 7 July 1990.

31. Mansfield manuscript, September 1984; Patricia Stewart, interview with author, 27 October 1983, Berkeley, California.

32. On women in labor unions see Milkman, *Gender at Work*, Nancy Gabin, *Feminism in the Labor Movement: Women in the United Auto Workers, 1935–1975* (Ithaca, N.Y.: Cornell University Press, 1990). For quote on Ella Baker, see Giddings, *When and Where I Enter*, 275. For other discussions of women in the civil rights movement, see Vicki L. Crawford, Jacqueline Anne Rouse, and Barbara Woods, eds., *Women in the Civil Rights Movement: Trailblazers and Torchbearers, 1941–1965* (Brooklyn, New York: Carlson, 1990); Garrow, *The Montgomery Bus Boycott;* Charles Payne, "Ella Baker and Models of Social Change," *Signs* 14 (1989): 885–899.

33. Mary Maples Dunn, "Women of Light," in *Women of America: A History*, Carol Ruth Berkin and Mary Beth Norton, eds. (Boston: Houghton Mifflin, 1979).

34. A number of major leaders of the women's rights and suffrage movements of the nineteenth and early twentieth centuries, such as Susan B. Anthony and Alice Paul, had been Quakers. Whether Quaker women continued to be as involved in feminist activities after 1920 demands further exploration. In the mid–nineteenth century the Hicksite branch of Quakerism nurtured stronger feminists than did the Orthodox branch. The relationship between the two branches and their respective

concerns with feminism await study. The Quaker tradition of separate business meetings for women came to an end, at least in the Philadelphia yearly meetings, during the 1920s. See Herbert M. Bradley, "Diminishing Separation: Philadelphia Meetings Reunite, 1915–1955," in *Friends in the Delaware Valley: Philadelphia Yearly Meeting, 1681–1981*, John M. Moore, ed. (Haverford, Pa.: Friends Historical Association, 1981).

35.   Author's interviews with the following: Nancy Duryee, 2 March 1984, Philadelphia; Eleanor Stabler Clarke, 7 March 1984, Kennett Square, Pennsylvania; Madeleine Stephenson, 25 January 1984, Santa Rosa, California; Cuthbertson, 2 March 1984; Babbitt tape, September 1984; Josephine Whitney Duveneck, *Life on Two Levels*.

36.   Graves interview, 11 November 1984.

37.   Osborne interview, 5 March 1984.

38.   Graves interview, 11 November 1983.

39.   Cuthbertson interview, 2 March 1984.

40.   Moffett interview, 8 March 1984.

41.   Cott, *The Grounding of Modern Feminism*, 75–76.

42.   The Women's Bureau coalition included the YWCA, the National Women's Trade Union League (which disbanded in 1950), the National Consumer's League, the National Council of Jewish Women, the National Council of Catholic Women, the National Council of Negro Women, the League of Women Voters, the American Association of University Women, and women's affiliates of the AFL and the CIO.

43.   Harrison, *On Account of Sex*, 89–105.

44.   Rupp and Taylor, *Survival in the Doldrums*, 136–144; Harrison, *On Account of Sex*, 19–21.

45.   Augusta Roberts, interview with author, 6 March 1988.

46.   Cuthbertson interview, 20 February 1988.

47.   Ellen C. Dubois, "Eleanor Flexner and the History of American Feminism," *Gender and History* 3 (Spring 1991), 84.

48.   Young Men's Christian Associations, *Interracial Practices in the YMCA* (New York: Associated Press, 1953); Galen M. Fisher, *Public Affairs and the YMCA: 1844–1944, with special reference to the United States* (New York: Association Press, 1944), 8; C. Howard Hopkins, *History of the YMCA in North America* (New York: Association Press, 1951); Nina Mjagkij, "A History of the Black YMCA in America, 1853–1946" (Ph.D. diss., University of Cincinnati, 1990).

49.   Jesse Howell Atwood, *The Racial Factor in YMCAs: A Report on Negro-White Relationships in Twenty-four Cities* (New York: Association Press, 1946), 56.

50.   . Dodson, *Role of the YWCA*, 85–86.

51.   Robert Wuthnow and William Lehrman, "Religion: Inhibitor or Facilitator of Political Involvement Among Women?" in *Women, Politics, and Change*, Louise A. Tilly and Patricia Gurin, eds. (New York: Sage, 1990), 302.

52.   Paul Limbert, *New Perspectives for the YMCA* (New York: Association Press, 1964), 79, 86.

53.   Further research is needed on the different organizational styles of the two associations. Some of these observations are based on impressions of YWCA activists and scholars. Guild interview, 7 July 1990; Charlotte Bunch, interview with author, 2 April 1991; Adrienne Lash Jones, telephone conversation, 14 April 1991; Height interview, 13 June 1990; Persinger interview 6 May 1989.

54. I thank Elizabeth Norris, archivist and librarian of the National Board of the YWCA, for information on the class composition of the YWCA board structure. On the contrast between working-class involvement in the YW and the YM, see Kenneth Fones-Wolf, "Gender, Class Relations, and the Transformation of Voluntary Organizations: Labor Reform in the Philadelphia YM and YWCAs, 1890–1930" (Paper presented to the Organization of American Historians Annual Meeting, Washington, D.C., 1990).

55. Maureen A. Flanagan, "Gender and Urban Political Reform: The City Club and the Woman's City Club of Chicago in the Progressive Era," *American Historical Review* 95 (1990): 1032–1050; Dolores E. Janiewski, *Sisterhood Denied: Race, Gender, and Class in a New South Community* (Philadelphia: Temple University Press, 1985), 83.

56. A number of staff members of the AFSC commented on this tendency for women to be more active than men at the community level, including Jean Fairfax, in reference to race relations programs in the South; Red Stephenson, discussing North Richmond Neighborhood House; and Frank Quinn and Wes Huss, who worked with California Indians. Fairfax interview, 4 March 1984; Red Stephenson, interview with author, 25 January 1984, Santa Rosa, Calif.; Frank Quinn, interview, 15 November 1984; Huss interview, 9 October 1984.

57. Osborne interview, 23 May 1989.

58. Alice G. Knotts, "Methodist Women Integrate Schools and Housing, 1952–1959," in *Women in the Civil Rights Movement*, Crawford et al., eds., 251–258; on the Women's Emergency Committee for Public Schools, see Julia Kirk Blackwelder, "Race, Ethnicity, and Women's Lives in the Urban South," in *Shades of the Sunbelt: Essays on Ethnicity, Race, and the Urban South*, Randall M. Miller and George E. Pozetta, eds., (Westport, Conn.: Greenwood Press, 1988); Fairfax interview, 4 March 1984; Marie Laberge, " 'We Are Proud of Our Gains: Wisconsin Black Women's Organizational Work in the Post World War II Era" (Paper presented at the 8th Annual Berkshire Conference on the History of Women, Douglass College, 9 June 1990).

59. Giddings, *When and Where I Enter*, 284; Crawford et al., *Women in the Civil Rights Movement*; Garrow *The Montgomery Bus Boycott*;, C. Payne, "Ella Baker," 885–899; Dianetta Gail Bryan, "Her-Story Unsilenced: Black Female Activists in the Civil Rights Movement," *Sage* V (1988): 60–63.

60. Charles Payne, "Men Led, But Women Organized: Movement Participation of Women in the Mississippi Delta," in *Women in the Civil Rights Movement*, Crawford et al., eds., 1–11. There is some debate about the question of whether women were less likely to be subjected to physical violence. Charles Payne dismisses this claim, while Jean Fairfax supported it. Fairfax interview, 6 July 1990.

61. In a study of union organizing efforts at Duke University Medical Center in the 1970s, Karen Sacks observed similar gender differences between men and women activists: "Women created the detail, made people feel part of it, and did the menial work upon which most things depended, while men made public pronouncements, confronted, and negotiated with management." Karen Brodkin Sacks, *Caring By the Hour: Women, Work, and Organizing at Duke Medical Center* (Urbana: University of Illinois Press, 1988), 120.

62. Graves interview, 11 November 1983.

63. Joan W. Scott, "Gender: A Useful Category of Historical Analysis," *American Historical Review* 91 (1986): 1073.

6   New Sprouts from Old Roots

1.   C. Wright Mills was a leftist sociologist who wrote about the relationships between the U.S. economic and political system and the cultural patterns based on mass communications and conformity. Paul Goodman's analysis of the malaise of affluent youth who lacked genuine opportunities for authenticity and useful work spoke to a generation of young people. The beatnik subculture developed in the late 1950s among poets and artists who rejected most mainstream values of U.S. society. James Miller, *Democracy Is in the Streets: From Port Huron to the Siege of Chicago* (New York: Simon & Schuster, 1987); Todd Gitlin, *The Sixties: Years of Hope, Days of Rage* (New York: Bantam, 1987).
2.   Guild interview, 7 July l990.
3.   National Student Council of the YWCA, "Our Interracial Concerns: Report for the Program Year, 1961–1962," RFC.
4.   National Student YWCA Race Relations Workshop, 1963, RFC.
5.   National Student Council of the YWCA, "College Camp, 30 August to 2 September, 1964," RFC.
6.   National Student Council of the YWCA, "Civil Rights Project, 1966," RFC.
7.   National Student Council of the YWCA, "Civil Rights Resolution," September 1963, RFC; National Student Council of the YWCA, "Human Relations Annual Report for Program Year 1962–63," RFC.
8.   "Historical Record of Desegregation and Integration," 10 May 1964, San Antonio, Texas, YWCA, RFC; minutes of the National Board, 6 April 1960, RFC.
9.   Minutes of the National Board, 2 October 1963, RFC.
10.   Minutes of National Board, 3–7 May 1965; "Letter to Community YWCA's," from Mrs. Lloyd J. Marti, president, Mrs. Earl D. Thomas, vice-president at large, and Edith M. Lerrigo, general secretary, 17 June 1965; "Report by Mr. Oze Horton, Chair, Subcommittee on Racial Integration, Community Division Committee," 18 October 1966; "Workshop on Racial Integration," 13–16 December 1965, Interracial Action Program, Southern Region, Atlanta, RFC.
11.   Minutes of the National Board, 1–4 February, 5 May, and 16–20 May 1966, 5 October 1967, RFC; "Proposed Plan for the Work of the Office of Racial Integration," RFC.
12.   Tracey A. Fitzgerald, *The National Council of Negro Women and the Feminist Movement, 1935–1975*, Georgetown Monograph in American Studies, 1985; Bettye Collier-Thomas, *National Council of Negro Women, 1935–1980* (Washington: National Council of Negro Women, 1981).
13.   Young Women's Christian Associations of the U.S.A, 25th Triennial Convention, 1970, *Proceedings*, RFC.
14.   Graham interviews, 7 November and 12 December 1990.
15.   Charlotte Bunch, *Passionate Politics: Feminist Theory in Action* (New York: St. Martin's, 1987), 3.
16.   Bunch, *Passionate Politics*, 3.
17.   Bunch interview, 2 April 1991.
18.   Casey Hayden, "The Women's Movement and the Nonviolent Direct Action Movement Against Segregation, 1960–1965," manuscript in the author's possession.
19.   Mary King, *Freedom Song: A Personal Story of the 1960s Civil Rights Movement* (New York: Morrow, 1987), 59–61.

20. Margarita Mendoza de Sugiyama, interview with author, 10 July 1991, Olympia, Washington.

21. Ibid.

22. Ibid.; YWCA of the U.S.A., National Board Committee to Study the Purpose, "The Purpose Study Session with Marilyn Whaley Winters" (videotape).

23. Mendoza de Sugiyama interview, 10 July 1991.

24. Ibid.

25. Ibid.

26. Minutes of the Community Relations Round-Up, 28 February to 4 March 1960, AFSC Archives.

27. Minutes of the Community Relations Committee, 20 February 1962; minutes of the Southern Programs Committee, Community Relations Division, 3 October 1964, AFSC Archives.

28. Helen Baker to Jean Fairfax and Will Hartzler, 20 June 1961, Records of the Community Relations Division, AFSC Archives.

29. Jean Fairfax to Southern Programs Committee, "AFSC's Prince Edward Program Proposal for 1963–64," 1 October 1963, AFSC Archives.

30. Raymond Wolters, *The Burden of Brown: Thirty Years of School Desegregation* (Knoxville: University of Tennessee Press, 1984), part 2.

31. Minutes of the Executive Committee, 23 March 1964; minutes of the Southern Programs Committee, Community Relations Division, 21 January 1964 and 1–3 May 1964, AFSC Archives.

32. Fairfax interview, 4 March 1984.

33. Minutes of the Southern Programs Committee, 3 October 1964, AFSC Archives.

34. Constance Curry, interview with author, 13 April 1991, Louisville, Kentucky.

35. Ibid.

36. Ibid.

37. Winifred Green (Falls), interview with author, 17 September 1991.

38. Constance Curry to Jean Fairfax, "Report #6," 14 June 1964; Constance Curry to Jean Fairfax, "Report #7, 7 July 1964; Constance Curry to Jean Fairfax, "Report #9, Mississippians for Public Education," 22 August 1964; Constance Curry to Jean Fairfax, "Report #10, Mississippians for Public Education," 2 November 1964, AFSC Archives.

39. Moffett interview, 24 May 1989.

40. Ibid.

41. Green interview, 17 September 1991.

42. Minutes of the Community Relations Executive Committee, 27 October 1964; "Schools and Desegregation," 1965; Community Relations Executive Committee, "Summary Sheet—Southern Programs," 22 January 1965; Minutes of the Southern Programs Committee, 30 April to 2 May, 1965; Minutes, Community Relations Executive Committee, 25 May 1965, all in AFSC Archives.

43. Connie Curry to Barbara Moffett re: Washington Visit, 1–2 February and 3 February 1966, AFSC Archives.

44. "Memorandum to Honorable John W. Garner, Department of HEW, from AFSC and NAACP Legal Defense and Education Fund, Report on Implementation of Title VI of Civil Rights Act of 1964 in Regard to School Desegregation," 15 November 1965, AFSC Archives.

45. Minutes of the Community Relations Executive Committee, 27 March 1966, AFSC Archives, AFSC.

46. Curry interview, 13 April 1991.

47. Ibid.

48. Fairfax interview, 4 March 1984.

49. Moffett interview, 24 May 1989.

50. "AFSC Family Aid Fund Program, March 1967–October 1972, By Connie Curry"; Minutes of the Community Relations Executive Committee, 22 March 1966; "AFSC Family Aid Fund Program, March 1967–October 1972," AFSC Archives.

51. Moffett interview, 24 May 1989.

52. Fairfax interview, 4 March 1984.

53. Fairfax interview, 6 July 1990.

54. Morris, *Origins of the Civil Rights Movement*, 139–140.

55. Meacham interview, 14 July 1989.

56. Curry interview, 13 April 1991; Green interview, 17 September 1991.

57. Meacham interview, 14 July 1989; M. Ho'oipo DeCambra, interview with author, 14 July 1989, Santa Rosa, California.

58. Charles DeBenedetti, *An American Ordeal: The Antiwar Movement of the Vietnam Era*, Charles Chatfield, assisting author (Syracuse, N.Y.: Syracuse University Press, 1990), 21–23.

59. CNVA sponsored civil disobedience actions at the Atomic Energy Commission test site in Nevada in 1957, a missile base in Cheyenne, Wyoming, in 1958, and Mead Air Force Base in Omaha, Nebraska, in 1959. The 1958 voyage of "The Golden Rule," a small ship that entered the South Pacific nuclear test site area to dramatize the issue of nuclear testing, was also sponsored by CNVA. See Jo Ann Robinson, *Abraham Went Out; A Biography of A.J. Muste* (Philadelphia: Temple University Press, 1981), 162–166.

60. Paul Boyer, "From Activism to Apathy: The American People and Nuclear Weapons, 1963–1980," *Journal of American History* 70 (1984): 821–844.

61. Boyer, "From Activism to Apathy."

62. Weinstein, *Ambiguous Legacy*,134–141; DeBenedetti, *An American Ordeal*, 110–112.

63. *Peace in Vietnam: A New Approach in Southeast Asia* (New York: Hill and Wang, 1966).

64. Minutes of the Peace Education Committee, 26 April 1967, 22 November 1967, AFSC Archives.

65. "National Public Affairs Program: A Program of Study and Action, 1961–1964," adopted by the 22nd Triennial Convention of the YWCA of the U.S.A., Denver, 8–18 May, 1961, 2–3; "National YWCA Emphases, 1964–1967," adopted by the 23rd Triennial Convention of the YWCA of the U.S.A., Cleveland, 23–25 April 1964; "National YWCA Emphases, 1967–1970," as adopted by the 24th Triennial Convention of the YWCA of the U.S.A., 6–7 April 1967, Boston; minutes of the National Board, 30 October to 3 November 1961, all in RFC.

66. Minutes of the National Board, 18 May 1966, RFC.

67. "National YWCA Public Affairs Priorities," 1970–1973, as adopted by the 25th National Convention of the YWCA of the U.S.A., April 1970, Houston, 6–7, RFC; "Public Affairs—A Continuing Program," as amended by the 26th National Convention of the YWCA of the U.S.A., March 1973, San Diego, 7, RFC.

68. Duryee interview, 9 November 1987.

69. Graves interview, 9 December 1987.

70. Hayden, "Women's Movement," 1–12; Evans, *Personal Politics*; King, *Freedom Song*.

71. Bunch interview, 2 April 1991; see also Bunch, *Passionate Politics*.

72. Harrison, *On Account of Sex*.

73. "Guidelines for the Development of a YWCA Program With Mature Women," produced by a subcommittee of YWCA's Vistas Steering Committee of White Plains, New York, and Bureau of Personnel and Training, YWCA National Board, June 1966, RFC; "Vistas for Women: Report of a Special Project, 1963–1965, Laura C. Gardner, Project Director, n.d., RFC.

74. Telephone conversation with Mildred Persinger, 14 December 1991; Jean Whittet, letter to author, 22 January 1992.

75. Roberts interview, 6 March 1988; Whittet interview, 7 March 1988.

76. "National YWCA Public Affairs Priorities, 1970–1973," as adopted by the 25th National Convention of the YWCA of the U.S.A., April 1970, Houston, 10, RFC.

77. Ibid. The YWCA Public Affairs Program first expressed support for family planning services and "adequate child care services for children who need them" in 1967. See "National YWCA Emphases, 1967–1970," as adopted by the 24th National Convention of the YWCA of the U.S.A., April 1967, Boston, 10, RFC.

78. "Public Affairs—A Continuing Program," as amended by the 26th National Convention of the YWCA of the U.S.A., March 1973, San Diego, 22, RFC.

Index

gion *(see* religion, and social reform); and separate women's organization vs. mixed-sex organizations, 121–122, 125; student participation in, 45, 66; theory of, 186–187n16; and women *(see* women activists)

Socialist party, 17, 22, 24, 29, 30, 34–35; and feminism, 130; and the peace movement, 21, 22, 99; and racial reform, 22–23; and the Social Gospel, 18–19, 35

Society of Friends, *see* Religious Society of Friends

Southeast Asia, 167, 170

Southeastern Public Education Program, 164

Southern Christian Leadership Conference (SCLC), 93, 124–125, 164, 198n12

Southern Interagency Conference, 160

Southern Student Human Relations Project, 159

Southern Tenant Farmers Union, 23

Soviet Union, 26, 35, 100, 101, 104, 107

Spanish civil war, 21–22, 99, 196n18

Speak Truth to Power (AFSC), 101–102

Stalin, Joseph, 102, 141

Stephenson, Madeleine, 127

Stephenson, Red, 87, 127

Steps to Peace (AFSC), 107

Steward, Annalee, 97

Stewart, Patricia, 124

Student Christian Movement, 29, 35, 36, 188n25

student movement, 141–142, 145

Student Nonviolent Coordinating Committee (SNCC), 93, 125, 142, 151, 152, 159–160, 165, 198n12

Student YMCAs, 14, 114, 133, 134, 188n25

Student YWCAs, 35, 36, 41, 49, 143, 152, 155, 156, 159; African-American women in, 57, 66 ; and the AFSC, 74; and the civil rights movement, 143–144, 145; on college campuses, 29, 114–115; Executive Committee of, 42; and feminism, 118, 120, 172, 173, 175; funding status of, 45; leadership of, 114–115, 119; mentoring in, 149–150,

151; National Field Staff of, 53; and the peace movement, 23, 104; racial integration of, 42–43, 44, 45, 57, 66, 188n2, 191n34; and racial reform, 22, 24, 42–43, 56, 63–64, 65–66, 134, 149, 153, 154; and religion, 14, 24, 188n25; role models in, 31; and the Social Gospel, 24, 66; and socialism, 24; southern, 42–43, 66; and the Student YMCA, 114

Students for a Democratic Society (SDS), 141, 142, 169–170, 173

Sugiyama, Masao, 153

suffrage: women's, 3, 17, 98, 112, 199–200n34

Sweeney, Odille, 41

Taft-Hartley Act (1947), 7

Talmadge, Herbert, 32

Test Ban Treaty (1963), 4. *See also* nuclear testing

Thiermann, Stephen, 86

Thomas, Norman, 24, 34–35

Thompson, Java Mae, 143

Tillich, Paul, 77

Treaty of Versailles, 20

Truman, Harry, 63, 89, 94

Turner, Dorothy, 58

UAW, *see* United Auto Workers

UCYM, *see* United Christian Youth Movement

Unitarian Universalist Association, 164

United Auto Workers (UAW), 124, 183n3

United Christian Youth Movement (UCYM), 14, 15

United Farm Workers of America, 83, 155

United Nations Day, 108

United Nations Organization, 65, 107, 159, 171, 179; and the AFSC, 9, 101; and liberal internationalism, 101, 102–103, 104, 105, 106, 107, 171; and the YWCA, 2, 9, 105–106, 107, 108, 171

United States: and foreign aid, 104, 106, 107; foreign policy of, 95, 101, 170 *(see also* Cold War); and the Spanish civil war, 22